DIAMONDS
IN THE
DUST

ADVANCE PRAISE FOR THE BOOK

'*Diamonds in the Dust* is a wonderful book for people who want to grow and maintain their wealth. With a number of solid research findings, the book explains why investing in companies' equity is the path to investment success. The process of analysing companies is explained in a systematic and clear way. The authors also reveal the most damaging myths of investing. They explain how to evaluate firms' competitive advantages and capital allocation. I particularly liked the various checklists giving all the important items needed when studying companies. Finally, the use of specific investor case studies bring to life all the principles given in the book. This book will certainly help you find those investment diamonds in the dust!'—**Mark Mobius, founder, Mobius Capital Partners**

'The translation of deep competitive advantages into wealth creation for shareholders is one of the most appealing aspects of equity investing. This book from the team at Marcellus lays out with great clarity how this process unfolds. If you care about wealth creation in modern India, you should read this book.'—**Harsh Mariwala, chairman, Marico Ltd**

'*Diamonds in the Dust* is an eye-opener, on a subject of great relevance. Through the pages of this lucidly written book, the team at Marcellus explains why investing in clean, well-managed companies selling essential products to 1.4 billion Indians is a simple and sound path to wealth creation. The authors present their well-researched arguments with great conviction, in a manner that is so easy to understand. A compelling read, indeed.'—**Harish Bhat, author of *Tata Log* and *#Tata Stories***

'If you are a direct stock picker or would like to be, here is a book that gives you a to-do and a not-to-do checklist along with a method to the process.' —**Monika Halan, author of *Let's Talk Money: You've Worked Hard for It, Now Make It Work for You***

'Wealth creation via the construction of powerful franchises is one of the most exciting facets of a fast-growing economy. The team at Marcellus has simplified and amplified this narrative better than anyone else in India. The result is an engrossing book which lays out the fundamental principles of successful equity investing in India.'—**Sanjeev Bikhchandani, co-founder and vice chairman, Info Edge (India) Ltd**

DIAMONDS IN THE DUST

CONSISTENT COMPOUNDING FOR EXTRAORDINARY WEALTH CREATION

SAURABH MUKHERJEA
RAKSHIT RANJAN
SALIL DESAI

BUSINESS
An imprint of Penguin Random House

PENGUIN BUSINESS

USA | Canada | UK | Ireland | Australia
New Zealand | India | South Africa | China

Penguin Business is part of the Penguin Random House group of companies whose addresses can be found at global.penguinrandomhouse.com

Published by Penguin Random House India Pvt. Ltd
4th Floor, Capital Tower 1, MG Road,
Gurugram 122 002, Haryana, India

Penguin Random House India

First published in Penguin Business by Penguin Random House India 2021

10 9 8 7

The views and opinions expressed in this book are the authors' own and the facts are as reported by them which have been verified to the extent possible, and the publishers are not in any way liable for the same.

ISBN 9780670095308

Typeset in Adobe Caslon Pro by Manipal Technologies Limited, Manipal
Printed at Replika Press Pvt. Ltd, India

www.penguin.co.in

To all the remarkable people, who together help Marcellus Investment Managers look after the assets of many thousands of hardworking Indian families

Disclaimer

The following stocks mentioned in the book are part of one or more portfolios managed or advised by Marcellus:

Asian Paints	Maruti Suzuki
HDFC Bank	Page Industries
Abbott India	Garware Technical Fibres
Divi's Labs	HDFC Asset Management Company
TCS	GMM Pfaudler
Pidilite Industries	Dr Lal Pathlabs
Kotak Bank	Info Edge (India)
Nestlé India	Titan Company

Contents

Foreword

I have known Saurabh Mukherjea for more than twenty-five years, since—newly graduated—he joined my economic consulting business. I have watched his subsequent career with pleasure and pride, as he became interested in equity research, and we were involved together in a London venture, Clear Capital. And then followed his return to India and rise to become one of the leading figures in India's asset management community and a regular commentator on investment matters.

Saurabh and I share the firm belief that successful investment requires a knowledge of business. This sounds obvious, and yet it does not seem to be obvious to most people who manage their own money or other people's. They are interested in securities markets, not product markets; in stocks, not companies. They are fixated on the idea that businesses should make the numbers, but wiser investors are fixated on the idea that businesses should make goods and services that people will want to buy and want to go on buying for years to come. The dichotomy was well expressed for me in an exchange with a well-regarded London fund manager, as we tried to persuade him to take an interest in business strategy. 'I don't care about competitive advantage,' he said. 'I just want to know which stocks are going to go up.' I knew that I would not want to trust any money to his management or want any of my friends, or encourage any funds I advise to do so.

Marcellus is founded on the principle that, to understand the stock, you must first understand the company. Not only does competitive advantage matter, in the long run, it is the only thing that matters. In this book, you will learn that successful investors look to fundamental value. Real businesses with real capabilities. As I write this, I am bombarded with invitations to buy meme stocks, baseball cards, cryptocurrencies and non-fungible tokens. But the tendency for price to revert to fundamental value is a basic law of investment. And it is a core tenet of 'coffee can investing'. As Warren Buffett puts it, if you aren't willing to hold it for ten years, do not hold it even for ten minutes. Long run stock returns are asymmetric—a small number of stocks account for a high proportion of overall market returns. Appreciation of the underlying economics of the business gives you the best, indeed the only, chance of holding these outstanding stocks.

No one said successful investment was easy. But this book will lead you carefully through the underlying principles. You will learn how to see through deceptive accounting. You will not learn how to time the market, but you will learn that even if you were able to do it, by some prescience no one else has yet achieved, the returns from market timing are far less than the returns from effective stock picking. You will learn the nature of competitive advantage, and how to identify sources of competitive advantage that are appropriable and sustainable. To invest well, you must understand these things—or entrust your funds to someone who does, like Marcellus. I hope this book will encourage many people to take control of their own wealth management. And if for you that is a leap too far, as it is for many people, this book will certainly enable you to ask the right questions of your financial adviser.

London
4 June 2021

Sir John Kay

Introduction

Test Cricket and Investing: A Classic Analogy

'Amidst the cacophonous tumult of India, there is a tendency to look for greatness and leadership amongst those who have flair, flamboyance and a certain sense of extroversion. But perhaps because the country is so prone to major upheavals . . . those who achieve long-lasting success in India are often those who are unflashy, introverted, determined and intelligently tenacious . . . in cricket, no one exemplifies this more than Rahul Dravid . . . the Coffee Can companies are the Rahul Dravids of the business world—rare, determined and constantly seeking to improve the edge or the advantage they enjoy vis-à-vis their competitors.'

—Saurabh Mukherjea, in Chapter 9 of *The Unusual Billionaires* (2016)

Peak performance in Test cricket requires not just technical proficiency but also intelligence and immense powers of concentration. In that regard, Test cricket and investing in Indian equities have interesting parallels, an appreciation of which can help newcomers understand the process of investing and the toolkits required to build a durably successful investment portfolio.

WHY EQUITY INVESTING IN INDIA PARALLELS TEST CRICKET

As a group of cricket lovers, we at Marcellus are not just crazy followers of the sport, but from time to time also find inspiration from it and its heroes in our personal and professional lives. And, given that ours is an entire nation of cricket lovers, we have also found cricketing analogies to be the most effective in communicating our investing approach.

Many people perceive investing as something involving constant action, including watching share prices all the time and reacting quickly to news flow and market movements. The general belief is that such 'active' investing yields result in the immediate future. However, it seldom works like that. Investing is not like a T20 match where you attempt to hit every ball out of the park. It is more like Test cricket, where you do not even attempt to play every ball, let alone try to hit it to the boundary. In Test cricket, you choose your shots carefully, leave the deliveries outside the off stump alone, score your ones and twos regularly, and dispatch the occasional loose ball to the boundary. The key to successful investing, therefore, is to first leave the risky stocks alone, then to identify the ones that can grow earnings and cash flows steadily, and once you find such stocks, to bet big on them. Also, as in Test cricket, investing requires the player to not just possess the relevant skills and training but also the mental conditioning and discipline to apply those skills and training consistently. More crucially, investing requires the patience to play a long innings, which, as in Test cricket, is the assured way to victory. The difference between successful and unsuccessful investing is, in many ways, the difference between Test cricket and T20.

The skill-building process for an investor starts ten years later compared to that of a budding batter. Most investors are in their early twenties when they first learn the analysis of financial statements and valuation techniques. While these are the foundational concepts of investing, the young investor tends to understand only the superficial aspects of these concepts. In other words, in her formative years, she learns the language of investing but doesn't, as yet, fully understand or appreciate its deeper significance.

Then, as she grows older and becomes a more experienced investor, she learns how to go deeper into these concepts and appreciates what they really mean. For example, she understands how companies deliberately cook their books so that investors end up overvaluing them and paying more for their shares than they really should. She also comprehends better why a small minority of companies is able to create competitive advantages so powerful that no rivals are able to effectively compete with it for years, even decades, on end.

While the time taken by an individual cricketer or investor to mature and then peak varies from person to person, a very small minority of players/investors is able to excel over long periods of time. To go deep and truly excel for ten and twenty years requires talent in cricket and intelligence in investing. At the same time, both call for deep thinking, alongside a growth mindset (which pushes you to address your deficiencies), focused hard work and a multi-disciplinary skill-set (rather than a one-dimensional, inflexible mindset).

And, if investing is akin to Test cricket, who better to emulate than Rahul Dravid, the greatest Test batter to play for India and one of the greats of the game across all eras and all countries. His skill-set, which on the face of it looks simple, is actually very hard to acquire.

IF INVESTING IS LIKE TEST CRICKET, INVESTORS SHOULD AIM TO BE LIKE RAHUL DRAVID

> 'By any meaningful reckoning . . . he was India's greatest match-winning batsman, with 24 away wins (Sachin Tendulkar has 20) where he averaged nearly 70. When imponderables are introduced into the equation, with such things as the ability to absorb pressure and match impact, he is the greatest series-defining batsman in the history of Test cricket, his count of eight series-defining performances greater than anybody else's.'
>
> —Suresh Menon[1]

> 'Rahul's batting was poetic, with flowing follow-throughs that capitalised on exceptional footwork and a rock-solid base. His head was like the statue of David, allowing for perfect balance.'
>
> —Steve Waugh[2]

ADELAIDE, 2003

When the Indian cricket team toured Australia in 2003-04, memories of the repeated hammerings that India had received in that country through the 1990s were still fresh in everyone's mind. In fact, as India was going into the series, cynics in the country were talking in terms of celebrating if the Indian side even managed to take a single Test match into the fourth day. Since this was to be Aussie legend Steve Waugh's final Test series, the consensus view was that the Aussies would go the extra mile to defeat India and seal Waugh's already legendary status as the most successful captain in Test history.

Rahul Dravid, the Indian team's vice-captain in the 2003-04 series, had had a traumatic tour to Australia in India's previous outing there in 1999-2000, with scores of 35, 6, 9, 14, 19 and 0 in the four tests played there. He had a poor run of form, and India were whitewashed 3-0 in that Test series. As Dravid later admitted,

> The whole phase was quite tough for me. Three tests against Australia and then hardly a break before we played two tests against South Africa at home. I had more doubts about my game in that period than I've ever done . . . I was out of form . . . I was not batting well. I was not getting into good positions. I got out to balls that I had lost track of. I didn't feel confident . . . Let's just say that I wasn't good enough and they were too good for me . . . [3]

After Dravid began unimpressively in the first Test of the 2003-04 series—which India managed to draw thanks to a century from their captain, Saurav Ganguly—Indian cricket lovers started fearing a repeat of the 1999-2000 horror show. Then came the second Test in Adelaide, which shook the world and took Dravid's game and his reputation to a different level.

The second Test at the Adelaide Oval began on 12 December 2003 with the Australian batsmen taking the Indian bowling to the cleaners. At the end of the first day, Australia had put 400 on the board with only 5 wickets down. They added a few more runs on day two to finish their first innings at 556. In next to no time, India collapsed to 85 for 4, with both Tendulkar and Ganguly back in the pavilion. It was at that point that Rahul Dravid stepped forward to play a seminal innings, which not only swung that Test match towards India but also ended an era of Australian domination over visiting Indian sides.

Dravid's 233 runs in the first innings of the 2003 Test in Adelaide took exactly ten hours. As a result of Dravid's epic effort, India trailed Australia by only 33 after both sides had finished their first innings. Australia then collapsed for 196 in the second innings, with Ajit Agarkar taking 6 wickets. Set 230 to win the match, a nervous Indian batting line-up stuttered to 170 for 4 (once again with Tendulkar and Ganguly back in the hut). Dravid again came to the fore, with 72 not out, and once he had smashed a Stuart MacGill final long-hop past cover—Dravid 'roared and kissed the India crest on his cap.'[4] India thus attained their first Test victory in Australia since 1981. If you watch the video of this memorable Test match, you can see the wild celebration among the Indian supporters, commentators and cricketers and understand how much this victory meant to the nation.[5]

As Aakash Chopra, who opened the batting for India in that series, said many years later, 'The Australians have the habit of forcing batsmen into making a mistake. But Rahul did not make a single mistake during that innings. They were trying to force him, but he was in no mood to oblige.'[6]

The Australians have similar recollections of the Adelaide Test match. Nine years later, Jason Gillespie, who led the Australian attack in the Adelaide Test match, said:

> . . . in Adelaide there was good bounce and carry, and we thought that if we stuck to our plans, we could get anyone out. But the way Dravid played, essentially, he was more patient than us bowlers. We became impatient, especially when he scored that double-century, because we could not get him out, and that made us go away from our game plan. That in turn worked for him because his plan was to wait for the bowler to lose patience.[7]

A few weeks after the Adelaide epic, Rahul Dravid told writer and journalist Rohit Brijnath in an interview that in the second innings, as he steered India to a historic win, 'I didn't feel in much control. I had to fight through periods, refocus, reminding myself of what I wanted to achieve. My goal was to not get out, to make it as difficult as I could.'[8]

Dravid then talked about his frame of mind on the final morning of the Adelaide Test match:

> We had a quiet confidence. We knew we had a great chance to win and we knew we could do it. Of course, we were a bit nervous, and it was natural. We had lost a lot of matches we should have won in the past. I was quite determined to not let that happen again . . . We had worked so hard . . . so we had to win . . . I told myself that I needed to do whatever it took, that whatever happened I would try to be there at the end. I had to give it all I had.[9]

The final word on Dravid's superhuman effort in Adelaide in 2003 belongs to his then captain, Saurav Ganguly, who said, 'Rahul batted like God.'[10]

THE GREATEST NUMBER 3 IN TEST CRICKET

Besides his Herculean feats in famous Test matches—like those of Adelaide in 2003, Eden Gardens in 2001, Headingley in 2002, Rawalpindi in 2004 and Jamaica in 2006—the distinctions of being the fourth-highest run getter in Test cricket, with 13, 288 runs (the second-highest Indian run scorer after Sachin Tendulkar), and of having faced more Test deliveries than any other (31, 258 to be precise i.e. 5, 210 overs) batter, are also his.

Batting at number three, Rahul Dravid scored more Test runs—10,524—in that position than any other batter in the history of the game. His sixteen-year international career has an often overlooked but significant statistic—in that period, Dravid scored more runs than Sachin Tendulkar. Dravid made an incredible 23 per cent of the runs scored by India in the twenty-one Test victories under Ganguly's captaincy, at a 'Bradmanesque' average of 103.[11] Those victories put India on the road to becoming the number one Test team in the world in the late 2000s.

During his Test career, whilst Dravid was at the crease, the Indian cricket team scored over 32,000 runs, which amounts to 35.6 per cent of the total runs that India made in the Tests which Dravid played. No other Indian player has a score of over 30 per cent for this metric. Dravid is also the only batter in Test cricket history to have batted in more than 700 partnerships; in fact, no other batter has recorded even 650 partnerships so far.[12]

Outside India, Rahul Dravid averaged 53.03 runs per innings. That is the second best 'away-from-home' average achieved by any Indian Test batter (Tendulkar leads with an away average of 54.7).[13] In all, eight of Dravid's eleven man-of-the-match awards were won in overseas Tests, and five in overseas wins. In contrast, Tendulkar won only five of his fourteen man-of-the-match awards overseas, and only one in a win (excluding Tests in Bangladesh). In fact, no Indian cricketer has won as many match awards overseas as Dravid has done.[14]

WHAT MADE DRAVID SO GOOD?

On the face of it, if you ask other Indian players who played alongside or under Dravid, or if you read what leading cricket writers had to say about him, it appears that what Dravid did was pretty 'simple'. Broadly speaking, the feedback on Dravid's recipe for success has three dimensions to it:

Firstly, as has been described in the opening paragraphs of this section, Dravid spent a lot of time in the middle playing more deliveries than anybody else has ever played in Test cricket. How was he able to do this? As Dravid himself told cricket writer Samir Chopra in 2011, 'My attitude towards batting was simple: the bowler had to earn my wicket. I told myself that I had to bat at least 30 overs in a Test. If I didn't do that, I had failed. I would do it one way or the other.'[15]

As the late Peter Roebuck, one of the world's greatest cricket writers, put it, 'Dravid has a very simple game founded upon straight lines. Reasoning that runs cannot be scored in the pavilion, he sets out to protect his wicket. Curiously, this thought does not seem to occur to many batsmen . . .'[16]

In the words of Jason Gillespie, who led the Aussie attack in the 2003-04 series in Australia, which we discussed earlier:

> Dravid had a simple game plan and he stuck to it. It comes back to patience: he had the patience to grind out long innings and wait for the right ball to hit. He had his specific shots that he wanted to play, and he would wait for the bowler to pitch in the area where he was comfortable playing an attacking shot. That made him very difficult to get out . . . The special thing about Dravid was when he got a bad ball, he would be waiting for it and he had the ability to put it away. He did not miss those opportunities to score. This is sometimes the difference between a very good player and a great player: the ability to score when you get the chance to score.[17]

Secondly, one could clearly see that, his patience aside, Dravid was technically a very accomplished player, someone who was a living cricket textbook. As Sambit Bal, editor of *Cricinfo*, said: 'Dravid's batsmanship was often taken for granted because it is so firmly rooted in time-worn traditions—leaving the good balls, not hitting in the air and on the up, and because it was so utterly comprehensible and lacking in mystique.'[18]

And, thirdly, as Dravid's career progressed and his fame grew, it became apparent to cricket aficionados that here was a devoted cricketer who was committed to his game and worked hard to stay fit. According to John Wright, the Indian cricket team's coach from 2000-05, Rahul Dravid was 'in the top 10% when it comes to physical training'. This, we are told, meant that in a typical Indian cricket squad of sixteen, Dravid was number one or two when it came to physical fitness.[19]

Dravid's teammate for many years in the Indian team, Virender Sehwag, made a similar point, but in his own inimitable way. Sehwag said: 'What can a youngster learn from Rahul Dravid? For starters, his discipline—waking up early, meditating and then working out and training.'[20]

However, if this is all that it takes to succeed, then why don't dozens of other determined men and women in India emulate Dravid? Why is it that nearly a decade after Dravid's exit from Test cricket, India has only one batter in men's cricket, Cheteshwar Pujara, and one in women's cricket, Mithali Raj, who can claim that they can approach Dravid's exalted standard? Why is it so hard to be like Rahul Dravid? We will take up this matter further on in this book. In doing so, we will also try to understand why successful investing at its heart is more about human behaviour than it is about technical skills.

In the first chapter of this book, we discuss the challenges faced by Indian households in deciding where to invest their life's savings. In chapters 2, 3 and 4, we have laid out the basic concepts for successful investing (analogous to the basic techniques required to be a good batter). In these chapters, we focus on how to understand which companies have poor accounting quality and which ones have sustainable competitive advantages (the cricketing analogue of learning how to appreciate the line and length of a delivery and the quality of the opposition).

Then, in chapters 5 and 6, we take you deeper and focus on more advanced concepts, such as capital allocation, valuation and the totality of the investment process. The cricketing analogue for this would be the mental conditioning and visualization skills that allow the greatest cricketers to raise their game when they are under most pressure, when the odds are most comprehensively stacked against them. The distinction we are seeking to draw is between the more psychological skill-sets (addressed in the final two chapters) and the more practical/technical skill-sets (addressed in chapters 2 to 4).

In the Appendices, we have provided a checklist to guide investors through the investing process, and we have also tried to summarize and simplify the critical concepts contained in the book so that someone who doesn't want to take the professional road and master the classic investing techniques can still build a decent portfolio for herself. The cricketing equivalent of this would be to play fantasy cricket online, rather than grinding it out in the middle of the cricket ground for years on end under the baking heat of the Indian sun.

However, just as there is no shame in playing fantasy cricket online whilst admiring legends like Dravid from afar, there is nothing wrong in understanding and appreciating the skill-sets of professional investors without being a practitioner of the same art. In fact, a full life can only be lived if we appreciate the T-shaped paradigm laid out in Chapter 2 of Saurabh and Anupam Gupta's book, *The Victory Project: Six Steps to Peak Potential*:

> . . . regardless of whether you are a cricketer, a politician, a fund manager, a dancer, or a film star, it is hard to believe that a unidimensional expert or an incompetent expert will reach the summit in the rapidly evolving flux of a complex and competitive society. The mental-model for achieving success in complex 'wicked' societies such as ours therefore resembles the letter 'T', i.e., broad-based knowledge alongside deep, focused expertise.

* * *

CHAPTER 1

The Four Most Damaging Myths in Indian Investing

'. . . most of all we worry about emergencies and hoard cash. The cash accumulates, and then some sharpshooter comes along and offers this fantastic deal. He's persistent; pushy; throws numbers; works on your fears, emotions, guilt. And gets your money. This ends in several ways. In a total loss, a partial loss or simply a bad investment that gives you returns worse than a bank fixed deposit.'

—Monika Halan[1]

Investing on the basis of grandmothers' stories and advice from snake oil salesmen means that the vast majority of affluent Indians have parked most of their wealth in assets that do not and cannot deliver returns in excess of the rate of inflation. This skewed portfolio allocation means that millions of Indian families are heading into retirement with investment portfolios that are being swiftly depleted. How did this happen? And what can be done to retrieve the situation? Let us understand the behaviour of most investing Indians with the help of the following fictional cases.

HOW INDIANS INVEST: CASE STUDIES OF DEVIKA AND RAJVEER

DEVIKA PATEL: 'THE SYSTEM IS RIGGED AGAINST ME'

Having shattered the glass ceiling at her workplace, Devika Patel took over as the CEO of Shineda Industries at the relatively young age of forty-one in 2007 as the Indian economy enjoyed its first period of sustained high growth since Independence in 1947. Shineda was a Thane-based company in Maharashtra, specializing in exporting medical fabrics to Africa and the Middle East.

Patel, now in her mid-fifties, had reaped the fruits of a very successful career. Her base salary had been a seven-figure sum for as long as she could remember, and her bonuses had also been hefty as Shineda had prospered.

She began investing her large bonuses from 2010 onwards, focusing largely on the booming residential real estate market in Mumbai, believing, like millions of other affluent Indians, that it would bring her lifelong benefits. Taken in by the slick pitch put forward by one of the multinational real estate broking firms, Devika invested in two luxury flats in upcoming residential high-rises in the suburbs of Mumbai.

Unfortunately, with the developer repeatedly running out of money, it was 2017 by the time the apartment blocks were delivered to Devika. By then, however, the government's attack on black money, in addition to the glut of residential apartment blocks in the market, had not only dented the resale value of

Devika's flats, were she willing to sell at the prevalent market price, but her compounded annual rate of return from the investment also would be in the low single digits. Still, Devika considered herself extremely fortunate to have got delivery of her flats; many others in her social circle had not been so fortunate.

Alongside real estate, jewellery in general and gold in particular were also Devika's longstanding fascinations. Her staunch belief in investing in gold came from her grandmother, who had passed on gold coins that had come down the generations to Devika's mother. Harbouring the noble ambition of sustaining the family's traditions, Devika had invested heavily in gold bars from the day she became the CEO of Shineda. Sadly, she reaped little monetary benefit from this, as the post-tax return on gold was only a little better than the rate of inflation.

Disappointed by her inability to compound her wealth from buying physical assets, Devika turned to fixed deposits. A wealth manager told her that a suburban co-operative bank in Mumbai, MCC Bank, was giving 8 per cent returns on fixed deposits. Having parked around Rs 1 crore in the bank over the course of a decade, Devika was horrified to read in the *Times of Worli* in late 2019 that the bank in question had gone bust as local politicians, working in cahoots with the bank's chairman, had run away with the savings of thousands of depositors.

Now, in the sunset years of her corporate career, Devika was a worried woman. She not only had her own retirement to fund, but her elderly mother was also dependent on her. Over the past twenty years, her compounded returns on her consolidated corpus—across real estate, gold, fixed deposits—had been close to zero. Effectively, Devika's investment decisions—based as they were on cocktail party gossip, planted articles in the financial press and 'advice' from financial intermediaries—had taken away much of the wealth generated by her hard work as the CEO of Shineda.

Her net worth, excluding the property in which she resided, was Rs 9 crore. Her assets consisted of real estate (i.e., flats in Lower Parel, an upmarket locality in Mumbai) worth Rs 6 crore, physical gold worth Rs 2 crore and fixed deposits of Rs 1 crore. To maintain her lifestyle post-retirement, Devika needed at least Rs 20 crore a decade hence, implying an annual post-tax required rate of return of 9 per cent on her current assets.

Devika now believed that the system was rigged against people like her—who, although wealthy, did not know how to navigate their monies through the complex corridors of India's financial system. How will Devika now recover from her mistakes? Can she actually generate sufficient returns to fund a happy retirement?

RAJVEER BHATIA: 'I KNOW HOW TO TRADE IN THE STOCK MARKET'

A class topper from IIM and bright as a button, Rajveer Bhatia had from a young age a knack for numbers. Nobody in his peer group was therefore surprised when he was hired straight off the campus by McIntyre Capital. Entering the firm as an associate at the age of twenty-three, he became a vice-president at thirty. Rajveer's parents, who had seen their own aspirations dashed in the socialist milieu of the India of the 1970s and 1980s, could not be prouder of their upwardly mobile son.

Although, as a corporate financier, Rajveer had earned a significant seven-figure sum each year, he knew better than anybody else that if he were to fulfil his dream of building a villa in Goa, in addition to his two-bedroom flat in Bandra, he needed to make his financial investments sweat harder. After all, Rajveer had seen first-hand how little his hardworking parents had got out of their fixed deposits and their life insurance policies.

So, Rajveer chose to invest his money in small-cap stocks. Having heard from his venture capitalist friends about a new discount broking platform, he opened a broking account there. With his knack for numbers, he built a substantial small-cap portfolio in next to no time. And, first in 2014 and then in 2017, Rajveer's small-cap portfolio rocketed in value, doubling Rajveer's initial investment. Wealth is a ticket to fame in Mumbai, and Rajveer soon became known as a master stock-picker in his social circle.

But then, 2018 came along and knocked a third off Rajveer's portfolio. As if that wasn't bad enough, 2019 compounded Rajveer's losses. By the time COVID-19 hit India in 2020, Rajveer's portfolio had halved, and six years after he had started investing in small caps, Rajveer was back to where he had started in 2014.

Finance 101 in college had taught Rajveer the merits of diversification. So, through his years of small-cap trading, Rajveer had been convinced by a wealth manager to invest in the Credit Risk funds managed by a multinational mutual fund house. As this mutual fund consistently generated 10–12 per cent returns per annum, Rajveer convinced his retired parents also to invest a large part of their retirement corpus in these funds. Whilst other mutual funds suffered in 2018 and 2019 from defaults in their underlying portfolios, the multinational fund house kept urging millions of investors like the Bhatias to keep increasing their investments in their funds. Rajveer and his parents dutifully followed the advice—with not just a little moral support from their wealth manager.

And then, one day in the summer of 2020 came the news that turned the Bhatias' world upside down: the multinational fund house froze all the monies invested in the Credit Risk fund by the Bhatias and tens of thousands of others like them. Rajveer's parents' dream of a post-retirement world trip lay in tatters. Rajveer could barely comprehend how, a full decade out of college, he had not only not managed to generate any wealth for himself but had also destroyed the financial foundation of his retired parents' lives.

Thirty-five-year-old Rajveer and his parents' total assets, excluding their primary residence, today amounts to Rs 5 crore, consisting of small-cap stocks worth Rs 3 crore and fixed deposits, owned by Rajveer's parents, worth Rs 2 crore. Can Rajveer now finance his parents through retirement over the next fifteen years and still buy his holiday home in Goa?

THE PERILS OF BEING AN INDIAN HNI

AN RBI REPORT ACTS AS A WARNING BELL

The investment and wealth profiles of Devika and Rajveer are very similar to that of a large number of individuals, particularly high-net-worth Indians. In August 2017, Reserve Bank of India published its 'Indian Household Finance Survey'.[2] The report said:

> The average Indian household holds 84% of its wealth in real estate and other physical goods, 11% in gold and the residual 5% in financial assets. Retirement accounts play a very limited role in household balance sheets, even at the top of the wealth distribution . . . Households in advanced economies hold substantially more financial assets than their Indian counterparts, are much more likely to finance home purchasing with a mortgage, and allocate a sizeable fraction of their wealth to retirement savings over the course of their lifetime . . . The model also cannot explain the observed prominence of physical assets in middle-age, exactly when the potential for the accumulation of financial wealth would be largest . . .

In spite of the extraordinary nature of the findings of the report, back in 2017, no one paid too much attention to it. However, over the last couple of years, having met over 10,000 high net-worth individuals (HNIs), the enormity of RBI's 2017 report has hit us, as we have seen first-hand that most Indians—including affluent Indians—have allocated the vast majority of their wealth (over 95 per cent, according to the RBI report)—to assets which do not and cannot generate a real rate of return. These assets include gold, real estate, low-quality debt mutual funds and low-quality stocks. The stage is therefore set for a whole generation of Indians, who began working in the early 1980s and who will retire in the next ten years, to struggle mightily through retirement. How did this disaster take place? And what can be done to mitigate the problems that millions of seemingly affluent Indian families will face as they head into retirement?

FOUR MYTHS ABOUT INVESTING IN INDIA

The challenge for affluent Indians who are trying to get their financial planning on track arises from two different sources. Firstly, manufacturers of financial savings products and the intermediaries of such products are marketing proactively, and sometimes aggressively, to get a slice of the Indian HNI savings pot. Often, these marketing/advertising campaigns have little to do with the facts on the ground. The second challenge facing well-intentioned Indian HNIs is themselves—most affluent investors live in an environment where myths around the pros and cons of various investments proliferate. These myths are often the biggest driver of the investment decisions affluent Indians make. We now highlight the four myths that we encounter most often in our discussions with HNIs.

MYTH 1: GOLD WILL HELP ME PROTECT MY WEALTH

As mentioned earlier, an RBI report found that next to real estate, gold, at 11 per cent, accounts for the largest share of the wealth of Indian households. An 11 per cent allocation to any asset is a reasonably large chunk by any standard. How has such a material asset allocation worked for Indian households? Over the last ten/twenty/thirty years, the price of gold (in rupee terms) has compounded at an annualized return of 9.2 per cent/12.7 per cent/9.3 per cent, respectively (columns 1–3 in Exhibit 1). Over the same time periods, an investment in the equity markets, represented by an investment in the BSE Sensex index, retuned 10.4 per cent/15.0 per cent/14.8 per cent, respectively, higher than gold in each time period. If we consider returns from gold in each of the three decades separately over the last thirty years, we see that gold has underperformed the Sensex by a wide margin (columns 4–6 in Exhibit 1). In the decade 1990–2000, gold prices grew at an annualized return of just 2.8 per cent, not even beating inflation (column 6 of Exhibit 1). The narrowest margin by which gold underperformed was in the decade of 2010–2020, when gold prices compounded at 9.2 per cent per annum, against 10.4 per cent of the Sensex. However, in this decade, gold prices were more volatile (measured by the standard deviation) than equities, suggesting that on a volatility-adjusted basis, there wasn't a compelling reason to own gold.

Exhibit 1: Comparative returns and volatility of gold and Indian equities

	Cumulative periods			**Decadal periods**		
Asset	**2010-2020 (10-years)** (1)	**2000-2020 (20-years)** (2)	**1990-2020 (30-years)** (3)	**2010-2020** (4)	**2000-2010** (5)	**1990-2000** (6)
Annualized returns						
– Gold	9.2%	12.7%	9.3%	9.2%	16.3%	2.8%
– BSE Sensex	10.4%	15.0%	14.8%	10.4%	19.9%	14.4%
Standard deviation						
– Gold	15.8%	15.2%	14.9%	15.8%	14.1%	11.9%
– BSE Sensex	14.1%	27.9%	36.3%	14.1%	35.7%	48.5%

Source: BSE; RBI; returns in CAGR for each calendar year (January to December)

Even though gold does not fetch returns superior to equity, it could improve the risk-adjusted returns of your portfolio if it were negatively correlated to equities (thus allowing you to diversify your returns). The widespread public perception is that gold is negatively correlated to equities. However, the data on this is actually mixed, as seen in Exhibit 2. Whilst gold has been negatively correlated to the Sensex over the past ten years, over longer periods of time, namely twenty and thirty years, the negative correlation drops away and actually becomes a mild positive correlation. This means that over the last twenty-year and thirty-year periods, the prices of gold and the BSE Sensex have moved more or less in tandem. Further, if we break down the last thirty years into three decades, we see that gold has, for the most period, been positively correlated to equities. This means that using gold as a diversifier of wealth also does not work consistently. On the whole, it is difficult to make a case for gold forming a significant part of the portfolio of an Indian investor.

Exhibit 2: Correlation between gold and equities

	Cumulative periods			**Decadal periods**		
Asset	**2010-2020 (10-years)**	**2000-2020 (20-years)**	**1990-2020 (30-years)**	**2010-2020**	**2000-2010**	**1990-2000**
Correlation	-61.1%	-3.2%	8.7%	-61.1%	16.1%	39.1%

Source: Marcellus Investment Managers; RBI; BSE; correlation of monthly year-on-year returns from equities represented by the BSE Sensex Total Return Index and gold prices in INR

The RBI report referenced above also corroborates these findings and makes a case for reallocation of wealth from gold to other financial assets. The reports states:

> For households that hold more substantial amounts of gold, i.e., those in the top third of the cross-sectional distribution, the ongoing annual income gain from re-allocating a quarter of their gold holdings to financial assets is 3.4%, which when capitalised, translates into an upwards movement of roughly 5 pp along the Indian wealth distribution. These projected gains are almost always above zero, even when we account for volatility which may lead to different realisations of returns on gold and financial assets.

MYTH 2: REAL ESTATE WILL HELP ME GROW MY WEALTH

Over the last five years, if one were to look at the return rate from real estate in metropolitan cities in India such as Mumbai, Delhi and Bengaluru, one would see that returns have been around 3–4 per cent per annum; i.e., house prices have at best kept pace with consumer inflation. Real estate in major markets like the National Capital Region has not even accomplished that.[3] However, there is a school of thought in India which says that because residential real estate returns have been weak over the last five years they will be better going forward. This point of view cannot be sustained when one compares Indian house prices with the prices prevalent in other markets. The first problem is affordability. As shown in the chart below, Indian residential house prices, expressed as a proportion of GDP, are 6–10x the prices prevalent in some comparable Asian economies.

Exhibit 3: Indian residential house prices in India are among the highest in the world (based on 2020 data)

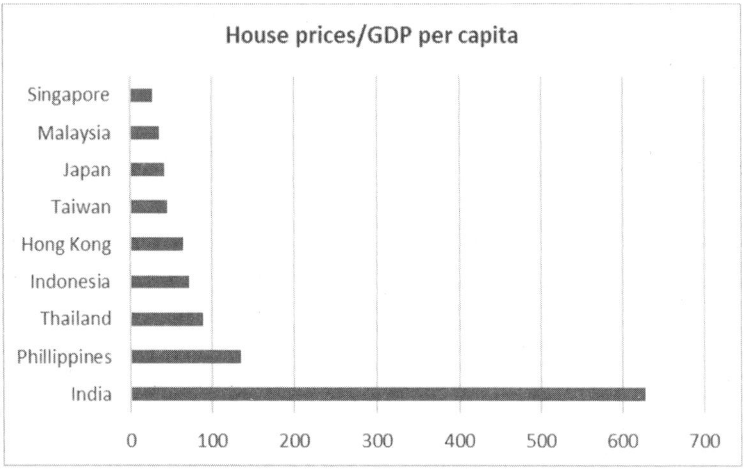

Source: Marcellus Investment Managers, Global Property Guide, https://www.globalpropertyguide.com/Asia/price-gdp-per-cap

Secondly, Indian residential rental yields are around 2–3 per cent in most Indian cities, whereas the cost of a home loan for prime residential real estate customers is around 7 per cent. The disparity between these numbers suggests that Indian residential real estate still has room to correct from its highs before it becomes an attractive asset class.

Thirdly, comparing Indian residential rental yields with yields in other countries suggests that the Indian residential property market is significantly overvalued. Other markets whose rental yields are comparable with India's—say, Singapore and the USA—have costs of borrowing in the range of 2–3 per cent. In contrast, as mentioned above, in India, the cost of a home loan for even a prime customer is much higher, around 7 per cent. In fact, the cost of a home loan in India is significantly higher than it is in Indonesia (7 per cent vs 5 per cent), even though rental yields in Indonesia are much higher than in India.[4] Clearly, investing in real estate in India does not make much economic sense. Add to it other factors—such as high transaction costs (broking, stamp duty, etc.), illiquidity (your property is pretty useless in funding emergency cash calls) and the lack of transparency in finding the true value or price—and investing in real estate becomes cumbersome and risky.

MYTH 3: DEBT MUTUAL FUNDS OFFER DECENT RETURNS WITH LOW VOLATILITY

Salespeople who earn a living by selling mutual funds have popularized the idea that HNIs should invest in debt funds, which give industry-beating returns. In spite of the repeated high-profile reverses suffered by prominent mutual fund houses who have high-risk, low-quality paper in their debt funds, the intermediary community continues to sell such products. So, why are debt funds far riskier to invest in than many investors believe (and many intermediaries let on)? Personal finance guru Monika Halan has provided an excellent explanation for this:

> Remember, when you lend money, the interest is the reward you get for postponing your consumption, to take care of the effects of inflation on the money you get back and for the risk of the borrower not returning your money. The government is considered to have no risk of default and therefore the rate at which the government borrows is called the risk-free rate. As the credit-worthiness of firms falls, the interest they offer rises. When you invest in a debt fund, the scheme goes out and buys bonds and other fixed return instruments. The risk in debt funds comes from several sources. I will discuss the three most important aspects for this conversation.

> The first is interest rate changes, or an interest rate risk. This is the risk of your fund manager's interest rate call going wrong . . .
>
> The second is the risk of default by the borrower—or a credit risk. Funds are allowed to invest in debt papers that are rated investment grade by credit ratings agencies. But within this band of investment grade, it is possible for fund houses to invest in lower-rated papers than the safest paper in the market. When things go wrong for the firm that borrowed money from the mutual fund, the credit ratings can drop sharply and the value of the fund suffers. When such an event happens and there is a big redemption pressure, the third risk kicks in: lack of liquidity—or the lack of a market when you want to exit. The non-government Indian bond market is not very liquid, that is, fund managers may not find buyers if they need to sell in distress.[5]

In Chapter 7 of *Coffee Can Investing: The Low-Risk Route to Stupendous Wealth* (2018), Saurabh Mukherjea, Rakshit Ranjan and Pranab Uniyal explained the issue in the following manner: A debt mutual fund's return is a function of: 1) Yield to Maturity or YTM, 2) Mark to Market or MTM, and 3) Expense Ratio. Let's delve into each of these:

MTM and the expense ratio should not differ markedly between debt mutual funds. That brings us to the YTM, which refers to the total return earned on a bond if it is held until maturity with the interest received reinvested at the same rate. The YTM of a debt fund is the weighted average yield of all its investments. The yield of a debt fund depends on the credit quality of its portfolio. All corporate debt is 'rated' basis the probability of the corporate defaulting on its debt obligations. These ratings are provided by credit rating agencies who, the world over, are conflicted because the issuer of the debt pays the credit rating agency its fees. The debt issuers with the strongest balance sheets get a rating of 'AAA', implying that their probability of default is similar that of the government. In contrast, the companies with poor debt management may get a rating of 'B'.

There tends to be an inverse correlation between the rating enjoyed by the debt issuer and the YTM on the issuer's bonds, i.e., companies with the strongest ratings enjoy the lowest YTMs. That, in turn, means that a fund manager who stuffs his debt fund full of highly rated bonds will have a fund with a low YTM, and hence the debt fund will give low returns. However, that will make the fund unpopular with the army of salespeople who sell such products. So, fund managers who want to earn big bonuses tend to stuff their debt funds full of bonds with low credit ratings. Such funds deliver high returns for a few years, but when defaults occur (low-rated bonds have high default risk) the whole thing blows up and millions of investors find that their savings in debt funds are worth much less than they thought they would be. For the following few years, HNWs steer clear of debt funds, but as the memory of the last debt fiasco fades, the intermediary gets to work again, and the cycle of wealth destruction repeats itself.

MYTH 4: GDP GROWTH DRIVES THE STOCK MARKET. SO, IF I (OR MY WEALTH MANAGER) CAN TIME THE ECONOMIC CYCLE, I CAN TIME THE STOCK MARKET

Exhibit 4: Nifty50 EPS growth vs the nominal GDP growth

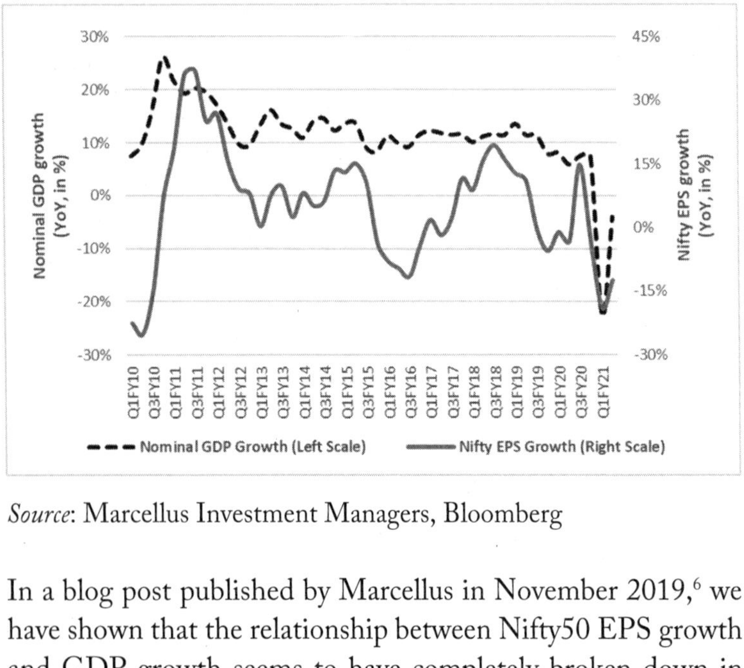

Source: Marcellus Investment Managers, Bloomberg

In a blog post published by Marcellus in November 2019,[6] we have shown that the relationship between Nifty50 EPS growth and GDP growth seems to have completely broken down in the last five years. Do note two things in the chart above: (1) the growing gap between the two lines; and (2) the fact that the lines often go in opposite directions.

To understand why the Nifty50 no longer captures the dynamism of the Indian economy, a good place to start is the index as it stood ten years ago. The ten-year (2011–2020) share price return from investing in the Nifty50 is 9 per cent (on a total return basis), i.e., significantly lower than India's nominal

GDP growth, which, over the same decade, has been around 12 per cent per annum.

More generally, across the world there tends to be low or no correlation between stock markets and GDP growth, implying that timing the stock market is not possible on a systematic basis. Ben Inker of the fund management house GMO, in an article in 2012, concluded that 'Stock market returns do not require a particular level of GDP growth, nor does a particular level of GDP growth imply anything about stock market returns.'

The valuation guru Aswath Damodaran says that the causal relationship, instead of running from GDP growth to the stock market, instead runs the other way round, i.e., stock markets are predictors of GDP growth (rather than being 'reflectors of GDP growth'). He highlights a 30 per cent correlation between stock market returns in the US in the period 1961–2019 and GDP growth four quarters hence.[7]

REALITY: EQUITIES ARE A BETTER WAY TO BUILD WEALTH

If gold, real estate, bank deposits and corporate debt (through mutual funds) do not optimally balance risk, returns, diversification and financial objectives for Indian savers, then what other options do they have to invest in and build their wealth? Are equities the answer?

Over the last twenty years, equities have generated a 13 per cent compounded return (measured by the returns on the Nifty50 Total Return Index). And some selected portfolios, such as the ones shown in the book *Coffee Can Investing: The Low-Risk Route to Stupendous Wealth*, have generated compounded annual returns in excess of 20 per cent over a twenty-year period. However, investments in equities also suffer from some of the same problems discussed above, the main being the lack of access to sound and trusted advice. This leads to investors taking on undue risk while building their equity portfolios. Chasing stocks in sectors that are in favour, buying cyclical stocks without appreciating the underlying drivers of cyclicality, and trading in and out of stocks based on punts on the outcome of short-term events, are some of the ways these risks manifest in investors' portfolios. A key reason for this is the reliance on conventional financial theory, particularly the capital asset pricing model (CAPM), which has shaped the world view of many investment advisors.

HOW CAPM HAS HURT A GENERATION OF INDIAN INVESTORS

There are many delusional theories in finance. One of these is the Efficient Markets Hypothesis (EMH), which contends that since stock prices efficiently discount all the available information in the market, it is impossible to beat the market. Another is the Capital Asset Pricing Model (CAPM), which claims that the returns from a stock will be directly proportional to the systematic risk (or beta) represented by the stock.

Whilst Warren Buffett's rubbishing of the EMH in a celebrated speech delivered in 1984 at Columbia University is well-known,[8] CAPM is still taught in classrooms across the world—thanks to the pseudo-science peddled by business schools—including in India, a country where CAPM is even less applicable than it is in America.

So, what is CAPM and just why is it so damaging? Investopedia explains CAPM this way:

The Capital Asset Pricing Model (CAPM) describes the relationship between systematic risk and expected return for assets, particularly stocks. CAPM is widely used throughout finance for pricing risky securities and generating expected returns for assets given the risk of those assets and cost of capital.

The formula for calculating the expected return of an asset given its risk is as follows:

$ER_i = R_f + \beta_i (ER_m - R_f)$
where
ER_i =expected return of investment
R_f =risk-free rate
β_i =beta of the investment
$(ER_m - R_f)$ =market risk premium

Investors expect to be compensated for risk and the time value of money. The risk-free rate in the CAPM formula accounts for the time value of money. The other components of the CAPM formula account for the investor taking on additional risk.

The beta of a potential investment is a measure of how much risk the investment will add to a portfolio that looks like the market. If a stock is riskier than the market, it will have a beta greater than one. If a stock has a beta of less than one, the formula assumes it will reduce the risk of a portfolio.

A stock's beta is then multiplied by the market risk premium, which is the return expected from the market above the risk-free rate. The risk-free rate is then added to the product of the stock's beta and the market risk premium. The result should give an investor the required return or discount rate they can use to find the value of an asset.[9]

Using CAPM—An Example

Let us understand, with an example, how to calculate the expected rate of return on a stock using the CAPM. We use State Bank of India (SBI) for this purpose.

Risk-free rate: This is the interest rate on an investment that has no default risk and no reinvestment risk. Therefore, a government bond that is held until its maturity can be considered as carrying the risk-free rate. The prevailing rate (early 2021) on the Indian government security maturing in ten years is about 6.5 per cent and becomes our risk-free rate (R f).

Beta: SBI's beta is calculated as the covariance of the return on the stock with the return on the market, divided by the variance of the return of the market (the benchmark) over a certain period. We consider the Nifty50 as the benchmark and monthly returns of SBI and Nifty50 for a period of ten years from March 2010 to March 2020. This gives us the beta of SBI as 1.5x (β i).

Market return: Over the ten-year period considered above, the return on the Nifty50 was approximately 10.4 per cent, which is the market return (ER m).

Calculating the expected return on SBI using these numbers, we get the result:

ER i for SBI = 6.5% + 1.5 * (10.4% – 6.2%) = 12.35%

Following CAPM in India leads investors to cause self-damage. The investor ends up believing that higher returns are proportional to higher risk (measured in CAPM by higher beta). This simply is not true. Consider the evidence:

> If you take the top ten return-generating stocks from the Nifty50 over the twenty, ten, five and three years ending March 2020, the average beta of these stocks is between 0.8 and 0.9, i.e., clearly below the market beta of 1, in spite of the fact that each of these groups of top ten stocks drawn from the Nifty50 (as it stood twenty, ten, five and three years ago) has significantly outperformed the index.
>
> Within these four groups of ten stocks for each of the Nifty50 cohorts (from twenty, ten, five and three years ago), the correlation between beta and returns is either mildly positive (0.22 correlation between beta and returns from the Nifty50 cohorts of twenty years ago) or strongly negative (-0.45 and -0.47 correlation between beta and returns for the Nifty50 cohorts from three and five years ago, respectively).
>
> If you take the ten Nifty50 stocks with highest beta as of 31 March 2020 (Axis Bank, Bajaj Finance, Hindalco, ICICI Bank, IndusInd Bank, JSW Steel, M&M, Maruti Suzuki, Tata Motors, UPL), the average beta is 1.4, i.e., well above the market beta of 1. And yet, over three, five, ten and twenty years, these stocks—as a group—have underperformed the index.
>
> Finally, if you study the correlation between beta and returns inside this group of the highest beta stocks in the Nifty50 (as of 31 March 2020), you find that over twenty, ten, five and three years, the correlation is negative, usually strongly so (-0.35 and -0.39 correlation between beta and returns for the Nifty50 over the past three and five years, respectively).

In short, not only is there NO POSITIVE relationship between beta and stock-level returns, there seems to be strong evidence that lower beta leads to higher returns. This finding also holds if, rather than using beta as a proxy for risk, one uses share price volatility (as measured by the standard deviation of monthly returns divided by the compounded annual returns over the corresponding time period). To be specific, there is STRONG NEGATIVE correlation between share price volatility and returns, i.e., companies whose share prices are less volatile give significantly better returns over twenty, ten, five, and even three years.

The data therefore shows that CAPM is completely useless in India—not only do the highest-risk stocks (high-beta stocks) NOT deliver the highest returns, the stocks which do deliver the best returns are actually low-risk stocks (i.e., low-beta stocks with low share price volatility).

So, why doesn't CAPM work in India? Because the assumptions underlying CAPM are unrealistic, even in a developed market like the US. In an emerging market like India, these assumptions are on the verge of being delusional. For example, CAPM assumes that all investors have free access to all information at no cost. This obviously makes no sense in a market like India where even institutional investors have little or no idea of the extent of accounting fraud that most companies engage in (see the next section and see Chapter 10 of *The Unusual Billionaires* for more details). Another example of a nonsensical assumption embedded in CAPM is that there are no taxes and there are no transaction costs. In reality, short-term capital gains tax is 15 per cent, and even for Nifty50 stocks, brokerage costs plus price-impact costs[10] are around 0.5 per cent for institutional investors.

So, if CAPM does not work in India, what does? *Crushing risk* works in India.

CRUSHING RISK IS THE KEY TO GENERATING HIGHER RETURNS IN INDIA

You need to minimize four types of risks if you want to generate steady and healthy investment returns in the Indian stock market:

ACCOUNTING RISK: Whilst we all now know how prominent public and private sector banks in India fudged their bad-debt figures for years on end until the RBI's Asset Quality Review in 2015 forced them to come clean, the same problem still exists with several housing finance companies. The accounts of a leading cement manufacturer don't stack up. Neither does the annual report of a high-flying retailer make sense. Ditto with a prominent petchem company and a prominent pharma company. In fact, the majority of the companies in the BSE500 have annual reports that don't pass scrutiny. Using twelve forensic accounting ratios and a financial model which contains time-series data on 1,300 of India's largest listed companies, we seek to identify that 20 per cent of the Indian stock market whose books are actually believable. The next chapter of this book focuses on this subject in more detail.

REVENUE RISK: At around US$2100, India's per capita income is still very low (nearly half the level of Sri Lanka's, less than one-fifth of Malaysia's and about one-fourth of Thailand's).[11] As a result, beyond the basic essentials of life—FMCG products, medicines, basic apparel and basic financial services products—most other products in India are luxury items for most Indians. As a result, even for small cars or entry-level two-wheelers, demand in India fluctuates wildly. For example, if we consider the sales volumes reported by Maruti Suzuki, we see that the company typically experiences six to seven years of strong demand growth (growth well above 15 per cent per annum—example, 15.2 per cent CAGR in volumes over FY2004–11) followed by three to four years of famine (growth well below 5 per cent per annum—example, 0.4 per cent CAGR in volumes over FY2011–15). Whilst its cross-cycle average growth tends to be around 12 per cent, the stock price volatility reflects the volatility of Maruti's top-line growth. In contrast, a company selling essential products, like Asian Paints or Marico, tends to see steady revenue growth—between 10 per cent and 20 per cent per annum—pretty much every year. Investing in companies selling essential products in India therefore reduces risk.

PROFIT RISK: As the cost of capital is still pretty high for India, it is rare to find Indian companies who spend heavily on genuine R&D. Understandably therefore, the Indian economy is characterized by rapid imitation—one company spots a niche (say, gold loan finance) and within a decade it has dozens of imitators. This rapid entry of new companies in a business squeezes the profitability of the first mover and thus creates risk for its shareholders. In order to reduce such risk, we look for sectors where, over extended periods of time, one or two companies cumulatively account for 80 per cent of the sector's profit pie. Such monopolies have lower volatility in their profit margin.

LIQUIDITY RISK: Liquidity is a measure of how easily an asset or security (like stocks) can be bought or sold in its markets. Liquidity is usually measured in terms of the average daily traded volume (ADV) of a stock. The higher the ADV, the easier it is to buy or sell the stock without materially impacting its price. India is one of the least liquid of the world's top eight stock markets, largely because promoters own more than half of the shares outstanding in the Indian market. As a result of this, beyond the top thirty or so stocks in India, liquidity drops rapidly. By the time you are in the lower reaches of the BSE100, the ADV tends to fall to as low as Rs 10 crore per day. Such low liquidity creates stock-price gyrations, as investors go through their cycles of election-induced euphoria followed by accounting-fraud-induced panic. Tilting the portfolio towards liquid stocks reduces this risk.

THE CONSISTENT COMPOUNDING FORMULA

In this book, we elaborate on the key elements necessary for crushing risk to generate steady and healthy returns from equities in India. Our approach is to buy clean, well-managed Indian companies selling essential products behind very high barriers to entry. We call this approach to investing Consistent Compounding, and have seen, both in theory and in practice, that it works. This approach has three key elements—Credible Accounting, Competitive Advantage and Capital Allocation. They are the foundational pillars of Marcellus's investment philosophy, which will help investors generate healthy returns without taking extra risk (or loading up on beta).

The first pillar, Credible Accounting, uses a set of forensic accounting ratios and techniques to identify companies with the least accounting risk and the highest reliability of reported financial statements. Competitive Advantage is the search for companies that possess strong and durable pricing power, enabling them to be leaders in their markets and consistently earn returns higher than their cost of capital. This mitigates their revenue and profit risk. The third pillar, Capital Allocation, is about finding companies that make the best use of their excess returns (the difference between return on capital and cost of capital, akin to free cash flow) in order to grow their business as well as to deepen their competitive advantages. Knowing what stocks to buy using the three pillars is what we call the Consistent Compounding Formula.

Exhibit 5: The Consistent Compounding Formula

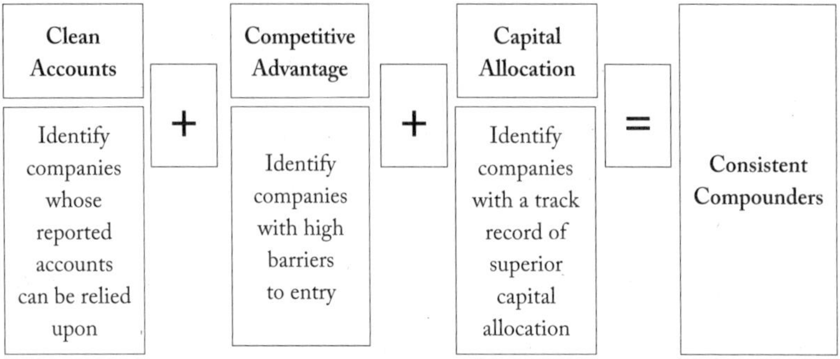

Source: Marcellus Investment Managers

In the first part of the book, we discuss the Consistent Compounding Formula to understand 'what to buy'. In the later part, we discuss 'when to buy', and focus on two key areas that regularly confound investors—the timing of stock purchases (or sales) and the valuations at which to buy (or sell) them.

Before we dive into these topics, let us also understand what this book is *not* about.

THE ABC OF INDIAN STOCKS

The Consistent Compounding approach to investing, as we will see in subsequent chapters, is simple to understand, but not easy to practise. A key challenge investors face at the very outset is that 'consistent compounder' stocks are few and far between in the Indian stock market. This book is not about the vast majority of stocks that do not possess the three foundational pillars of consistent compounding mentioned above. In this section we discuss the kind of stocks that make up this vast majority of the Indian stock market and also the kind of stocks that are the small minority of 'consistent compounders'.

> Given the way price multiples have expanded for high-quality companies over the last decade, should investors be concerned about the sustainability of stock returns from such companies if they buy at current levels? Our answer is a resounding NO . . . whether we look at bull market phases of the Indian stock market or bear market phases, all the evidence points in one direction—starting-period valuations have very little impact on long-medium-run investment returns in India. The lack of correlation between starting-period valuations and long-term holding period returns seems to be specific to India.[12]

Eighty years ago, Benjamin Graham and David Dodd introduced to the investing world the then revolutionary and interlinked concepts of 'value investing' and 'margin of safety' in their book *Security Analysis*[13]. In an era ravaged by the Great Depression, the two men pointed out that the way to make money in the stock market with a high degree of certainty is to buy companies with low P/B, low P/E multiples and low debt. Such investments meant that your purchase price would be significantly below the fair value of the stock, thus providing a 'margin of safety' for the investor.

In the years since the publication of *Security Analysis*, numerous academics have shown that value investing does generate superior results in the US market and elsewhere. Even more famously, Warren Buffett in his celebrated 1984 speech at Columbia University—which we referenced earlier in this chapter—reaffirmed the superiority of value investing to other investing approaches:

> The common intellectual theme of the investors from Graham-and-Doddsville is this: they search for discrepancies between the value of a business and the price of small pieces of that business in the market. Essentially, they exploit those discrepancies without the efficient market theorist's concern as to whether the stocks are bought on Monday or Thursday, or whether it is January or July, etc. Incidentally, when businessmen buy businesses, which is just what our Graham & Dodd investors are doing through the medium of marketable stocks . . . Our Graham & Dodd investors, needless to say, do not discuss beta, the capital asset pricing model, or covariance in returns among securities. These are not subjects of any interest to them . . . The investors simply focus on two variables: price and value.[14]

In India, too, one could argue that for the majority of stocks, value investing (i.e., buying companies when they are inexpensive on P/E) makes sense. In fact, one can divide the Indian stock market into broadly three sets of companies:

TYPE A stocks comprise around 80–90 per cent of the Indian market. Such companies find it difficult to grow earnings over extended periods of time as they have no sustainable competitive advantages and hence no ability to generate a Return on Capital Employed (RoCE) in excess of the Cost of Capital (CoC). Lacking sustainable free cash flows, such companies struggle to invest in growing their businesses. Examples of such companies are India's telecom providers and its airlines—companies with never-ending volume growth but with no sustainable competitive advantages and hence no earnings growth.

If you assume that you make returns from investing in any company from two sources—either the P/E expands or the earnings expand—with Type A stocks, your only hope of making money is that the P/E expands (since the earnings are unlikely to expand). If you find a fund manager who can double the Type A company's P/E over a decade, your returns will compound at 7 per cent CAGR. If the fund manager you have found has mistimed his investment, i.e., he entered when the P/E was high (he wasn't a value investor) and exited when the P/E had halved, your return will be -7 per cent CAGR.

TYPE B stocks account for a further 5–10 per cent of the Indian market, and this segment includes good franchises like Maruti or HUL, which have meaningful competitive advantages. As a result, in most years, these companies will have an RoCE higher than the CoC. Reinvestment of the free cash flow will allow these companies to grow their business at around 10–12 per cent CAGR, i.e., the same rate as nominal GDP growth on a cross-cycle basis.

Here too, value investing works. If you can find a fund manager who enters Maruti Suzuki at 13x P/E and exits a decade later at 26x P/E, the stock would give you returns of around 18–19 per cent (10–12 per cent from earnings growth and 7 per cent from P/E doubling). If, on the other hand, your fund manager has mistimed your investment, i.e., he entered when the P/E was high (he wasn't a value investor) and exited when the P/E had halved, your return will be 3–5 per cent CAGR (10–12 per cent from earnings minus 7 per cent from P/E compression). With Type B stocks, a committed value investor like Warren Buffett can generate high-teens returns if he times his entry point well. In fact, this is exactly what Buffett's legend is built around.

If we were living in America (or in any other large economy, barring India), Type A & B stocks would form our entire investment universe. However, in the Indian stock market there exists a third subset of stocks—**Type C.**

This book is all about Type C stocks. Such stocks constitute less than 1 per cent of the Indian stock market (if measured by the number of stocks). So, why are we writing a book about a handful of companies which make up less than 1 per cent of the Indian stock market?

India is perhaps the only large economy where several industries are dominated by one or two players, and these dominant players make returns on capital employed (RoCE—earnings generated on each unit of capital employed on the balance sheet) that are significantly higher than the cost of capital (CoC) for several decades. For instance, it is not hard to find global players who dominate their industries—Walmart dominates US grocery retailing, Carrefour dominates French grocery retailing, Toyota dominates the mid-segment car market in Japan, Hanes dominates Europe's innerwear market. However, none of these companies makes RoEs substantially higher than their cost of equity. On the other hand, there are several industries in India where one or two companies not only have a dominant market share, but their RoCEs have also remained substantially above the cost of equity for decades in a row.

We can call these Indian companies—whose RoCEs are a million miles above their CoC for decades on end—**Type C**. The vast free cash flows that these firms generate decade after decade allow them to not only pay generous dividends (dividend yields for such firms tend to be 2–3 per cent) but also reinvest in growing the business. Earnings growth for such firms tends to be around 25 per cent per annum.

With a Type C firm, if our fund manager is able to get the timing of his entry and exit right, the results are spectacular: 25 per cent earnings growth + 7 per cent from doubling of P/E + 2 per cent from dividend yield = 34 per cent per annum return. However, since many of these firms are trading at optically high P/Es, let's assume that their P/Es halve over the next decade. Even then, these the Type C firms produce a return of 20 per cent (25 per cent earnings growth—7 per cent for P/E halving + 2 per cent dividend yield). Interestingly, even with P/Es halving over ten years, Type C firms produce returns similar to Type B firms with P/E doubling (20 per cent vs 17–19 per cent].

For 99 per cent of Indian stocks, value investing provides the only route to decent returns (in the mid-high teens). The challenge that India's Type C firms pose to Graham & Dodd's value investment paradigm can be understood in the context of the investment framework that these legends had laid out in *Security Analysis*.

The value of a firm is nothing more than its future cashflows (discounted appropriately). These future cashflows are nothing more than the gap between RoCE and CoC. When a firm or firms in any industry are earning a return on capital far higher than their cost of capital, they attract new players into the industry who also wish to earn attractive returns. The more the number of players, the greater the competitive intensity in the industry, which puts pressure on profitability and returns for all players, including the incumbents. As a result, the gap between the RoCE and CoC keeps narrowing. If, however, the gap between the RoCE and CoC does not close (say, because the Indian economy is not as competitive as the US economy or the Chinese economy)—as often happens with Type C companies in India—the future cash flows of such firms remain healthy and drive a high value for the firm.

Such firms can therefore command very high P/E multiples. As we have said before, less than 1 per cent of the stocks in the Indian market fall in this category! For the remainder of the investment universe in India—as in America—the rules of Graham and Doddsville can be successfully applied. In this book, we discuss why Type C firms exist in India, how you can spot them, and how much money you can make from them. The table below summarizes the taxonomy of Types A, B and C that we have outlined above.

Exhibit 6: Marcellus's ABC framework

Type of company	Decadal earnings Compounding	Returns if fund manager doubles P/E in 10 years	Returns if fund manager halves P/E in 10 years
'A' is for Airlines	0%	7%	-7%
'B' is for Buffett	12%	7% + 12% = 19%	12% - 7% = 5%
'C' is for CCP (e.g. Asian Paints, HDFC Bank)	25%	7% + 25% = 32%	25% - 7% = 18%

Source: Marcellus Investment Managers; all returns are in CAGR

KEY TAKEAWAYS

- Most investors in India who follow the common myths around investment in asset classes like real estate, gold and debt mutual funds, fail to beat the rate of inflation in their wealth-compounding.
- Whilst equities as an asset class are better wealth compounders compared with real estate, gold and debt and real estate, investment in equities is also plagued with similar problems as the other asset classes, in the context of investors taking on undue risk while building their equity portfolios.
- An equity investor in India needs to minimize four types of risks if she wants to generate steady and healthy investment returns—Accounting risk, Revenue risk, Profit risk and Liquidity risk.

- The 'Consistent Compounding' approach to investing in equities in India has three key elements—Credible Accounting, Competitive Advantage and Capital Allocation, which help investors generate healthy returns without having to take extra risk (or loading up on beta).

* * *

CHAPTER 2

What to Buy—Part 1: Accounting Quality

'Over the years, Charlie and I have observed many accounting-based frauds of staggering size. Few of the perpetrators have been punished; many have not even been censured. It has been far safer to steal large sums with a pen than small sums with a gun.'

—Warren Buffet[1]

Forty per cent of the stocks in the BSE500 as at end-December 2009 have since exited the index, resulting in enormous erosion of wealth for their shareholders, both during and after their exit. The primary drivers of these exits were shoddy corporate governance and poor capital allocation (the two are linked). While choosing a great stock is important, avoiding dubious companies is equally important if you must generate healthy investment returns, more particularly given the relative abundance of shady companies in India.

The key points we elaborate upon in this chapter are:

- Why evaluating account quality should be a central part of investment research and analysis.

- How to identify the key traits of fraudulent companies/ management; and
- What Marcellus's forensic framework for avoiding dubious companies is.

IDENTIFYING CREDIBLE ACCOUNTING: THE FIRST STEP IN CONSISTENT COMPOUNDING

Till 2008, Satyam Computer Services Ltd (Satyam) counted among the top Indian information technology services companies, in the same league as Infosys Technologies, TCS, Wipro and HCL Technologies. Over the five-year period from FY2003 to FY2008, Satyam's revenues had grown at a CAGR of 31 per cent (the third highest among the large listed IT peers) and profit after tax (PAT) at a CAGR of 34 per cent (the second highest). Then, in January 2009, B. Ramalinga Raju, promoter and chairman of Satyam, in a letter to the company's board, admitted to large-scale falsification of the company's financial results, including inflation of revenues and profits, understating of liabilities and inflation of cash and bank balances. The reported cash and bank balances as on 30 September 2008 were Rs 5,361 crore, while the actual amount was lower by 94 per cent, at just Rs 321 crore![2] According to investigative agencies, Raju ostensibly siphoned cash out from Satyam to buy land and properties in his personal name using many different means, including creation of fake employees who were paid salaries.[3] At one point, when it became difficult to manage and supress the widening gap between actual and reported cash balances, Raju sought to merge two of his family-owned entities, Maytas Properties and Maytas Infrastructure, with Satyam. The plan was to pay for the acquisitions using the fictitious cash on Satyam's books. Since the cash was to be paid to Raju and his family, it did not matter whether any actual payments were made. In return, the assets of the Maytas companies could be used to clean up the fraud.

From the day Satyam announced its decision to buy the two group companies, until a day before the admission of fraud, Satyam's stock had declined by about 21 per cent. The relatively insignificant price decline meant that even after a bizarre acquisition proposal, investors did not suspect anything seriously wrong. Then, on the day of Raju's admission of fraud, the Satyam stock fell by close to 78 per cent in a single day! Surely, many investors in the stock would have seen a significant erosion in their wealth. And they would not have expected this from the fourth largest IT services company in India, audited by a Big-Four audit firm, and which was, right until the day the fraud became public knowledge, part of the Bombay Stock Exchange's flagship Sensex index. The sudden evaporation of wealth, leaving investors very little time to respond, is the typical outcome of accounting frauds getting discovered.

One can see why, before we even think of making money from equities, it is absolutely critical to be positioned to avoid such snap losses. And that makes investing in companies with **Clean Accounts** the first pillar of Marcellus's investment philosophy.

WHY EVALUATING ACCOUNTING QUALITY IS CENTRAL TO INVESTING

1. FINANCIAL STATEMENTS FORM THE FOUNDATION OF THE INVESTOR'S EFFORTS TO EVALUATE AND VALUE COMPANIES

Financial statements provide the critical window to understanding and evaluating the operating performance, competitive strengths and health of a company. Financial statements also form the basis for making future projections about companies and valuing them. Hence, if the financial statements themselves are inaccurate, the whole edifice of the analysis can come crumbling down. Therefore, building confidence in the sanctity of the financial statements and the broader corporate governance of the company should be the starting point for any stock analysis.

2. THE MAJORITY OF LISTED COMPANIES IN INDIA GIVE A RAW DEAL TO THE MINORITY SHAREHOLDERS

~50 per cent of BSE500 constituents (as at Dec 2009) have not been able to generate 'positive' returns over CY2010–19[4]

Given that greed is a common human trait, financial misreporting has been occurring in companies across the world for decades. However, given the high proportion of Indian companies engaged in manipulating their financial statements, evaluating accounting quality is the single most important component of researching Indian stocks. This is amply demonstrated in the quantum of churn in the BSE500 Index—a premier index representing the top 500 companies by market capitalization in India.

Between June 2003 and June 2020, the annual churn in the BSE500 was close to 12 per cent, which means on an average, nearly sixty companies exited the index every year. The high churn ratio implies that most incumbents are unable to sustain their place in the index, making way for more deserving candidates.

A closer analysis of the stocks exiting the BSE500 over the last five to ten years indicates that most of these exits had little to do with business downturns but were mainly on account of corporate governance/accounting lapses and/or capital misallocation at these firms. If one were to look at the BSE500 as it stood in end-December 2009, of the 500 member stocks, only 267 remained in the index by end-December 2019. Nearly 40 per cent of the stocks have exited the index over the last ten completed calendar years for reasons other than corporate action (delisting, acquisition, etc). On their way out, most of these stocks saw significant erosion in their shareholders' wealth. On average, the companies which exited the index in 2019 had lost 30 per cent of their December 2009 market capitalization.

Exhibit 7: High churn in BSE500 with existing firms witnessing enormous erosion in market capitalization

BSE 500	Numbers	% of total	Comments
Total constituents in Dec 2009	500	100%	
Companies exited by Dec 2019	233	47%	About 32 of these companies exited due to delisting or acquisition by other companies
Companies remaining in Dec 2019	267	53%	
Return CAGR (Dec 09-19)*			Only 50 of these delivered 20%+ CAGR
> 15%	85	18%	
0% to 15%	145	31%	
0% to (-) 15%	95	20%	Nearly 120 of these lost 20% CAGR (many even ceased to exist)
> (-)15%	143	31%	

Source: BSE, Marcellus Investment Managers; * data is for 500 companies less thirty-two that exited the Index due to mergers, delisting, etc

While the number of companies that have generated enormous wealth for their shareholders is bound to be a handful, the number of companies that have destroyed shareholder wealth is perturbingly high in India. Only 18 per cent of the December 2009 BSE constituents generated compounded annual returns in excess of 15 per cent over December 2010–December 2019. On the other hand, 51 per cent of the constituents generated negative returns for the same period. Hence, an investor's ability to stay away from dubious names is equally if not more important than her ability to discover a great company.

Exhibit 8: Superstar stocks which imploded

	Market Capitalization (Rs m)			Share Price (Rs)		
Name	**Dec 2009**	**Dec 2020**	**Decline**	**Dec 2009**	**Dec 2020**	**Decline**
63 Moons Technologies Ltd.	6,177	373	-94%	1,344	82	-94%
Educomp Solutions Ltd.	6,773	47	-99%	714	4	-99%
Housing Development & Infrastructure Ltd.	12,473	349	-97%	361	7	-98%
Lanco Infratech Ltd.*	13,914	139	-99%	58	0	-99%
Suzlon Energy Ltd.	14,065	5,479	-61%	90	6	-93%

Source: Ace Equity, Marcellus Investment Managers; the returns mentioned above are before any dividend; Suzlon has raised equity multiple times and hence the market capitalization has not declined as much as the share price; *market capitalization and stock price of Lanco Infratech are as on 12 September 2018, the day it last traded on the stock exchanges

3. CORPORATE FRAUDS OFTEN LEAVE THE INVESTOR WITH LITTLE TIME TO REACT AND TO EXIT THE STOCK WITHOUT MATERIAL FINANCIAL LOSS

As discussed earlier, when a fraud starts unravelling, the stock in question sees significant erosion in price. While the absolute destruction in market cap is enormous, the pace of destruction in most cases is equally devastating. For instance, going back to the Satyam case, we find that Satyam Computer Services, an Indian blue-chip and an investor favourite, lost Rs 10,000 crore, or 78 per cent of its market capitalisation, in a single day on 7 January 2009, when then Chairman Raju made the sensational revelation about its fraudulent accounts. However, this is not an isolated example. Exhibit 9 shows that when the underlying fraudulent intentions of the management get exposed, it is a matter of days or at most a few months before the building comes crumbling down. Hence, more often than not, when a scam breaks, investors don't get enough time to exit the stock of the company in question, largely because everybody decides to rush for the exit at the same time.

Exhibit 9: When accounting issues emerge, investors get very little time to react

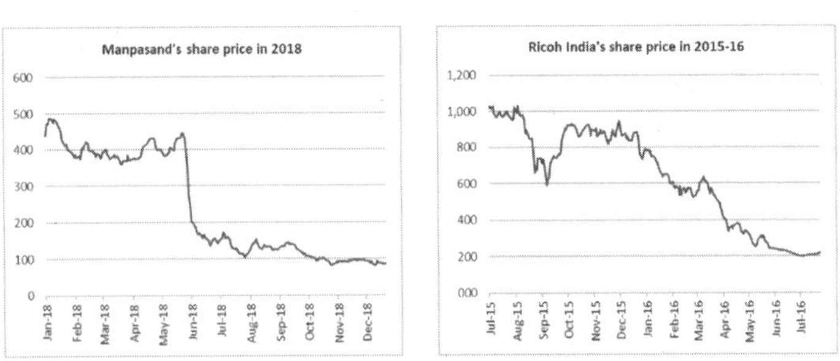

Source: NSE, Marcellus Investment Managers

When the fraud gets unearthed, the share prices decline sharply in most cases, as mentioned above. However, a similar or even more painful scenario is when the complete picture of the fraud is not yet out in the open but the accounting quality and practices of the company appear to be questionable. A typical feature of such stocks is that they appear to be significantly cheaper compared with their historical valuation multiples and relative to their peers. Gullible investors who are not able to recognize that such stocks are value traps keep buying the stock on every fall. However, the share price slide never stops, and what was perceived to be value hunting turns out be a falling knife.

CASE STUDY: RICOH INDIA

Ricoh India, a subsidiary of Japan's Ricoh, was a manufacturer and seller of printers and scanners. Through an acquisition in FY2011, Ricoh entered the IT services space, aiming to become a 'solutions' provider rather than just remain a hardware supplier. Over the subsequent four years, the company's revenues increased at a strong 53 per cent CAGR, from Rs 298 crore in FY2011 to Rs 1,638 crore in FY2015. Profitability, in the two years immediately following its entry in the IT services space, took a hit, with the company reporting a net loss of Rs 2.6 crore in FY2012 and Rs 1.3 crore in FY2013, which the management attributed to a weak Indian rupee. However, there was a turnaround in FY2014, when the company reported a net profit after tax of Rs 17.2 crore, which nearly doubled the next year to Rs 33.9 crore.*

The company's stock reacted favourably to the changing fortunes, increasing by approximately thirty times (about 2,900 per cent) in just twenty-eight months, from April 2013 to July 2015.^ The stock was, in market and investor parlance, a multi-bagger.

FY2015 saw the transition of statutory auditors at the company, in compliance with new regulations on the tenure of auditors. The new auditors for Ricoh India, BSR & Co. LLP, raised a number of concerns with the proposed financial results for the quarter and half year ending 30 September 2015. This led to an investigation by PricewaterhouseCoopers India (PwC) to resolve these concerns. In March 2016, some of Ricoh India's senior executives, including the managing director, chief financial officer and chief operating officer, were sent on leave. The managing director subsequently resigned in April 2016.[**]

The results for the September 2015 quarter were eventually filed only in May 2016, showing a net loss of Rs 147 crore. In November 2016, the FY2016 audited accounts were filed, showing a net loss of Rs 1,117.7 crore after an exceptional charge of Rs 693 crore, which included adjustments to profits of previous years. This adjustment was more than the total profit reported in FY2014 and FY2015 put together.

Exhibit 10: Ricoh India revenues and profits

Rs crore	FY11	FY12	FY13	FY14	FY15	FY16
Revenues	298	432	633	1,049	1,638	998
PAT	16	(3)	(1)	17	34	(1,118)
Net worth	132	881	123	140	169	(949)

Source: Marcellus Investment Managers; Ricoh India annual reports

That there was something amiss in Ricoh India's accounts could have been ascertained by using the methods highlighted in this chapter. For example, in FY2014 and FY2015, when the company reported a turnaround in profitability with profit after tax of Rs 17.2 crore and Rs 33.9 crore, respectively, cash flow from operations was a negative Rs 58.9 crore and a negative Rs 222.5 crore, respectively. Another check on debtor days would have revealed an increase in receivables, from 97 days of sales in FY2012 to 180 days in FY2015.

From its peak in July 2015, the Ricoh India stock had plummeted by close to 80 per cent by July 2016.^ It was suspended from trading on the Bombay Stock Exchange in December 2016. The company was eventually placed under Corporate Insolvency Resolution Process in May 2018.[***] A consortium of bidders was approved to acquire Ricoh India, and their proposal included an offer to pay public shareholders just Rs 52.49 crore in aggregate—much less than the value of their aggregate holding of Rs 228 crore in July 2016, when the stock had already wiped off 80 per cent of their wealth in the company. Unfortunately for minority investors, the selection of the consortium is being challenged, and they still await clarity on when, and how much of their investment they will be able to recover.[$]

Sources: * Ricoh India's annual reports for FY11–15
** Ricoh India's annual reports for FY16
*** Ricoh India's annual reports for FY18
^ Ace Equity and Marcellus Investment Managers
$ https://economictimes.indiatimes.com/news/company/corporate-trends/nclat-stops-consortium-buying-ricoh/articleshow/77400682.cms

KEY TRAITS OF A FRAUDULENT COMPANY/ MANAGEMENT

To build an effective fraud detection framework, the investor has to understand the modus operandi of fraudulent companies. Based on our collective experience of analysing the financial statements of thousands of companies over the last twelve years, we at Marcellus believe that the following are the most common traits of companies/managements engaging in accounting malpractices:

Exhibit 11: Some common tricks employed by companies to mispresent financial statements

Trait	Description
P&L reflects a different, and more often glossier, story than the balance sheet & cash flow statements	▪ The most common tool used to misrepresent financial statements, as it is relatively easy to manipulate income statement items like revenues, operating profits, etc. ▪ Also, the obsession of research analysts and investors with earnings, rather than the quality of earnings reflected in cash conversion, RoCE, etc., makes the P&L statement a common tool for misrepresentation of accounts
Promoters' interests outside of the listed entity	▪ Group companies involved in similar business as the listed company ▪ Extensive related-party transactions between the listed company and promoter-owned entities ▪ Listed entity used to support/finance promoter ventures ▪ Significant amounts of promoter holdings in the listed company are pledged, indicating stress in group companies ▪ Consistent reduction in promoters' shareholding in the company

Trait	Description
Off-balance sheet liabilities and complex holding structures	▪ Balance sheet of the listed company does not represent the true picture of liabilities/debt ▪ Holdings in step-down ventures deliberately structured to avoid consolidation of operationally weak/debt-laden investee companies ▪ Complex holding structures (for instance, a web of entities between standalone entity and operating subsidiaries) to create side pockets for the promoters
Company repeatedly engages investment bankers	▪ Frequently engaging in mergers and acquisitions ▪ Multiple rounds of fund-raise
A weak or less-than-ideal board of directors	▪ A weak board of directors or one stuffed with promoters' relatives and friends, indicating a lack of independent voices to question the promoters' decisions or judgement
Frequent changes in financial year-ends, auditors, chief financial officers	▪ Tell-tale signs of something fishy in the company's accounts

Source: Marcellus Investment Managers

We will discuss some of the specific case studies in detail in the subsequent sections.

MARCELLUS'S 3-LEVEL CHECK TO DETECT ACCOUNTING FRAUDS

Evaluating accounting quality and corporate governance is the cornerstone of Marcellus's investment process. This evaluation is covered in our research in three ways: Level 1 checks, where we use our forensic quantitative screens to rank companies on their accounting quality (we typically eliminate the companies which score low on our forensic model). Nearly 40 per cent of companies from broad-based stock exchange indices that we analyse are rejected by our quantitative screens.

The companies which make it through our forensic quantitative screens are the ones on which we conduct in-depth research and diligence. These companies are subject to two further levels of forensic checks: Level 2 checks, where we conduct in-depth reading of the financial statements to identify some of the traits mentioned in the preceding section; and finally, Level 3 checks, where we also try to gauge promoter/management integrity by doing primary data checks on the companies, wherein we speak with former employees, customers and suppliers of the company.

LEVEL 1 CHECKS: MARCELLUS'S CLEAN ACCOUNTING MODEL

Our first line of defence is our proprietary forensic accounting model. We have developed a model, using a set of twelve ratios, that helps us grade companies on their accounting quality. The selection of these ratios has been inspired by Howard M. Schilt's legendary book on forensic accounting, *Financial Shenanigans*.[5] This book draws upon case studies of accounting frauds (involving not only well-known frauds like Enron and WorldCom, but also numerous lesser known cases of accounting trickery), and from the lessons learnt, creates techniques for detecting frauds in financial statements.

Our twelve forensic accounting ratios cover checks across the key components of financial statements, including the profit and loss account (for revenue or earnings manipulation), balance sheet (for incorrect representation of assets and liabilities), cash pilferage and audit quality. Some of the key ratios and the rationale for using them are shown in the exhibit below.

Exhibit 12: Marcellus's forensic ratios to evaluate accounting quality of non-financial companies

Ratio		Rationale/remarks
Income statement checks	Cash flow from operations (CFO) as % of EBITDA	To check aggressive revenue and earning recognition practices
	Year-on-year volatility in depreciation rates	Being a non-cash charge, it is easy to manipulate earnings by changing depreciation policy and/or rates
	Change in reserves & surplus explained by the profit/loss for the year and dividends	To check direct knock-offs from balance sheet instead of routing through P&L
Balance sheet checks	Yield on cash and cash equivalents	To check cash balance misstatement or cash mis-utilization
	Contingent liabilities as % of net worth (for the latest available year)	Indicative of the extent of off-balance sheet risks
Cash theft checks	Capital work in progress to gross block[6]	High ratio may indicate unsubstantiated capex
	Free cash flow (cash flow from operations + cashflow from investing) to median revenues	To check if cash generated by business is being siphoned off or whether reported revenue/earnings are believable
Auditor objectivity checks	Growth in auditors' remuneration to growth in revenues	Faster growth in auditors' remuneration vis-à-vis company's operations raises concerns surrounding auditors' objectivity

Source: Marcellus Investment Managers

Using the sort of ratios shown in Exhibit 12, we first rank stocks on each of the twelve ratios and then give a final decile-based pecking order for them on the basis of accounting quality—with D1 being the best on accounting quality and D10 being the worst. The top five deciles, i.e., D1 to D5, are generally where companies with good accounting quality are found. Hence, we call D1 to D5 the 'Zone of Quality', whereas the bottom 30 per cent, i.e., D8 to D10, generally represents companies with questionable accounting practices. We have labelled these bottom deciles the 'Zone of Thuggery'. Companies in the D6 and D7 deciles lie somewhere in the centre of the quality gradient and are also best avoided.

OUR FORENSIC FRAMEWORK HAS PROVEN TO BE AN EFFECTIVE PREDICTIVE TOOL

There is a strong correlation between accounting quality, as indicated by our forensic model, and shareholder returns. For instance, the 'Zone of Quality' (the top five deciles) has outperformed the 'Zone of Thuggery' (the bottom three deciles) by a significant 7 per cent per annum over CY2016–20.

Exhibit 13: Strong correlation between accounting quality and shareholder returns

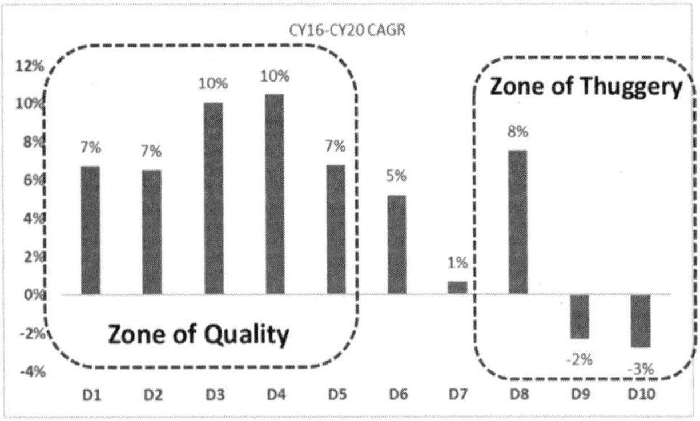

Source: Marcellus Investment Managers, Ace Equity

Exhibit 14: Quality wins, and wins big over the long term

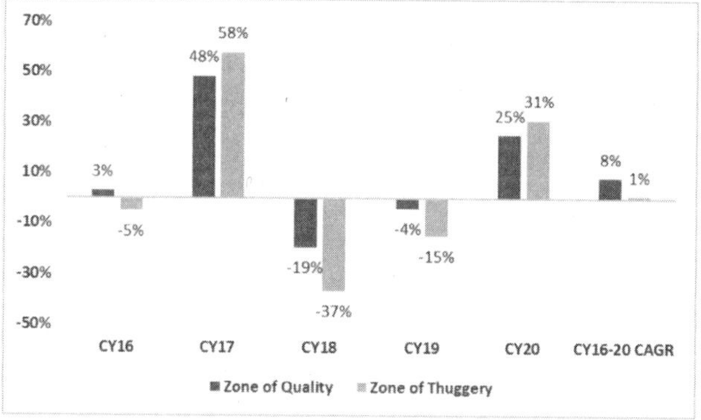

Source: Marcellus Investment Managers, Ace Equity

There is another way to understand the effectiveness of this forensic model—there are around fifty-three companies (out of the BSE 500) that constantly featured in the D8 to D10 rankings in our accounting model for the years FY2015–19. Over CY2016–20, these companies have on an average delivered negative CAGR of 14 per cent, against the benchmark BSE500's 11 per cent, i.e., an underperformance of nearly 25 per cent p.a.

Exhibit 15: Companies consistently falling in 'Zone of Thuggery' significantly underperform

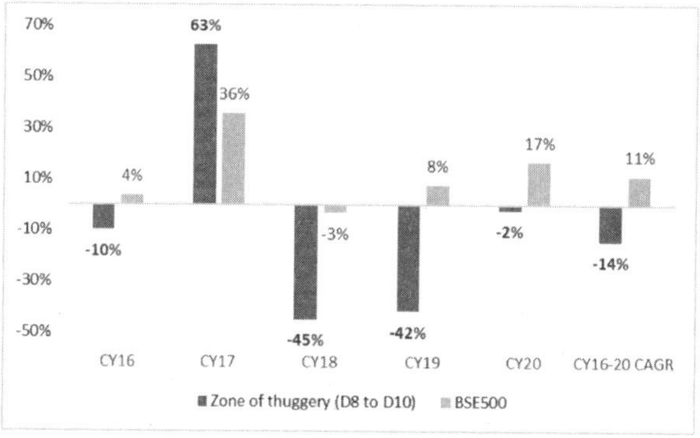

Source: Marcellus Investment Managers, Ace Equity

CASE STUDY: DECCAN CHRONICLE

Deccan Chronicle Holdings Ltd.(DCHL) started a newspaper publishing business in 1938, first with the weekly *Deccan Chronicle*, followed by the daily *Deccan Chronicle* in 1947. Over the years, the company went on to emerge as the leading English daily in Hyderabad and undivided Andhra Pradesh (AP), and one of the largest selling English newspapers across India. The company, then run by brothers T. Venkatarram Reddy (chairman) and T. Vinayaka Ravi Reddy (managing director), had a successful IPO in late 2004, raising Rs 148.6 crore. In 2005, DCHL acquired a majority stake (67 per cent) in *Asian Age* newspaper for Rs 17.1 crore (it already owned 23 per cent before). In FY06, it acquired 100 per cent equity share capital of Odyssey India Ltd (which was partly owned by the promoters), which owned a chain of bookstores, for a total cash consideration of Rs 61.35 crore. Further, it bought the Hyderabad franchise of the Indian Premier League (IPL) for US$107 million* in 2008 (the franchise, named Deccan Chargers, would go on to win the IPL title in 2009). While Odyssey's and Deccan Chargers's financial performances were not encouraging (both were loss-making in FY10), it was more than eclipsed by the strong performance of the core newspaper business (revenue and PAT CAGR of 40 per cent and 57 per cent, respectively, over FY2004–10 and a healthy consolidated RoCE, pre-tax, of 27 per cent in FY2010).

DHCL's fortunes started reversing soon thereafter, with PAT plummeting by 38 per cent in FY2011. The company attributed this to weak macros, political uncertainties in Andhra Pradesh (due to the Telangana agitation), high raw material prices and the merger of subsidiaries, viz., Odyssey

India, Deccan Chargers and Netlink Technologies. In retrospect, the weak FY11 performance proved to be a relatively small setback in the context of the events that were to unfold. In late July 2012, the promoters disclosed that they had pledged 54 per cent of their DCHL shareholding, confirming their heavy indebtedness, the news of which had been doing the rounds in the media for some time. This coincided with the resignation of Managing Director N.K. Krishnan around the same time. Further, almost all the independent directors of the company resigned in December 2012. It became clear that there were serious issues in the company/group.

After extending its year-end from March 2012 to September 2012, DCHL finally published its financial results (no results had been declared since the quarterly results for December 2011) in early 2013, reporting a massive net loss of Rs 1,040.4 crore for the eighteen months ended September 2012, and declaring ~Rs 4,000 crore worth of debt—a ~5x increase from the FY11-end levels. In the annual report that followed, the company attributed the large operating losses to the launch of newspaper editions in other parts of south India (beyond its stronghold in AP) and the ensuing revenue-cost mismatches. Further, 'intangible assets under development' worth Rs 2,905.3 crore pertaining to the acquisition of brands from undisclosed parties had been created, with a corresponding increase in liabilities (explaining the jump in debt)—all accounting entries having the effect of bringing off-balance sheet liabilities into the books. The poor financial results coincided with controversies in Deccan Chargers, where a player, in 2012, was accused of spot-fixing scams, and the franchise was terminated for failing to furnish the requisite bank guarantee.

DCHL's shares were suspended for trading from 23 January 2013, but by then the company's share price had already fallen by ~97 per cent from its peak in March 2010.

While identifying off-balance sheet liabilities is one of the toughest parts of forensic accounting analysis—some of the red flags raised by DCHL's accounts/governance practices could have been useful: (i) Sub-par capital allocation decisions, such as buying Odyssey India which was partly promoter-owned at relatively high valuation multiples (price paid per store at Rs 4.7 crore vs Shoppers Stop's acquisition of Crossword at a relatively lower valuation of Rs 1.32 crore around that time), and investment in Deccan Chargers, a clearly unrelated business; (ii) in FY08, both promoters 'gifted'** one-third of their shares each to Executive Director P.K. Iyer, making him an equal owner (20 per cent). In hindsight, this unprecedented transaction clearly warranted much closer scrutiny; (iii) DCHL's superior P&L, but much weaker balance sheet compared with those of its peers—DCHL's standalone EBITDA margin averaged 45 per cent over FY06–10, more than twice peers DB Corp's 20 per cent and Jagran Prakashan's 21 per cent. On the other hand, DCHL's average gross block turnover over FY06-10 was only 1.1x vs DB Corp's nearly 3x and Jagran's 2x.

Sources: DCHL Annual Reports

* https://www.business-standard.com/article/beyond-business/twist-in-the-tale-115022701227_1.html

** https://www.thenewsminute.com/article/deccan-chronicles-vc-arrested-timeline-when-trouble-started-media-house

CASE STUDY: MANPASAND BEVERAGES

Manpasand Beverages started off with its first product, Mango Sip, in 1997. The company chose to focus on the relatively underpenetrated rural and semi-urban areas, and in later years expanded its product portfolio to include fruit drinks in other flavours, as well as carbonated fruit drinks.*

Manpasand had marquee private equity investors, like SAIF Partners and Aditya Birla Private Equity Fund, who invested Rs 116 crore in the company in FY2012 and FY2015. The company went public in 2015, raising Rs 400 crore, mainly to fund expansion plans and repay debt. In the run-up to the IPO, the company had reported extremely strong financial results, with sales over FY2012–14 (FY2012 from December 2010 to March 2012) showing a CAGR of 85 per cent, EBITDA showing a CAGR of 81 per cent and PAT a CAGR of 83 per cent.*

All seemed hunky dory, until the company's auditors, Deloitte, Haskins and Sells, quit midway through the audit of FY2018, citing that the management was not sharing 'significant information'**. The company's share price fell 20 per cent on the day it announced the news. Manpasand then appointed another firm, Mehra & Goel, as statutory auditors, who certified the FY2018 annual results.

In May 2019, the company's managing director and CFO were arrested by the GST department after results of an investigation found evidence of tax evasion. In searches conducted at various locations, the authorities discovered that several fake business units were set up by the company across the country, and that purchase and sale transactions were showed between these units for claiming input tax credit. Such fake transactions amounted to Rs 300 crore, resulting in a fraudulent input tax credit claim of Rs 40 crore.[@] In the twelve months between the resignation of Deloitte and the GST-related arrests, Manpasand's market capitalization had declined by 84 per cent. Following the arrests, four independent directors of the company resigned within the same week. Two months later, in July 2019, the statutory auditors, Mehra & Goel, resigned, and another couple of months later, the company secretary quit too.

Meanwhile, to pay the GST dues, Manpasand's promoter, Dhirendra Singh, approached Finquest Financial Solutions Pvt Ltd (Finquest), a financial services company, for a loan of Rs 100 crore. A forensic audit commissioned by Finquest is alleged to have found revenues inflated by 7.6 times. After an acrimonious meeting of the board of directors in September 2019 on the matter, Mr Singh filed a criminal complaint against Finquest, accusing them of a hostile takeover bid.[^]

In October 2019, Batliboi & Purohit, the auditors appointed in place of Mehra & Goel, also resigned. Among the reasons cited by Batliboi & Purohit for their resignation was the denial of entry to their audit team members to the company's factory at Vadodara for conducting the statutory audit.[$]

The company's shares have been suspended from trading on the stock exchanges, and their last recorded market price was on 29 June 2020. At a market capitalization of a mere Rs 70.3 crore, the company has lost 99 per cent of its value from its peak market capitalization of Rs 5,567 crore recorded in January 2018.

The question is, could a forensic analysis have foreseen the events that subsequently unfolded in the case of Manpasand? The answer is, yes. In December 2016, 2Point2 Capital, a SEBI-registered provider of portfolio management services (PMS) wrote a detailed note on Manpasand, raising concerns on the reported financials, using a mix of accounting, governance and primary data checks.[#]

Sources:

[*] Manpasand's Prospectus
[**] https://www.bloombergquint.com/business/auditor-quit-as-manpasand-beverages-didnt-share-significant-information
[@] https://www.moneycontrol.com/news/business/how-a-rs-40-crore-gst-fraud-unfolded-at-manpasand-beverages-4049591.html
[^] https://www.businesstoday.in/current/corporate/is-manpasand-beverages-the-biggest-corporate-fraud-post-satyam/story/383726.html
[$] Letter dated 3rd October 2019 from Batliboi & Purohit to Manpasand's Board of Directors filed with Bombay Stock Exchange
[#] https://2point2capital.com/blog/index.php/a2016/12/06/the-curious-case-of-manpasand-beverages/

LEVEL 2 CHECKS: FURTHER ACCOUNTING AND CORPORATE GOVERNANCE CHECKS

These checks are over and above the forensic screens and are usually employed during our deep-dive diligence on individual companies. Our forensic framework helps us weed out companies with dubious accounting quality. It also helps us identify the key accounting red flags for a company. That being said, there are several qualitative aspects of accounting and corporate governance which our forensic model may not be able to pick up due to lack of uniformity in data across companies, or where there is subjective judgement involved. Such areas can only be evaluated through a deep dive into historical financial statements and through primary data checks around management integrity.

We have developed the following checklist for deeper accounting and corporate governance checks beyond the forensic model. This checklist should form an essential part of qualitative assessment of any stock.

Exhibit 16: Some deep dive forensic and corporate governance checks beyond the quantitative screens

Advanced accounting checks	Corporate governance checks
Comparative common-sized income statement vs peers to analyse any significant divergence in P&L items vs peers	Related-party transactions and their significance
Comparative Dupont analysis vs peers	Other business interests of promoters (any significant stress in those businesses, etc.)
R&D capitalization vs charge to P&L	M&A with promoter-owned entities
Goodwill as % of net worth	Significant litigation surrounding promoters
Frequent changes in auditors	Promoter family structure, succession, etc.
Any significant adverse comment in the auditor's report	Pledge of promoter shareholding
Any significant portion of company's operations (such as subsidiaries) not audited by the principal statutory auditor	Insider buying and selling
Quality of audit committee (whether chaired by an independent director)	Remuneration to promoters
Frequent changes in accounting periods	Frequency and necessity of equity dilution

Source: Marcellus Investment Managers

LEVEL 3 CHECKS: EXTENSIVE DILIGENCE THROUGH PRIMARY DATA CHECKS

The next level of accounting quality checks is assessment of the integrity of a company's promoters and management, through detailed discussions with our primary data sources. We seek corroboration of the picture reflected by the company's financials with the primary data sources who understand the company and have worked with or dealt with it. Such sources include consumers of the company's products, their channel partners, raw material suppliers, competitors, etc. This is especially important in the case of small caps with a relatively shorter operating history and where the propensity to fudge accounts is high. Similarly, visiting the branches of the company, visiting the factories or even a plant under construction helps build conviction regarding the company's financials.

CASE STUDY OF DEEP-DIVE FORENSIC ACCOUNTING: COX & KINGS

Exhibit 17: C&K India—a fateful ride for the company's minority shareholders and lenders

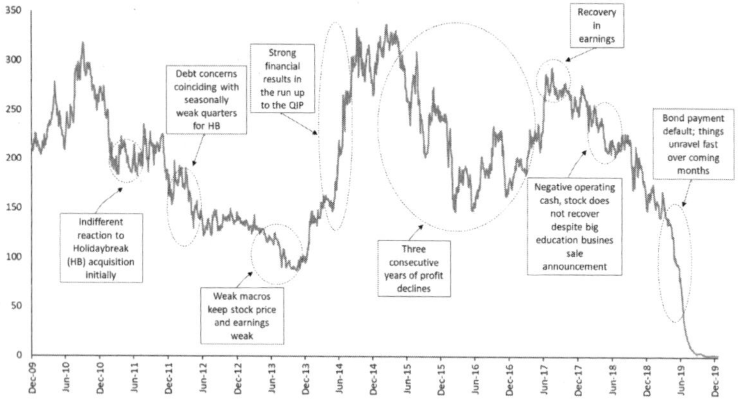

Source: NSE, Marcellus Investment Managers

As is evident from the share price chart shown above, Cox & Kings (C&K) was listed for about ten years before disaster struck. Throughout these ten years, i.e., from end-2009 to mid-2019, most participants in the Indian stock market regarded C&K as a professionally managed listed entity with a solid business. Yet, for most of this period, our forensic accounting score on this stock was D10, i.e., the stock was in the bottom-most decile in our forensic accounting model. So, why did our forensic accounting models start flashing red so early on in case of C&K? To explain that, let us go 250 years back, to the time when the East India Company was establishing itself in India.

A CHEQUERED HISTORY

CENTURIES OF EXISTENCE UNDER BRITISH OWNERSHIP . . .

The origin of Cox & Kings dates to 1758, when Lord Ligonier, Colonel of the 1st Foot Guards, appointed Richard Cox as his regimental agent for handling the affairs, pay and sundry obligations of the officers stationed overseas. Over the nineteenth century, the firm became agents and bankers to large parts of the British Army. In 1909, Cox & Co. was incorporated as an unlimited company under the Companies (Consolidation) Act, 1908 in London. In October 1922, Cox & Co. absorbed the business of Henry S King & Co., a small bank with Indian interests, following which the name Cox & Kings came into being. In February 1923, the company's banking business was taken over by Lloyds Bank Limited. In 1960, Lloyds Bank sold this acquired business to National and Grindlays Bank Limited (later renamed Grindlays Bank in 1975). In the year 1980, Grindlays Bank Limited divested its non-banking activities because of government regulations. This interest in the travel business was bought by two British citizens, A.B.M. Good and John Norman Romney Barber, who continued to operate it as a specialized tour operator.

. . . BEFORE THE KERKARS BECAME OWNERS OF THE INDIAN BUSINESS UNDER CONTROVERSIAL CIRCUMSTANCES

In 1980, the Reserve Bank of India (RBI) permitted Cox & Kings (Agents) Limited to transfer its Indian business to Cox and Kings (India) Limited (C&K India). In consideration of this purchase of business, C&K India issued 40 per cent of its outstanding shares to Cox & Kings (Agents) Limited. However, as a condition for Indianization imposed by the RBI, nearly 60 per cent of the shares were issued and allotted to certain resident Indians (57 per cent) and to the Staff Gratuity Trust Fund (3 per cent). There is no document available with us which lays out the exact names of the allotees and numbers of shares issued to them. However, on the basis of analysis of various news articles, subsequent shareholding patterns and share transfers, it seems the bulk of the allotments were made to certain subsidiaries of Indian Hotels Limited (part of the Tata/Taj Group), Ajit Kerkar (then chairman of Indian Hotels and the man credited with expanding the Indian Hotels empire in India) and other executives of Indian Hotels. News articles say that while Indian Hotels was one of the largest clients of C&K India, it did not outright acquire a majority stake in C&K India, due to restrictions under the prevailing competition rules of the time (Monopoly & Restrictive Trade Practices Act).[7]

Nevertheless, Ajit Kerkar and his family (his son Peter, daughter Urrshila and wife Elizabeth, first became shareholders via share transfers from some of the original allottees in 1981) increased their grip on C&K India over the years through share transfers from the original allottees and subscription to renunciations in multiple rounds of rights issues. However, in 1997, the Tata Group (under Ratan Tata, who had ousted Ajit Kerkar from Indian Hotels) claimed that the Kerkars increased their control in C&K India through dubious means. It was also alleged that C&K India unduly benefited from many long-term business deals with Taj Group companies (including Indian Hotels), at terms which were prejudicial to the latter.[8]

THE TULIP STAR CONTROVERSY

After his exit from Indian Hotels in 1997, Ajit Kerkar moved towards building a hotel empire (his children Peter Kerkar and Urrshila Kerkar were largely running the show at C&K India). For this the following group companies (collectively referred to as Tulip Group hereon) were used:

- Tulip Star Hotels Limited (renamed from Cox & Kings Finance Limited in September 2000), a listed company;
- Tulip Hospitality Services Private Limited (a company newly incorporated in September 2000; name changed to V Hotels Limited in November 2006); and
- Tulip Hotels Private Limited, incorporated in 1997.

The shareholding and inter-se holding between the three companies stood as below:

Exhibit 18: Tulip Group holding structure as on 31 July 2009

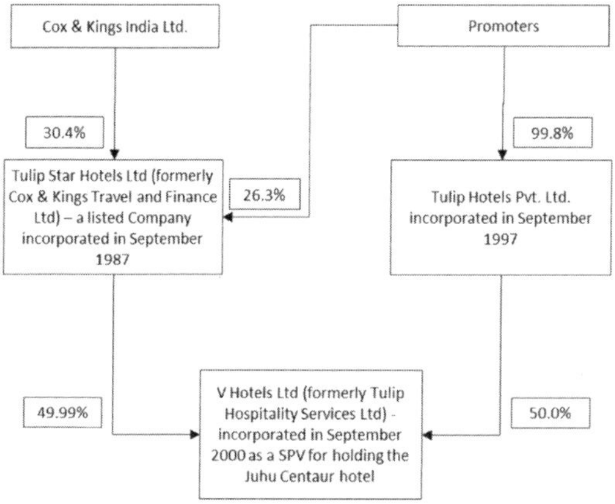

Source: C&K India IPO prospectus 2009, Marcellus Investment Managers

In 2001, in a highly contentious deal, the Kerkars (through Tulip Hospitality Services) were awarded the Centaur Hotel in Juhu, Mumbai, under the disinvestment process of the NDA government for about Rs 153 crore—considered a throwaway price for a sea-facing luxury hotel property with more than 350 rooms (it was owned by Hotel Corporation of India, a subsidiary of Air India). The deal escaped scrutiny during the initial years. However, after the new UPA government took charge in New Delhi in 2004, the Comptroller & Auditor General (CAG)'s report on this transaction in May 2005 raised several questions. This included the low reserve price (arrived at through questionable valuation assumptions), the absence of any financial bidder other than the Tulip Group (out of a total of twenty parties who initially submitted bids, only one eventually made the financial bid), the lack of adequate financial evaluation of the bidder (the deal was to be financed by Tulip through a bank loan, which had not been firmed up at the time of the bid submission) and multiple extensions granted for payment, that too without the charging of interest (the bid amount was to be deposited by 22 December 2001; however, extensions were granted until the amount was finally paid on 11 March 2002). The central government ordered a Central Bureau of India (CBI) investigation in July 2005.

In 2003, as its losses started to mount, the Tulip Group entered into a series of agreements with Nirmal Lifestyles Limited, granting the latter the licence to develop a shopping mall in the basement, ground floor and first floor of the Centaur property. However, due to non-receipt of approval from the consortium of banks with whom the property was mortgaged, the developments proposed under the agreements could not proceed. Both parties went into protracted legal proceedings, which are yet to reach finality.

Separately, in March 2005, Tulip Group entered into an agreement with Siddhivinayak Realities Pvt. Ltd. (a joint venture between the Vikas Oberoi-run Oberoi Constructions and Shahid Balwa and Vinod Goenka, co-promoters of DB Realty Limited) for sale of the Centaur property for about Rs 349.06 crore. Around Rs 73 crore in initial payment was received by Tulip Group under this deal. However, with the central government ordering a CBI inquiry into the acquisition of Centaur in July 2005, the proposed buyer insisted on a clean chit from the CBI to make further payments. Again, this matter went into legal proceedings and is currently pending closure.

Whilst the CBI enquiry subsequently exonerated the Centaur disinvestment process in 2008, there were multiple attempts to sell the property over the years. However, the pending legal proceedings impeded the sale of the property at every juncture, resulting in mounting losses for the Tulip Group companies over the years.

Exhibit 19: Tulip Group Companies' huge losses over the years

Profit/(loss) After Tax (Rs crore) Cumulative	FY06-10	FY11-15	FY16-19
Tulip Star Hotels Ltd.	15.5	(22.5)	(25.7)
Tulip Hotels Pvt. Ltd.*	(20.0)	(7.7)	(1.2)
V Hotels Ltd	(176.4)	(383.7)	(170.9)
Total	**(180.9)**	**(414.0)**	**(197.8)**

Source: Ministry of Corporate Affairs, Marcellus Investment Managers; *financials available only till FY2017 for Tulip Hotels Pvt. Ltd., and hence figures shown under column FY2016–19 are only for FY2016 and FY2017

DESPITE THE MANY CONTROVERSIES, PETER AND URRSHILA KERKAR HAD STEERED C&K INDIA TO A RESPECTABLE SIZE BY 2009

Cutting back to C&K India, the dispute with the Tata Group faded over time, with Indian Hotels completely exiting their stake in C&K India by end-2007. Further, the controversies surrounding Ajit Kerkar in the case of Tulip did not impact the performance of C&K India, which was essentially run by his children Peter and Urrshila. C&K India was overall headed by Peter Kerkar (based out of London), who had joined its London office in 1986 as a young executive and had graduated to become an executive director in 1994. Peter was credited with turning around the business by taking hard decisions, such as closing the cargo business and streamlining operations and strategy. On the other hand, his sister Urrshila was in charge of the Indian operations. She is credited with the successful foray into the outbound travel business (i.e., Indians travelling abroad), which was helped by Indian families' rising wealth, alongside their fondness for visiting European or American locations where many song-and-dance sequences in Bollywood movies have been shot.

In 2007, C&K India went on to acquire Cox & Kings Limited UK (CKUK, which was its original parent, with ownership of 40 per cent in C&K India at the time of its inception in 1980; this stake had come down significantly over the years due to renunciation of rights). C&K India also acquired CKUK's wholly-owned subsidiaries Cox and Kings (Japan) Limited and Cox and Kings Travel Ltd. Further, between 2006 and 2009, the company also made a series of acquisitions of small- to mid-sized companies viz., UK-based Clearmine Limited, Australia-based Tempo Holidays Pty Ltd., visa processing company Quoprro Global Services Pvt. Ltd. and East India Travel Company Inc., a US-based company.

By the end of FY2009 (the last completed financial year before the IPO), the consolidated 'net' revenues of the company were close to Rs 286.9 crore and its adjusted net profit at about Rs 62.8 crore. Just before the IPO, the Kerkars directly and indirectly owned close to 78 per cent of the company's outstanding share capital (an additional 6.4 per cent stake was held by ABM Good).

Exhibit 20: By FY09, C&K India was amongst the biggest and most profitable Indian travel companies

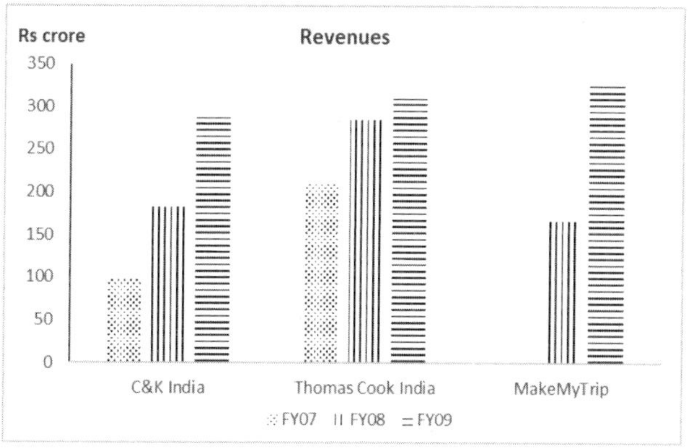

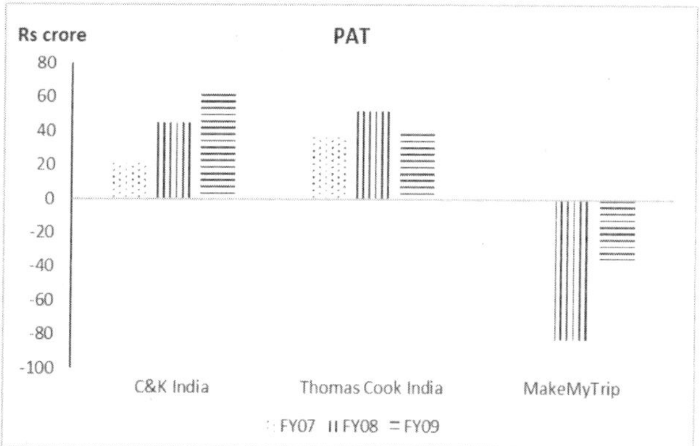

Source: Ace Equity, Companies, Marcellus Investment Managers (Note: Thomas Cook has December year ending and hence CY2006 for Thomas Cook = FY2007 for other companies and so on. Thomas Cook had a fourteen-month period for the year ending December 2006, which has been annualized in the above chart.)

THE BIG LEAP . . .

Over the next three years (FY2010–12), C&K India displayed exponential growth relative to what was seen in the preceding three decades under the Kerkars. In November 2009, the company successfully concluded its initial public offer, raising Rs 509.85 crore (before issue expenses) by diluting a ~29 per cent stake. The 2009 IPO was oversubscribed more than six times. This was followed up by a US$65 million (Rs 304 crore before issue expenses) GDR issue in August 2010. By FY2011-end, the company had a net cash surplus of Rs 304.4 crore owing to these two equity issues (unutilized cash of Rs 1,157 crore and gross debt of Rs 852.6 crore).

Then, on 27 July 2011, C&K India announced the big-bang acquisition of European holiday specialist Holidaybreak Plc. for an all-cash equity consideration of GBP323 million (~Rs 2,770.7 crore). This price was at a nearly 36 per cent premium to Holidaybreak's then market price (the company was listed on the London Stock Exchange). Besides the equity cash consideration, C&K India also assumed the outstanding debt of Holidaybreak, totalling about GBP132 million (Rs 1,132.3 crore), pushing up the total enterprise value of the acquisition to GBP455 million or Rs 3,906.7 crore.

While C&K India's pursuit of an inorganic strategy was known (it was a stated objective of the IPO and subsequent GDR issues), the Holidaybreak acquisition was one that was much larger in relative size and, moreover, was a leveraged transaction. Holidaybreak generated an EBITDA of GBP41 million (Rs 289.6 crore, based on the average GBP-INR rate) in year ended September 2010. Compared to this, C&K was relatively a smaller entity, with consolidated EBITDA of Rs 222.7 crore in FY2011. Similarly, the Holidaybreak acquisition was concluded at an enterprise value of Rs 3,906.7 crore—nearly 9x the enterprise value of C&K India at the time the acquisition was announced. While the bulk of the equity cash consideration was paid by taking on debt, the existing debt of Holidaybreak also added to the overall debt burden. The result of this was that from a cash surplus company at FY2011-end, C&K India's net debt-equity shot up to 3.1x as at FY2012-end.

Exhibit 21: C&K India's debt shot up significantly since FY2012 when it acquired Holidaybreak

C&K India (Consolidated Rs crore)	FY10	FY11	FY12	FY13	FY14
Gross debt	507	853	4,699	4,692	5,586
Cash	616	1,157	1,042	1,293	1,403
Net debt/ (cash)	(109)	(304)	3,656	3,399	4,184
Equity (including minority interest)	810	1,208	1,192	1,868	2,575
Gross debt equity (x)	0.6	0.7	3.9	2.5	2.2
Net debt equity (x)	(0.1)	(0.3)	3.1	1.8	1.6

Source: Ace Equity, Companies, Marcellus Investment Managers

. . . AND THEN THE BUST

In the years that followed, the company simply could not get out of this debt trap despite multiple rounds of equity raises (at both C&K India and the subsidiaries) and the sale of many of Holidaybreak's acquired businesses. This was further accentuated by long periods of weak earnings performance. The gross debt equity stood at 0.9x and the net debt equity at 0.5x at FY2018-end.

On 27 June 2019, the company defaulted on a scheduled repayment of Rs 150 crore worth of commercial paper, despite having sufficient cash balance in the books (FY2018-end reported cash and liquid investments were to the tune of

Rs 1,667.6 crore). This was followed by a series of defaults in the subsequent months. In October 2019, the company's CFO, Anil Khandelwal, resigned. In the same month, the National Company Law Tribunal (NCLT) admitted a petition to commence insolvency proceedings against C&K, bringing to an end the centuries-old journey of Cox and Kings, including about forty years under the Kerkars. This was followed by Peter Kerkar's arrest by the Enforcement Directorate in November 2020.

From FY2009 to FY2018, the company had raised net borrowings (net of repayments) to the tune of Rs 2,493.8 crore and equity (through IPO, GDR and QIP of C&K and sale of minority stakes in subsidiaries) to the tune of Rs 3,432 crore (before issue expenses). As the company was put under insolvency, these lenders were left unpaid while the equity shareholders would be able to recover their investment only if and when all other creditors have been paid.

Exhibit 22: C&K's internal accruals could generate only a fraction of its total cash needs, resulting in over-reliance on debt and equity

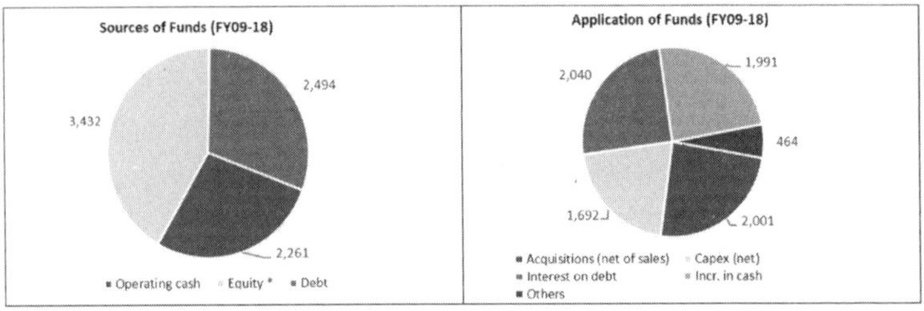

Source: Company, Marcellus Investment Managers; *equity above includes sale of minority stake in subsidiaries

THE MODUS OPERANDI

It can be argued that the company's downfall was a result of capital misallocation, as it could never come out of the debt emanating from the Holidaybreak acquisition. However, an analysis of the company's financials suggests that the company employed creative accounting tricks and questionable corporate governance practices that were, surprisingly, ignored by both lenders and equity investors. Specifically, the company seems to have inflated its revenues, profits and assets (using related-party transactions as one of the tools), used this misrepresented picture to raise money from lenders/investors and also made use of the complex group structure to siphon off the money.

We try to capture some of the key red flags from our analysis:

LESS THAN IDEAL DISCLOSURE OF REVENUES AND COSTS

There are two methods generally followed by companies in the business of tours and travels, forex and visa processing agency businesses, for recording/disclosing revenues and costs. One method (the 'gross basis' method) is to disclose both revenues and costs on tour packages/forex transactions separately (i.e., including tickets, forex, etc., in revenues as well as the cost of goods sold). The other method (the 'net basis' method) is to disclose only the net commissions on tour packages/forex transactions (thus the cost of goods sold will be netted off from the revenues and only the net amount will be disclosed as revenues). Amongst the large travel companies, while C&K, Thomas Cook and Hogg Robinson followed the 'net basis' method, Kuoni and MakeMyTrip followed the 'gross basis' method. While being perfectly compliant from an accounting perspective, recording revenue on a net basis makes discerning the profitability, working capital days and the fixed asset turnover ratios of the company difficult. This became particularly challenging in the case of C&K India, given: (i) the balance sheet items, such as trade receivables, were disclosed on a gross basis (even though the P&L was on a net basis); (ii) there was no proforma disclosure of gross revenues anywhere in the financial statements. However, this net method of revenue disclosure changed with the onset of IND-AS, which necessitated disclosure of gross revenues and costs.

The company's cash conversion was very weak, raising questions about the genuineness of the operating profits.

Irrespective of the revenue disclosure methods (pre- and post-IND-AS), C&K's conversion of operating profits to operating cash flows remained extremely weak throughout the last ten years of its existence. From FY2011 to FY2018, cumulative EBITDA to operating cash (before tax) conversion was only about 60 per cent.

Exhibit 23: C&K India's clear mismatch between the level of operating profits and operating cash

Consolidated cash flow (Rs crore)	**FY11**	**FY12**	**FY13**	**FY14**	**FY15**	**FY16**	**FY17**	**FY18**	**FY11–18**
EBITDA	223	167	718	890	1,011	822	688	901	5,420
(Incr)/decr in working capital	(81)	(353)	(373)	(18)	(387)	59	(441)	(663)	(2,256)
Trade & Other receivables	(113)	(60)	(191)	(203)	(77)	(308)	(426)	(423)	(1,802)
Inventories	(0)	4	(1)	0	(4)	(7)	9	4	6
Loans & Advances	(51)	(499)	(178)	(166)	(69)	(143)	26	(552)	(1,632)
Trade & Other payables	82	202	(3)	351	(238)	517	(49)	309	1,171
Other adjustments	8	75	(92)	66	36	9	147	(218)	32
CFO (before tax)	149	(111)	255	939	660	890	395	20	3,197
CFO (before tax) as % of EBITDA	**67%**	**-66%**	**36%**	**105%**	**65%**	**108%**	**57%**	**2%**	**59%**
Cash Tax outgo	(54)	(26)	(81)	(129)	(162)	(142)	(132)	(182)	(908)
CFO (post tax)	95	(137)	174	809	498	748	263	(161)	2,289

Source: Ace Equity, Marcellus Investment Managers

In particular, C&K India's trade receivables remained high and increased dramatically in the later years. Through FY2009 to FY2018, C&K India's debtor days averaged a whopping 176, meaning it was taking the company nearly six months to collect payments from its customers. Whilst, as explained above, due to the challenges surrounding net revenue accounting, the debtor days could look optically high during the pre-IND-AS year, even after the move to IND-AS accounting from FY2017, the debtor days averaged 86 from FY2016 to FY2018 (average debtor days was even higher, at 148, for the standalone entity)—a relatively high number for an industry where trips are generally paid for in advance. Furthermore, the debtor days for the same period were relatively lower, at 37 for Thomas Cook India and 25 for MakeMyTrip, suggesting that C&K's revenue recognition looked relatively aggressive.

THE SHEER QUANTUM OF RELATED-PARTY TRANSACTIONS

One of the most disturbing aspects of C&K's governance practices was the quantum of related-party transactions. It was difficult to analyse the gravity of related party-transactions in the earlier years, as these (particularly sales to and purchases from) were reported on a 'gross basis', whereas, as discussed earlier, overall revenues and purchases of C&K were reported on a 'net basis'. However as gross sales/purchases became available from FY2017 onwards (thanks to IND-AS requirements), the magnitude of the related-party transactions could be analysed better.

Whilst related party sales and purchases were significant in FY2016 and FY2017, they jumped to an altogether different level in FY2018. In that year, revenue from related parties accounted for 92 per cent of the total standalone revenues. Similarly, purchases from related parties were 81 per cent of total tour costs in FY2018 (at the consolidated level too, the revenue and purchase contribution were high, at 36 per cent and 26 per cent, respectively). Not just their size, the terms of the related-party transactions also appeared to be detrimental to C&K India—for instance, the payables due to the related parties were significantly lower compared to the trade receivables due from them. Besides the sale and purchase transactions and dues thereon, loans and advances were also given to promoter-owned entities.

The largest related-party transactions were with a promoter-owned entity called Ezeego One Travel & Tours Limited (more on this entity further on in this chapter). Further, amidst an exponential rise in related-party transactions, from FY2017 onwards the company also stopped the specific entity-wise disclosures of related-party transactions, a clear red flag on the corporate governance front.

Exhibit 24: C&K India's related parties had accounted for almost all its standalone sales and costs by FY18

C&K India Consolidated (Rs crore)	Standalone			Consolidated		
	FY16	FY17	FY18	FY16	FY17	FY18
Total Revenue	2,848	3,117	2,623	7,505	7,176	6,451
Total Revenue from related parties	886	885	2,416	840	851	2,333
% Revenue from related parties	**31%**	**28%**	**92%**	**11%**	**12%**	**36%**
Total debtors	953	1,226	1,789	1,398	1,820	2,242
Due from related parties	242	305	468	217	293	460
% due from related parties	**25%**	**25%**	**26%**	**16%**	**16%**	**21%**
Total Tour costs	2,250	2,465	1,889	5,098	4,997	4,051
Tour costs paid to Related Parties	1,079	1,210	1,524	743	738	1,037
As % of total tour costs	**48%**	**49%**	**81%**	**15%**	**15%**	**26%**
Total payables	254	140	162	460	311	420
Dues to Related parties	148	13	28	28	30	31
As % of total payables	**58%**	**9%**	**18%**	**6%**	**10%**	**7%**
Total Loans & advances given	2,168	2,182	2,433	592	665	990
Loans/advances to Related parties	1,744	1,781	1,593	154	167	167
As % of total loans & advances	**80%**	**82%**	**65%**	**26%**	**25%**	**17%**

Source: Ace Equity, Marcellus Investment Managers

INFLATED CAPEX FURTHER REDUCED THE ALREADY WEAK OPERATING CASH FLOWS

Compared to its peers, C&K's gross block turnover[9] was extremely low (we can calculate this reliably only for FY2016–18, as only during this period were gross revenue numbers disclosed uniformly across all the travel companies). The low gross block turnover raises questions about the capital expenditure shown in the books. Between FY2016 and FY2018, C&K India's gross block turnover averaged 1.7x. Even after excluding the high goodwill, the average gross block turnover for the above period was 3.1x—unusually low for a services business. As against this, MakeMyTrip's gross block turnover averaged significantly higher, at 9.7x from FY2016 to FY2018.

As discussed above, C&K's operating cash generation was already weak compared to the reported profits. And the high capex levels took away whatever little positive operating cash was generated. Between FY2011 and FY2018, C&K generated post-tax operating cash flow of Rs 2,289 crore. However, the capex for this period aggregated to Rs 1,640 crore, resulting in cumulative free cash (before acquisition pay-outs) of Rs 650 crore during the period. This capex excludes the cash paid for the inorganic acquisitions that were made by the company.

The result of weak operating cash generation as well as perennially high capex was that the huge debt that the company had taken on with the Holidaybreak acquisition had necessarily to be repaid and serviced through a recurring cycle of sale of assets/businesses, equity dilution and debt refinancing.

Exhibit 25: C&K India's weak cash flow generation

Consolidated cash flow (Rs crore)	FY11	FY12	FY13	FY14	FY15	FY16	FY17	FY18	FY11-18
EBITDA	223	167	718	890	1,011	822	688	901	5,420
(Incr)/decr in working capital	(81)	(353)	(373)	(18)	(387)	59	(441)	(663)	(2,256)
Trade & Other receivables	(113)	(60)	(191)	(203)	(77)	(308)	(426)	(423)	(1,802)
Inventories	(0)	4	(1)	0	(4)	(7)	9	4	6
Loans & Advances	(51)	(499)	(178)	(166)	(69)	(143)	26	(552)	(1,632)
Trade & Other payables	82	202	(3)	351	(238)	517	(49)	309	1,171
Other adjustments	8	75	(92)	66	36	9	147	(218)	32
CFO (before tax)	149	(111)	255	939	660	890	395	20	3,197
CFO (before tax) as % of EBITDA	67%	-66%	36%	105%	65%	108%	57%	2%	59%
Cash Tax outgo	(54)	(26)	(81)	(129)	(162)	(142)	(132)	(182)	(908)
CFO (post tax)	95	(137)	174	809	498	748	263	(161)	2,289
Capex	(88)	(131)	(169)	(266)	(181)	(320)	(207)	(276)	(1,640)
Free cash flow	7	(267)	5	543	317	428	55	(437)	650

Source: Ace Equity, Marcellus Investment Managers

AGGRESSIVE GOODWILL ACCOUNTING

While the Holidaybreak acquisition was a bold business call, its accounting appeared to be equally aggressive. Against the equity consideration of GBP323 million paid for Holidaybreak, 'identifiable' net tangible (including working capital) and intangible assets (such as software, brands, customer lists, order backlog) acquired amounted to only GBP87 million (basis Holidaybreak's March 2011 numbers). The balance GBP236 million of the purchase consideration was allocated towards 'goodwill'. Prior to the acquisition, Holidaybreak itself had a goodwill of GBP139 million in its balance sheet, which got marked up to GBP236 million (our estimate basis the calculations in Exhibit 26) due to the premium pricing paid over the existing reported values when it was acquired.

Exhibit 26: A large part of Holidaybreak's consideration could not be identified with specific assets, and hence were allocated to Goodwill

Goodwill on Holidaybreak acquisition	GBP mn	Rs crore
Purchase consideration—Equity (cash) paid (A)	323	2,771
Allocated towards:		
Tangible + intangible fixed assets + Investments	260	2,227
Current assets (excluding cash)	51	440
Less: current liabilities (excluding debt)	224	1,922
Net identifiable Tangible & intangible assets acquired (B)	87	745
Balance (Goodwill) (A) - (B)	**236**	**2,025**

Source: Company, Marcellus Investment Managers

After the acquisition was completed, goodwill accounted for nearly 45 per cent of C&K's consolidated capital employed by

FY2012-end. Moreover, after the acquisition, Holidaybreak increased its stake in the European budget hotel chain Meinenger from the earlier 50 per cent (during its acquisition by C&K) to 100 per cent over FY2013 and FY2014. This, together with currency fluctuations, resulted in goodwill further increasing to 50 per cent of C&K's consolidated capital employed by FY2014-end.

Exhibit 27: By FY14-end, Goodwill accounted for nearly 50 per cent of C&K India's capital employed

C&K India Consolidated (Rs crore)	FY11	FY12	FY13	FY14
Goodwill	218	2,663	2,733	4,053
Capital employed (net worth + gross debt)	2,060	5,891	6,560	8,162
Goodwill as % of Capital Employed	11%	45%	42%	50%

Source: Company, Marcellus Investment Managers

The generation of goodwill is largely a function of the capital allocation decisions of the company—it represents the premium that the management of an acquiring company pays over the fair value of the identifiable tangible and intangible assets acquired. However, goodwill should be subject to rigorous impairment tests to affirm the sanctity of its carrying value, particularly when it accounts for a large part of the overall net worth or capital employed of a company. In the case of C&K India, the reported value of the goodwill appears to us to be too aggressive because:

- The camping business (a part of Holidaybreak) was sold for a total consideration of Rs 834.5 crore in FY2015. This division had a total book value of about Rs 1,184.5 crore, including goodwill of Rs 552 crore. This resulted in a significant loss of Rs 202 crore upon the sale of this business (i.e., the seller received a lower consideration relative to the book value). Hence, clearly, the goodwill of Rs 552 crore stated for this business appears to be overstated.

- Similarly, Superbreak (part of Holidaybreak) was sold for a consideration of GBP9.25 million in FY2016. Against this, the goodwill for this business itself was close to GBP71 million. Hence, the goodwill reflected for this business too seems to be on the higher side.

PROMOTERS' CONFLICTING BUSINESS INTERESTS

Besides the Tulip Group companies, which we have discussed in detail earlier, the Kerkars also owned a clutch of several entities, some of whose businesses conflicted with those of C&K India. We now discuss some of the significant businesses owned by the promoters of C&K:

- **Ezeego One Travel & Tours Limited (Ezeego1)**

Amongst the Kerkars' business interests outside of C&K, Ezeego1 was a prominent one. Ezeego, incorporated in 2006, operated an online portal for flight, hotel and other travel-related bookings. For the year ended March 2017 (the last year when its financials are available), the company's shareholding stood as follows:

Exhibit 28: Ezeego1 was owned by the Kerkars directly and possibly indirectly through a Mauritius-based entity

Ezeego1's Shareholding pattern	FY14	FY15	FY16	FY17
Coad Management Mauritius Ltd.	47.1%	47.1%	47.1%	47.1%
Urrshila Kerkar	41.1%	41.1%	41.3%	41.3%
Cox & Kings Ltd.	7.9%	7.9%	7.9%	7.9%
Peter Kerkar	2.9%	2.9%	2.9%	2.9%
Neelu Singh	0.4%	0.4%	0.4%	0.4%
Pratima Alvares	0.2%	0.2%	0.2%	0.2%
Peter Fernandes	0.2%	0.2%	0.2%	0.2%
Sunil Menon	0.2%	0.2%	-	-
Total	**100.0%**	**100.0%**	**100.0%**	**100.0%**

Source: Ministry of Corporate Affairs, Marcellus Investment Managers

We have not been able to ascertain the ownership of Coad Management, a company registered in Mauritius and which had the largest shareholding in Ezeego1. However, some recent press articles point to the Kerkars being the owners of the company.[10] C&K India owned just about 8 per cent of Ezeego1 but played a key role in Ezeego1's existence through related-party transactions. Due to Ezeego1's (like C&K's) net method of revenue accounting, it is not possible to ascertain the exact share of its transactions with C&K India. Nevertheless, the absolute amounts of sales and purchases were big, as shown in Exhibit 29. Besides, C&K India provided significant financial support in terms of loans to Ezeego1 (9 per cent of the total borrowings of Ezeego at FY2017-end) and trade payables (C&K accounted for almost 68 per cent of the trade payables of Ezeego1 at FY2016-end). It is hard to understand how the Kerkars' ownership of Ezeego was not a direct conflict of interest with those of C&K India's minority shareholder interests.

Exhibit 29: Ezeego1's highly symbiotic relationship with C&K India

Ezeego1 - C&K India's RP* transactions (Rs crore)	FY11	FY12	FY13	FY14	FY15	FY16	FY17
Revenue from C&K India	16	32	20	371	486	714	713
Purchases from C&K India	219	386	324	315	516	841	833
Trade receivable from C&K India	0	10	0	-2	54	12	NA
% of Total Trade receivables	**0%**	**12%**	**1%**	**-6%**	**58%**	**8%**	**NA**
Trade payables C&K India	34	58	61	97	92	215	NA
% of Total Payables	**27%**	**66%**	**86%**	**89%**	**86%**	**68%**	**NA**
Loan taken from Cox & Kings	21	256	224	62	34	101	67
% of Total Borrowings	**13%**	**69%**	**64%**	**14%**	**7%**	**15%**	**9%**

Source: Ministry of Corporate Affairs, Marcellus Investment Managers; * Related Party

Ezeego1's operating performance witnessed some improvement between FY2011 and FY2016 (before tumbling in FY2017). However, the business could not scale up to generate enough operating profits to meet interest costs, resulting in consistent net losses, erosion of net worth, and hence continuous reliance on debt.

Exhibit 30: Ezeego1 could never scale up enough to wipe out its net losses

Rs crore	FY11	FY12	FY13	FY14	FY15	FY16	FY17
Revenue	39	78	94	93	97	128	165
EBTDA	(21)	(8)	24	35	23	27	9
EBITDA margin	-54%	-11%	26%	37%	23%	21%	6%
EBIT (including other income)	(24)	(11)	19	30	19	35	26
PBT before exceptional items	(30)	(44)	(26)	(10)	(39)	(8)	(17)
Profit/ (loss) after tax	(30)	(44)	(26)	(10)	(39)	(8)	(17)
Net worth	(100)	(225)	(251)	(261)	(308)	(316)	(333)
Gross Debt	21	233	192	242	282	272	278
Net debt	17	228	188	138	267	255	257
Net debt/equity	NM	NM	NM	NM	NM	NM	NM
Net fixed assets	6	20	16	2	4	3	3
Net working capital (ex-cash)	(100)	(35)	(86)	(41)	(62)	(87)	(102)
Net working capital days	(929)	(165)	(333)	(161)	(234)	(248)	(225)
CFO (before tax)	(70)	(78)	72	88	(72)	42	28
CFO (before tax) as % of EBITDA	329%	923%	295%	254%	-318%	154%	305%
Free cash	(77)	(100)	70	88	(75)	40	26

Source: Ministry of Corporate Affairs, Marcellus Investment Managers; NM = Not Meaningful

o **Shoppe Till U Drop (STUD)**

Ezeego1's executives (not the promoters) had floated this company in April 2008 for carrying out the business of providing administrative support to customers related to visa, passport and consular application processes. As at FY2017-end, almost

90 per cent of STUD's equity was owned by Ms Neelu Singh, CEO & director of Ezeego1. The company shared both the same registered address and auditors as Ezeego1. The existence of STUD added an additional layer of complexity to the already complicated holding structure of the group. And with no revenues, STUD also raises doubts about the true nature of its incorporation.

The company did not have any meaningful operations, with revenues reported as being NIL until FY2017. On the balance sheet side, the company's assets primarily comprised capital work in progress, while its liabilities mainly comprised statutory payables and dues to Ezeego1.

Exhibit 31: STUD's as-good-as non-existent operations

Rs crore	FY11	FY12	FY13	FY14	FY15	FY16	FY17
Profit & loss							
Revenue	NIL	NIL	NIL	NIL	NIL	NIL	NIL
EBITDA	NIL	NIL	NIL	NIL	NIL	NIL	NIL
Profit after tax	NIL	NIL	NIL	NIL	NIL	NIL	NIL
Balance Sheet							
Net worth	(0)	(0)	(0)	(0)	(0)	(0)	(0)
Net debt	(0)	(0)	(0)	(0)	(0)	7.8	(0)
Capital work in progress	18	28	35	42	45	46	46
Other liabilities including payables to Ezeego1	(18)	(28)	(35)	(38)	(45)	(38)	(46)

Source: Ministry of Corporate Affairs, Marcellus Investment Managers

PLEDGE OF SHARES BY THE PROMOTERS

Within two years of the 2009 IPO, the promoters started pledging a significant portion of their C&K India shares. It is not clear from the annual reports what the reasons for the pledges were (while C&K's borrowings were secured by personal guarantees by the directors/promoters, there was no mention of any pledge of promoter shares). The QIP prospectus of 2014 mentions that shares were pledged by the promoters for their personal loans. The percentage of pledged shares kept increasing, reaching a peak of almost 70 per cent by June 2019 before the pledge was invoked by Yes Bank in the subsequent quarter. The promoters' holdings in a group company, besides those in C&K, were also pledged. This consistently high proportion of pledged promoter shares seems to have missed adequate scrutiny by the company's investors and lenders.

Exhibit 32: C&K India's promoters indulged in heavy pledging of their shares

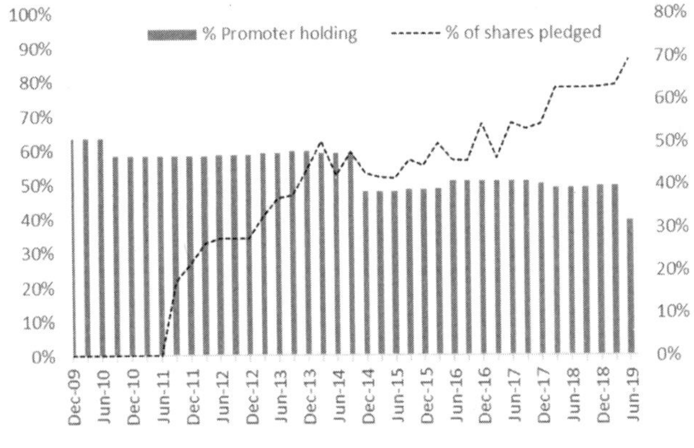

Source: BSE, Marcellus Investment Managers

Exhibit 33: A large percentage of group companies' shares were also pledged

As at March 2017	Total promoter holding %	% of promoter holding pledged
Tulip Star Hotel	57%	53.40%

Source: Ministry of Corporate Affairs, Marcellus Investment Managers

SIGNIFICANT LENDING ACTIVITIES DESPITE HUGE DEBT BURDEN

We are also perplexed by some of the disclosures in C&K's annual reports, particularly one related to its treasury operations. This disclosure was first reported in the FY2015 annual report as loans given to others (non-subsidiaries/associates, joint ventures) as part of the treasury operations of the company, bearing interest ranging from 12 per cent to 14 per cent. Under this mode, while the year-end outstanding balances were relatively low, the gross lending and repayment figures were astonishingly high, with no colour on how the company assessed the credit risks involved in such lending activities. This seems particularly damning for a company saddled with high amounts of debt.

Exhibit 34: Despite a weak balance sheet, C&K engaged in large lending transactions

Unsecured Short-term Inter-Corporate Deposits and other advances (Rs crore)	FY15	FY16	FY17	FY18
Opening Balance	334	101	307	335
Addition	3,261	1,867	1,922	807
Amount matured during the year	3,494	1,661	1,893	822
Closing Balance	101	307	335	320

Source: Company, Marcellus Investment Managers

BURGEONING CASH BALANCES NOT UTILIZED TO PAY OFF DEBTS

Another red flag in C&K's accounts was the existence of huge cash balances, particularly when the company also had a huge debt burden. Certainly, this situation warranted an explanation from the company's management as to why the cash had not been utilized for debt repayment. Furthermore, before the QIP of Rs 1,000 crore concluded in November 2014, C&K had almost Rs 1,402.5 crore in cash (including liquid investments) in its books (as per the March 2014 annual report). It was quite surprising how the company was able to justify and raise the additional equity when it already had a large cache of unutilized cash. Even more remarkably, this 'gross' cash balance kept increasing in the coming years, reaching Rs 1,667.6 crore by FY2018-end.

Exhibit 35: C&K India's cash balances were not utilized to pay off debts

C&K India (consolidated) **Rs crore**	**FY11**	**FY12**	**FY13**	**FY14**	**FY15**	**FY16**	**FY17**	**FY18**
Gross debt	853	4,699	4,692	5,586	3,803	4,132	3,713	4,003
Gross cash & cash equivalents	1,157	1,042	1,293	1,403	1,434	1,872	1,721	1,668

Source: Company, Marcellus Investment Managers

COMPLEX WEB OF ENTITIES CREATING MULTIPLE POCKETS WITH POTENTIAL FOR SIPHONING OF FUNDS

Every acquisition, big or small, added further complexity to C&K's already complex holding structure. C&K acquired and owned most of the operating entities (mainly subsidiaries) through a web of entities.

Exhibit 36: C&K India's complex web of entities creating several pockets to siphon off funds

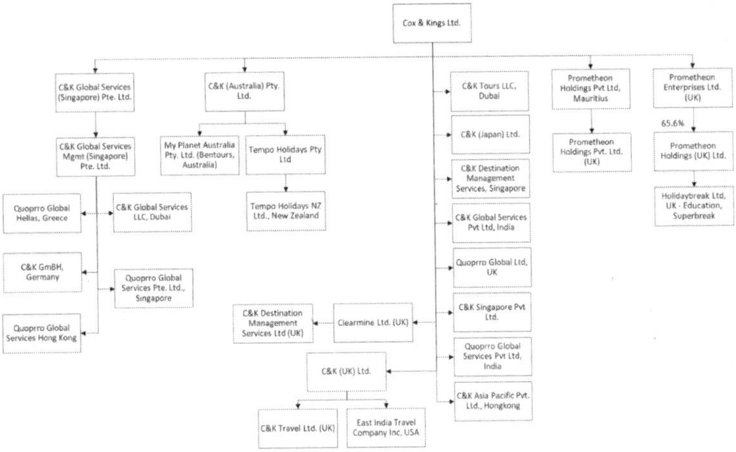

Source: Company, Marcellus Investment Managers; shareholding is 100 per cent in each subsidiary unless specified

- o Funds realized from the borrowings and equity raised at the standalone entity were advanced to the various subsidiaries in the holding chain. As at FY2018-end, advances worth Rs 1,468.8 crore were due, mainly from subsidiaries and to a smaller extent from the group companies. This was over and above the equity investments of Rs 231 crore made by the standalone entity in various subsidiaries as at FY2018-end.

Exhibit 37: Significant funds from standalone entity were routed to overseas subsidiaries and remained largely unreturned

Loans & Advances to Subsidiaries/ group Cos (Rs crore)	FY11	FY12	FY13	FY14	FY15	FY16	FY17	FY18
Opening Balance	127	279	1,339	665	503	1,131	1,744	1,780
Movement during the year	152	1,059	(674)	(162)	629	613	36	(312)
Closing Balance	279	1,339	665	503	1,131	1,744	1,780	1,469
As % of standalone net worth	26%	122%	58%	41%	48%	69%	62%	49%

Source: Company, Marcellus Investment Managers

- o Besides the money raised at the standalone level, C&K also sold stakes in the Holidaybreak businesses and sold minority equity stakes in key subsidiaries. For instance:
  - Rs 1,476.1 crore was raised through the sale of various Holidaybreak businesses, like Camping, Superbreak, LateRooms and Explore Worldwide, between FY2013 and FY2016.
  - Rs 1,270.3 crore was also raised through sale of minority stakes in Prometheon Holdings (UK) Limited (the key holding subsidiary for the Holidaybreak business)—in two parts—firstly a sale of 33.5 per cent in FY2013 to Citi Venture for Rs 649.9 crore, and secondly a 14.58 per cent stake sale in the same entity in FY2018 to SSG Capital Management for Rs 620.4 crore.

While some of this cash was used to repay debt taken at the level of the subsidiaries, a large part was shown in books as cash (Rs 1,094.8 crore) at FY2018-end and never repatriated to the standalone entity.

Exhibit 38: Cash at subsidiaries never made it back to the standalone parent

C&K India subsidiaries (Rs crore)*	FY11	FY12	FY13	FY14	FY15	FY16	FY17	FY18
Gross debt	425	3,493	4,077	4,754	3,285	2,900	2,418	2,006
Gross cash & cash equivalents	456	693	998	1,129	1,009	1,350	1,176	1,095

Source: Company, Marcellus Investment Managers; *arrived at by deducting standalone gross debt and cash figures from the consolidated figures

Further, in October 2018, C&K announced a significant divestment—the sale of Holidaybreak's education business to Midlothian Capital for an all-cash enterprise value of Rs 4,388.7 crore. By then, C&K India held a 51 per cent stake in Prometheon Holdings (UK) Limited—the holding subsidiary for Holidaybreak businesses—including the sold education business (the balance 49 per cent owned by SSG Capital Management). Hence, the amount accrued to C&K India was close to Rs 2,238.2 crore. However, this has not alleviated the troubles of the company.

The company submitted its standalone and consolidated financial statements for the year ended 31 March 2020 signed by the Resolution Professional (RP) appointed by the National Company Law Tribunal. The financials, severely qualified by both the RP and the auditors, disclosed drastically reduced revenue from operations (down ~87 per cent YoY), resulting in a massive consolidated PBT loss of Rs 957.2 crore for FY2020. Furthermore, heavy provisions/impairments made for most assets and some liabilities added an additional Rs 9,399 crore as exceptional loss. The company reported a negative net worth of Rs 7,293.1 crore as of 31 March 2020 (as against a positive Rs 4,732.2 crore as of 31 March 2019) and a significant upward revision in borrowings (excluding other financial liability), at Rs 5,532.2 crore as of 31 March 2020, vs Rs 2,944.3 crore as of 31 March 2019, bringing to the fore the extent of the misreporting of earlier years.

CASE STUDY: AMTEK AUTO

Exhibit 39: Amtek Auto's much more volatile ride vs BSE Auto index and the eventual collapse

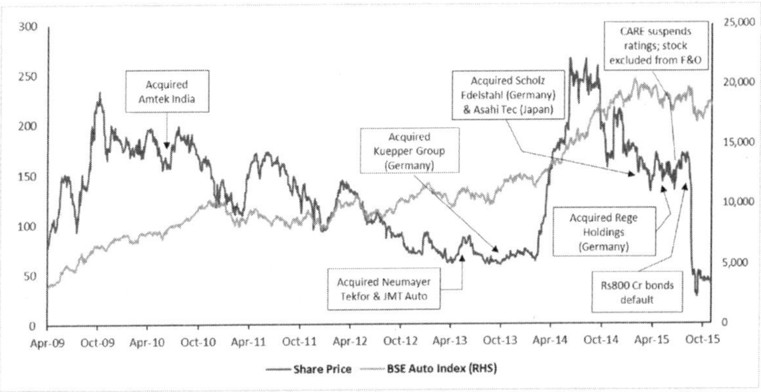

Source: Company, Ace Equity, Marcellus Investment Managers

Amtek Auto was founded in 1985 by the first-generation entrepreneur Arvind Dham as AM Metal Cast Limited (it was renamed as Amtek Auto Limited in November 1987).

Amtek Auto was one of the many auto component suppliers that sprang to life during mid-to-late 1980s to supply auto components to Maruti Udyog Limited (now Maruti Suzuki Limited). The company started with the supply of connecting rods to Maruti. Over the next decade, besides riding on the success of Maruti, Amtek Auto also made inroads with newer customers like Hero Honda, Eicher, etc., got into new products (forged and machined parts), and built multiple plants across India. The company also forged its first few JVs in the 1990s. In 1995, the company entered into a JV agreement with Benda Kogyo (Japan) and formed Benda Amtek Limited at Gurgaon for manufacturing flywheel ring gears. In 1999, it entered into a technical collaboration with Ateliers de Siccardi (France) and formed Amtek Siccardi India Limited at Manesar for manufacturing crankshafts. All these new initiatives were pursued through the organic route.

However, this approach changed by the dawn of the new millennium. In May 2001, the company made its first acquisition—a BIFR-registered company, Wesman Halverscheidt Forgings Limited (later renamed to WHF Precision Forgings Limited), a manufacturer of precision forgings in Madhya Pradesh. With this start, inorganic acquisitions, both domestic and more particularly global, would come to define Amtek Auto over the next fifteen years until the start of its collapse in 2015.

Between 2002 and 2015, Amtek Auto (including its subsidiaries) consummated more than fifteen acquisitions, one of the largest number by any Indian company in its operating history. Remarkably, despite going through a near existential crisis during the Great Financial Crisis of 2008-09, the group continued its pursuit of inorganic growth (while most of its auto component peers focused on consolidating their operations). In fact, even a few months before it declared bankruptcy,

Amtek Auto was still acquiring companies, in complete disregard of the health of its balance sheet.

Exhibit 40: Aggressive acquisitions despite ballooning debt became a key reason for Amtek's fall

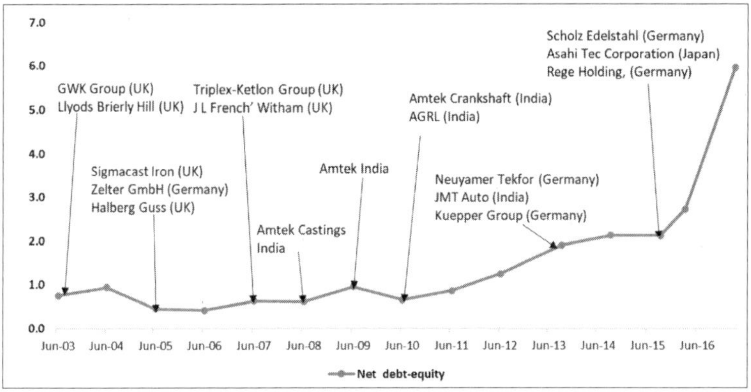

Source: Company, Marcellus Investment Managers

Driven by this inorganic pursuit, Amtek Auto's consolidated revenues increased sharply, by more than thirty times, from Rs 501 crore in the year ending June 2003 to Rs 15,454.6 crore in the year ending September 2014 (implying a CAGR of 36 per cent). However, the firm's adjusted net profit multiplied by only eighteen times. While Amtek Auto's income statement depicted a rosy picture, its balance sheets and cash flow statements conveyed a grim story. Amtek's reported revenues and earnings did not translate into commensurate operating cash flows (we discuss this in detail in a later section), resulting in heavy reliance on borrowings to finance its audacious organic capex and acquisitions. Shockingly, the company did not have a single year of positive free cash flow generation between June 2003 and September 2014. Hence, the consolidated net debt-to-equity rose from 0.8x as of

June 2003-end to 2.1x by September 2014 (high despite the denominator, i.e., net worth, being inflated; we will discuss this too in the later sections).

Exhibit 41: Amtek's internal accruals could provide for only a small portion of total capex & acquisition spends, resulting in heavy reliance on borrowings

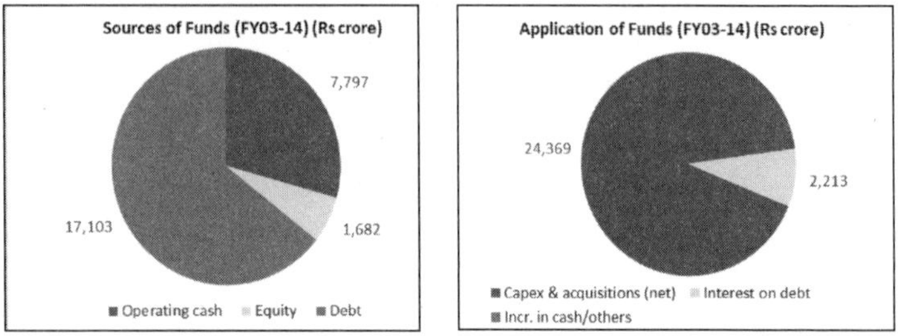

Source: Company, Marcellus Investment Managers; the above data is for Amtek Auto's consolidated accounts

The most widely cited reason for Amtek Group's failure is its aggressive capital allocation decisions (mainly acquisitions) going awry. Whilst this may be true, our analysis also suggests that its financial statements appeared to be misrepresented. In our earlier roles as research analysts on the sell-side, Amtek Auto came across as an interesting company that was delivering astonishingly high operating margins, yet it was amongst the cheapest front-line auto ancillary companies in terms of its price-earnings multiple. However, a deep-dive analysis of its financial statements threw up several red flags, and we therefore advised our clients to stay away from the stock. We present some of those red flags below. We restrict our analysis to the period until the year ending September 2014. The problems in the company started surfacing from 2015 onwards, and as kitchen sinking set in, its financials (and more particularly its profit and loss statement) started reflecting the true state of the company's affairs in the subsequent years.

OPERATING PROFITS AT ODDS WITH CASH GENERATION

A SIGNIFICANTLY HIGHER MARGIN VS PEERS NOT EXPLAINED BY ANY MEANINGFUL PRODUCT DIFFERENCES

Amtek Auto's standalone EBITDA margin was significantly higher than that of its peers like Bharat Forge and Mahindra CIE. In fact, Amtek Auto's standalone EBITDA margin was amongst the best in the Indian auto-ancillary space. While Amtek Auto's standalone raw material costs were significantly higher than for its peers, it had extremely low overheads, such as employee costs, power and fuel, etc. However, it did not appear from the company's financials that it was outsourcing a significant part of its manufacturing operations or otherwise buying finished goods (trading purchases), which could explain the low overheads. Furthermore, Amtek Auto's gross block turnover was significantly lower than its peers' (which we discuss in detail in a following section), which again suggested a reliance on in-house manufacturing and hence less likelihood of lower employee costs and other overheads vs peers. The significant divergence in margin vs peers was concerning.

Exhibit 42: Amtek's significantly lower overheads resulted in superior margin vs peers

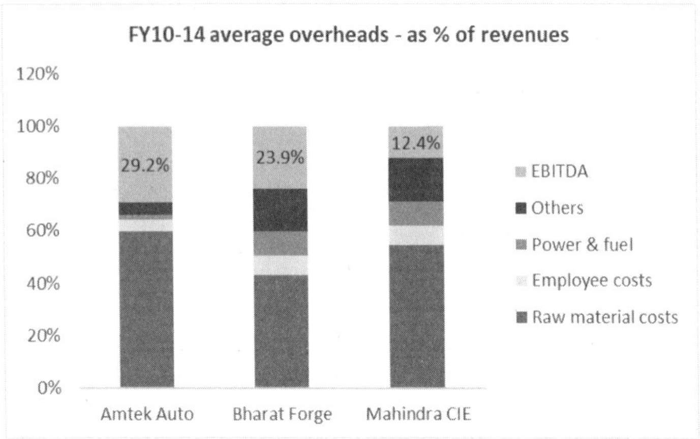

Source: Company, Marcellus Investment Managers; the above data is for standalone accounts for all the companies

SIGNIFICANTLY HIGHER WORKING CAPITAL DAYS VS PEERS

Amtek Auto's working capital cycle was significantly inferior to that of its peers. Inventory, trade receivables and loans and advances as percentage of revenues (or days) were significantly higher on a relative basis. Amtek Auto's higher trade receivable days relative to Bharat Forge was particularly worrisome, given the latter's much higher exposure to exports, where credit periods to customers tend to be typically higher. Also worrying was Amtek Auto's inordinately high loans and advances, which, to compound the concerns, were not sufficiently explained in the firm's annual reports. The consolidated working capital averaged an astonishing 200 days between these years (vs Bharat Forge's at an average of ten days on consolidated basis and an average of thirty-two days on standalone basis for FY2010–14), largely led by high inventory, debtors, and loans and advances. Amtek's loans and advances averaged particularly high, at sixty-seven days, reaching a peak of 183 days in June 2012 end. At the same time, Amtek Auto's trade payable days were much lower relative to peers.

Exhibit 43: Amtek Auto's significantly higher working capital days vs peers

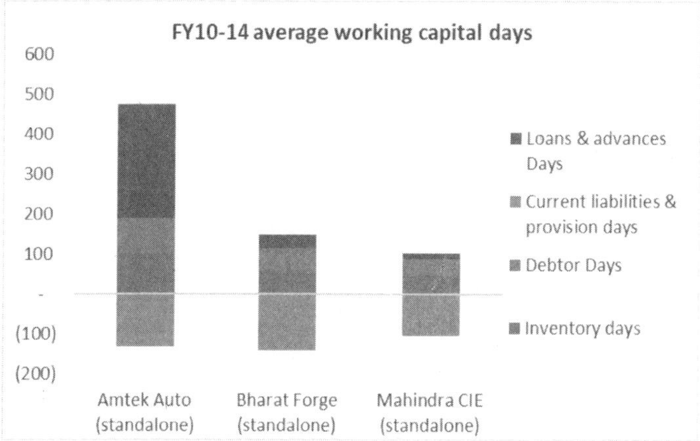

Source: Company, Marcellus Investment Managers

The high working capital levels led to Amtek Auto's cash flow from operations significantly lagging its reported operating profits. Between June 2003 and September 2014, Amtek Auto generated consolidated operating profits of Rs 12,974.1 crore. Against this, the operating cash (pre-tax) generated was only Rs 7,797.2 crore, or 60 per cent of operating profits—amongst the lowest cash conversion ratios in the auto ancillary sector, raising questions as to the sanctity of the company's reported operating profits.

Exhibit 44: High working capital restricted Amtek Auto's cash conversion

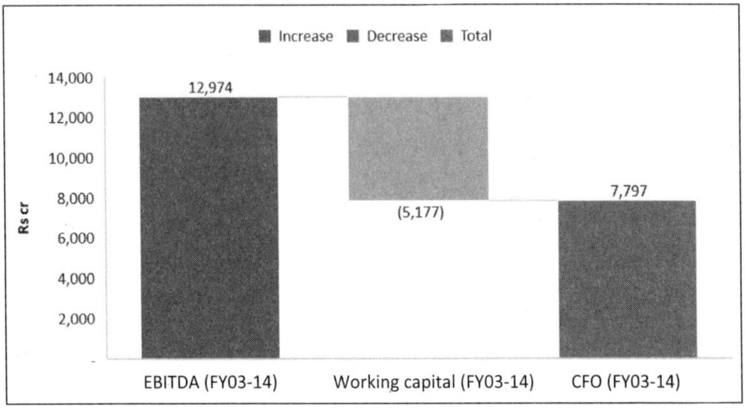

Source: Company, Marcellus Investment Managers; the above data is for Amtek Auto's consolidated accounts

A CONTINUOUS CAPEX CYCLE AND EXTREMELY LOW FIXED ASSETS TURNOVER

Amtek also lagged its peers in gross block turnover. In fact, Amtek's consolidated gross block turnover consistently remained below 1x since 2009. And this was not just due to the multiple acquisitions. Amtek's standalone gross block turnover fared even worse, not crossing 1x since June 2007 and falling to a low of 0.48x by September 2014. What was also confounding about Amtek's high capital expenditure was that the standalone entity incurred net cash capex of Rs 5,052.9 crore between June 2012 and September 2014, when the auto sector in India was clearly going through a down cycle and existing capacities were operating at abysmally low utilization levels. While Amtek Auto's standalone revenue growth was better than that of the industry—the incremental sales between the year ended June 2012 and the year ended September 2014 were only Rs 1,640 crore—it was less than a third of the capital expenditure mentioned above. This resulted in a massive decline in gross block turnover. Analysis of these numbers clearly raised questions about the genuineness of Amtek's capex. A likely inference is that the capex was potentially inflated (also termed as gold-plating) and the actual capacity (in physical terms) added was much lower relative to the amount spent. The excess, or inflated, amount then found its way to other destinations, possibly to the detriment of minority shareholders.

Exhibit 45: Amtek Auto's significantly lower gross block turnover vs peers

Company	F10	F11	F12	F13	F14	FY10–14 Average
Amtek Auto	**0.4**	**0.5**	**0.5**	**0.4**	**0.5**	**0.5**
Bharat Forge	0.7	1.0	1.2	0.9	0.9	0.9
Mahindra CIE	1.1	1.3	1.4	1.3	1.1	1.2

Source: Company, Marcellus Investment Managers; the above data is for standalone accounts for all the companies

The result of the weak operating cash flows (discussed above) as well as high capex was that Amtek Auto did not generate positive free cash in any single year between FY2003 and FY2014. This observation alone should have prompted lenders and shareholders to stay away from the company.

Exhibit 46: Low operational cash amidst high capex/acquisitions resulted in a massive shortage of positive free cash

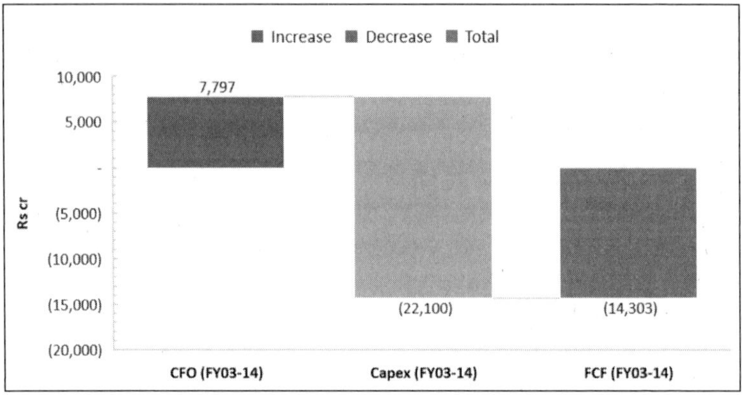

Source: Company, Marcellus Investment Managers; the above data is for Amtek Auto's consolidated accounts

A COMPLICATED GROUP STRUCTURE

Exhibit 47: Amtek Auto's complicated group structure, with several listed subsidiaries and a chain of entities for foreign subsidiaries

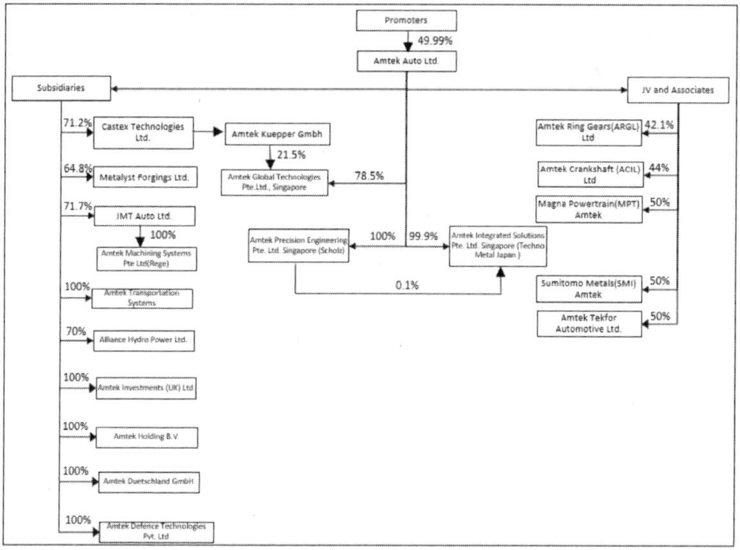

Source: Company, Marcellus Investment Managers

Amtek Auto owned interests in several auto component businesses in India and overseas through a web of entities, making it difficult to discern the performance of the company. The following aspects of the corporate structure raised significant concerns:

CONFLICTING BUSINESS INTERESTS AMONGST A FEW SUBSIDIARIES

As of 30 September 2014, Amtek Auto had three listed Indian subsidiaries—Castex Technologies (earlier Amtek India, 71.1 per cent stake as of September 2014), Metalyst

Forgings (earlier Ahmednagar Forgings, 64.8 per cent stake as of September 2014) and JMT Auto (71.8 per cent stake as of September 2014). An analysis of Amtek's product profile with these subsidiaries indicated an overlap with Metalyst Forgings for forged products, and with Castex Technologies for casting. In a scenario of wholly owned subsidiaries, this is usually not an issue, but given that these subsidiaries were partially owned, and moreover listed, it created a conflict-of-interest situation for the minority shareholders of these entities.

MULTIPLE ACQUISITIONS ALSO ADDED TO THE COMPLEXITY OF THE HOLDING STRUCTURE

Amtek's acquisition spree added to the complexity of the group structure by creating a chain of entities in the route to ownership of the ultimate operating entities. Further, unlike other overseas acquisitions, which were carried through Amtek Global Technologies (a special purpose vehicle [SPV] formed to hold overseas acquisitions), the Kuepper Group of companies (later renamed as Amtek Kuepper) was acquired through Castex Technologies in FY2014. This entity was later sold by Castex to Amtek Global Technologies, which further complicated the structure, since Castex ended up owning a 21.5 per cent stake in Amtek Global Technologies, besides Amtek Auto itself owning a 78.5 per cent stake in the company.

HOLDING STRUCTURE EXPLOITED TO MISLEAD LENDERS

In November 2014, Amtek Global Technologies (the holding SPV for the international subsidiaries) reached an agreement with global private equity firm KKR & Co LLP to obtain long-term funding of around Euro235 million for replacing some short-term bridge loans taken for the purpose of financing acquisitions.

The KKR agreement placed restrictions on Amtek Global Technologies making any payment/repayments to other group entities, including the Indian holding company (Amtek Auto). This prevented the lenders to the Indian entities, viz., Amtek Auto, Castex Technologies and Metalyst Forgings, who accounted for the bulk of the group's total consolidated debt, to have any recourse to Amtek Global Technologies' cash flows/assets, even though the businesses/acquisitions of the latter were largely financed by the debt taken at the Indian entities' level. Apparently, this critical detail about the restriction was not disclosed to the Indian lenders until the group started unravelling.[11]

Exhibit 48: Amtek's consolidated debt break-down

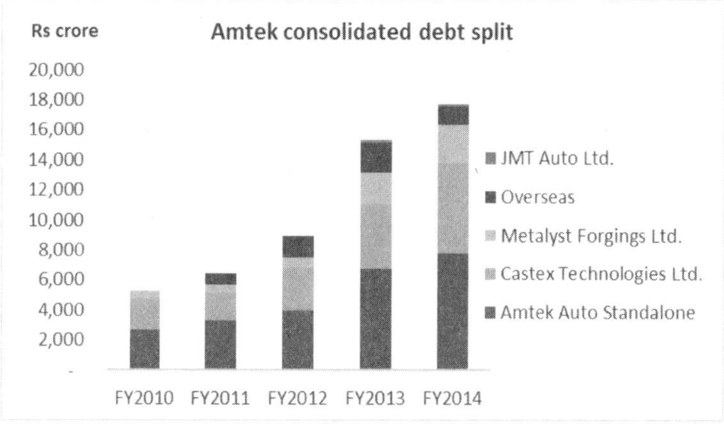

Source: Company, Marcellus Investment Managers

WEAK CORPORATE GOVERNANCE

PROMOTERS' OWN BUSINESS INTERESTS

Outside of Amtek Auto and its subsidiaries and joint ventures, the promoters also owned a sizeable business empire, which was as follows:

- The promoters had business interests in numerous real estate companies. Some of these companies were Garima Buildprop Pvt. Ltd, Brassco Estates Pvt. Ltd, Adhbhut Infrastructure Ltd, Forbes Builders Pvt. Ltd, Lotus Infraestates Pvt. Ltd, Dhanpat Properties Pvt. Ltd, Dilkhush Buildtech Pvt. Ltd, amongst several others.
- The promoters also seemed to have an eye for hospitality and food and beverages businesses. Through their listed packaging solutions company Rollatainers, the promoters acquired interests in, among other companies, the coffee chain Barista, acquired rights to develop and operate the Wendy's (the third largest burger chain in the world) brand across India, and acquired the Maple foods business, which supplied food to the Maple hotels as well as to Indian Railways.

In the context of the consistent negative free cash generation at Amtek Auto, the vastness of the promoters' personal business interests was clearly a red flag.

LACK OF CRITICAL DISCLOSURES IN THE FINANCIAL STATEMENTS

AMTEK'S ANNUAL REPORTS LACKED SOME CRITICAL DETAILS:

- In the consolidated financial statements, Amtek Auto only provided the names of the related parties but did not disclose the quantum of the company's transactions with these related parties. Further, the related-party names shared in the consolidated financial statements did not contain the names of some of the promoter-owned entities mentioned earlier in this chapter
- Lack of basic details, such as the total consideration paid for some of the key acquisitions well after the transactions were consummated, and details of goodwill computation, were

amongst the key information gaps in Amtek's financial statements, including the annual reports.

A RELATIVELY WEAK BOARD OF DIRECTORS

As of November 2014-end, Amtek Auto's board consisted of ten members, of which five were designated as independent directors, which indicates a well-balanced board. However, a closer look at the profiles of the independent directors raised several question marks:

Exhibit 49: Amtek's independent directors

Name	Designation	Name of other listed companies in which they hold directorships	Brief profile
Rajeev Thakur	Independent Director		Marine engineer and experience in the field of management consultancy.
B Lugani	Independent Director	Metalyst Forgings	Experience in the field of accounts, finance, management consultancy, income tax and setting up of new projects.
Sanjay Chhabra	Independent Director	Castex Technologies, JMT Auto	Experience in the field of technical, marketing and project implementation.
Raj Narain Bhardwaj	Independent Director	Technofab Engineering, Jaiprakash Associates, KSL & Industries, ABB	Long experience with LIC of India and in past served as the chairman of LIC Mutual Fund Trustee Company Pvt. Ltd
Sanjiv Bhasin	Independent Director	DBS Bank, Metalyst Forgings, Rollatainers	In past served as the CEO and general manager of DBS Bank Ltd.

Source: Company, Marcellus Investment Managers

- o Three of the independent directors, namely B Lugani, Rajeev Thakur and Sanjay Chhabra, did not have other directorships outside of the Amtek Group.
- o B Lugani, Rajeev Thakur and Sanjay Chhabra had been on Amtek Auto's Board for almost sixteen years, eighteen years and seventeen years, respectively, as of end-November 2014. Such a long tenure is not ideal for independent directors.
- o Certain independent directors were also on the boards of other promoter companies, as shown in Exhibit 50.

Exhibit 50: Independent directors held board seats in promoter-owned private entities—not an ideal situation

Name	Name of other group companies in which they hold directorships	
B. Lugani	Metalyst Forgings Ltd.	Castex Technologies Ltd.
Sanjay Chhabra	Castex Technologies Ltd.	JMT Auto Ltd.
	Adhbhut Infrastructure Ltd.	Barista Coffee Company Ltd.
Sanjiv Bhasin	Metalyst Forgings Ltd.	Castex Technologies Ltd
	Amtek Powertrain Ltd.	Rollatainers Ltd.
	Barista Coffee Company Ltd.	OCL Iron & Steel Ltd.
	Alliance Integrated Metaliks Ltd.	

Source: Company, Marcellus Investment Managers

LACK OF AUDITOR ROTATION

Amtek Auto's accounts were audited by the same auditor, M/s Manoj Mohan & Associates, at least since FY2002.

The same firm also audited the accounts of Castex Technologies, Metalyst Forgings and several other subsidiaries, including the promoter-owned entities like Rollatainers Ltd. Besides the Amtek Group, the firm did not have any other listed-company audits. The Amtek Group's dependence on one auditor, and that too an auditor who wasn't being rotated, was a red flag.

The poor accounting and governance practices at Amtek eventually caught up with the company, leading to invocation of the Corporate Insolvency Resolution Process against it in July 2017. The resolution process is not yet complete (as of December 2020), and with the stock suspended from trading by the stock exchanges, exit options remain elusive for those unfortunate shareholders who could not sell their holdings in the company in time.

THE WAY FORWARD FOR MINORITY INVESTORS IN INDIA

At Marcellus, we have a dozen chartered accountants and chartered financial analysts trained in this sort of detailed forensic accounting analysis. However, most individual investors simply won't have the resources to do this sort of analysis. So, how can they safeguard their wealth from corrupt promoters?

Firstly, if you do not have the time or the inclination to do any financial analysis, it is better to let a professional fund manager mange your wealth. Investing in Indian stocks on the back of tips from friends or brokers, or from the sundry advisors and investment consultants who dot the financial landscape, is a recipe for wealth destruction.

Secondly, if you can read the last three years of annual reports of the listed company that you are considering investing in, you will end up knowing more about that company than most other investors (retail and institutional). Every listed company is legally obliged to provide these reports on its website. Whilst reading a company's annual reports, you should ideally be conducting the analyses highlighted in Exhibit 12 and Exhibit 16 of this chapter. If you don't have the time or the training to go into such detail, then look out for the following in the annual report:

1. Is the board of the company largely made up of relatives of the promoter and his friends? If so, put one cross against the company.
2. In the cash flow statement in the consolidated financial statements of the company, you will find the cash flow from operations (CFO) and the cashflow from investments (CFI). The CFO should be a positive figure, as this is the cash that the company has generated from selling its wares. The CFI is usually a negative figure because these are monies that the company is spending on its plant and equipment. If CFO plus CFI is not greater than zero, then put a second cross against the company.
3. Does the section on related-party transactions (in the notes to the financial statements) show multiple large transactions between the promoter and his family-owned entities? If so, put a third cross against the company and move on to doing something more useful with your valuable time.
4. You should at least read the last three years of annual reports of any company to conduct the accounting checks highlighted in this chapter. If you do not have the time or the inclination to do any financial analysis, it is better to let a professional fund manager manage your wealth.

KEY TAKEAWAYS

- Several companies report inaccurate financial statements in India. Corporate frauds often leave the investor with little time to react, and even if they do, it's a slow burn to a sure negative outcome for the minority shareholders. Hence, building confidence in the sanctity of the financial statements and the broader corporate governance of the company should be the starting point for any stock analysis.
- Evaluating accounting quality and corporate governance is covered in Marcellus's research in three ways: a) Level 1 checks, where we use our forensic quantitative screens to rank companies on their accounting quality (we typically eliminate the companies that score low on our forensic model); b) Level 2 checks, where we conduct in-depth reading of the financial statements to identify some of the traits mentioned in the preceding section; and c) Level 3 checks, where we try to gauge promoter/management integrity by doing primary data checks on the companies, wherein we speak with former employees, customers and suppliers of the company.

* * *

CHAPTER 3

Accounting Quality: Spotting the Naughty Lenders

'You have to understand accounting and you have to understand the nuances of accounting. It's the language of business and it's an imperfect language, but unless you are willing to put in the effort to learn accounting—how to read and interpret financial statements—you really shouldn't select stocks yourself.'

—Warren Buffett[1]

The rewards for picking the right financial services company for investment are enormous, as these companies reinvest almost 100 per cent of their earnings back into the business. The reinvested earnings are then used to raise more debt and the company is then able to earn returns on this larger capital base. While this can prove to be a virtuous cycle and lead to extraordinary results for a well-run financial services company, poor accounting quality and dishonest promoters of financial services companies are an existential threat for a bank or non-banking financial company (NBFC).

The key questions we seek to answer in this chapter are:

- How can minority investors differentiate between companies with poor accounting quality and well-run financial services companies with high-quality accounting?
- What is the relationship between share price returns and accounting quality, and what are the benefits of investing in companies with high-quality accounting?
- Why is accounting quality central to investing in financial companies?

WHY IS ACCOUNTING QUALITY CENTRAL TO INVESTING IN FINANCIAL COMPANIES?

For a lending business, capital is its raw material. A lender raises equity capital, then raises debt, which is as high as five to ten times the equity, and lends it out. The profits generated from this increase the bank's net worth, allowing it to raise more debt and increase the quantum of loans it can give out. For some exceptionally able Indian lenders, this dynamic has created a virtuous cycle and has generated extraordinary returns for their shareholders. However, poor accounting quality and dishonest promoters are an existential threat for a bank or NBFC. Unfortunately for Indian investors, about 70 per cent of banks and NBFCs have poor quality accounting and have destroyed wealth over CY2016–20.[2] As seen in Exhibit 51 below, there is a strong correlation between accounting quality and shareholder returns—shareholder returns over CY2016–20 have been the lowest for companies with the poorest quality of accounting and the highest for companies with the best quality of accounting.

Exhibit 51: Strong correlation between accounting quality and shareholder returns (CY16–20)

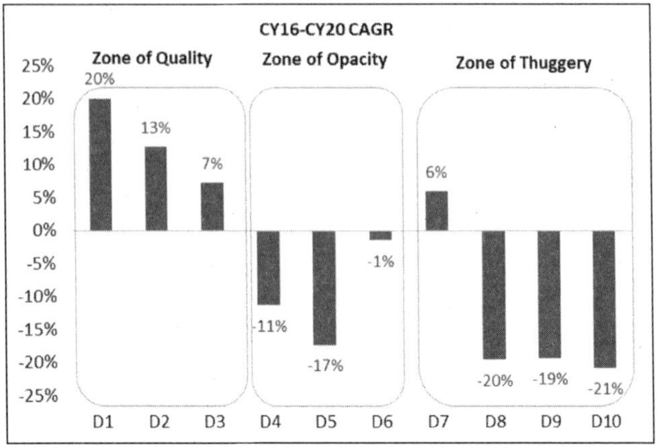

Source: Marcellus Investment Managers, NSE; Universe of 95 financial services companies with market capitalization of over Rs 1,000 crore

IN THE CASE OF FINANCIAL SERVICES COMPANIES WITH POOR QUALITY OF ACCOUNTING, DESTRUCTION OF SHAREHOLDER WEALTH IS A QUESTION OF 'WHEN' AND NOT 'IF'

In line with the tripartite framework we described in the previous chapter, we can break down the timeline of corporate fraud and accounting jugglery in financial services companies.

STAGE I: WHEN INVESTORS DO NOT KNOW WHICH COMPANIES HAVE A POOR QUALITY OF ACCOUNTING

As seen in Exhibit 51, there is a strong correlation between accounting quality and shareholder returns, irrespective of whether the sub-par accounting practices of companies are common knowledge or not. Therefore, in this chapter (see Exhibit 53) we have given details of Marcellus's proprietary forensic accounting model to identify financial services companies whose accounting quality is poor. This framework will help investors clearly demarcate financial services companies with high-quality accounting from those which have poor-quality accounting.

STAGE 2: WHEN INVESTORS KNOW WHICH COMPANIES HAVE POOR-QUALITY ACCOUNTING, BUT THEIR ACCOUNTING FRAUD IS NOT PUBLIC KNOWLEDGE YET

In some cases, shareholders decide to invest in financial services companies despite being aware about their sub-par accounting quality. Such investors are of the view that either: (i) the fraud won't come to light, or (ii) they will be able to exit the stock before the fraud becomes public knowledge, or (iii) they will have enough time to exit the stock once the fraud is public knowledge. None of these arguments hold true. As illustrated in Exhibit 52, even if the accounting fraud is not public knowledge, there is a gradual decline in shareholder value in some cases. In other cases, once the fraud becomes public knowledge, there is an overnight destruction of wealth and shareholders are left with no time to react to such events. For instance, both Yes Bank and DHFL saw a 40 per cent crash in their share prices within a month of their accounting issues becoming public knowledge. Even their credit ratings saw accelerated downgrades once their accounting issues start emerging. It took just six months for DHFL's AAA rating (in January 2019) to be downgraded to D, which is default grade.

STAGE 3: WHEN ACCOUNTING FRAUD IS PUBLIC KNOWLEDGE

Even after a fraud is public knowledge, retail shareholders have a tendency to go bottom fishing, i.e., investing in fraudulent companies at low prices in the hope of witnessing a miraculous turnaround story. As seen in Exhibit 52, the retail shareholding in Yes Bank and DHFL more than doubled once their frauds became public knowledge and share prices declined. Many investors end up falling prey to the anchoring bias—their attraction towards such companies is stoked by the fact that shares of these companies can be bought at a fraction of the price they had earlier traded at. However, turnaround stories in the case of financial services companies are rare, and even when such miracles do happen, the minority shareholders get substantially diluted before the new management is able to achieve the turnaround.

Therefore, the most prudent approach for investors would be to not invest in companies which have poor quality accounting, irrespective of whether such accounting malpractices are public knowledge or not.

Exhibit 52: Overnight destruction of shareholder wealth once fraud becomes public knowledge

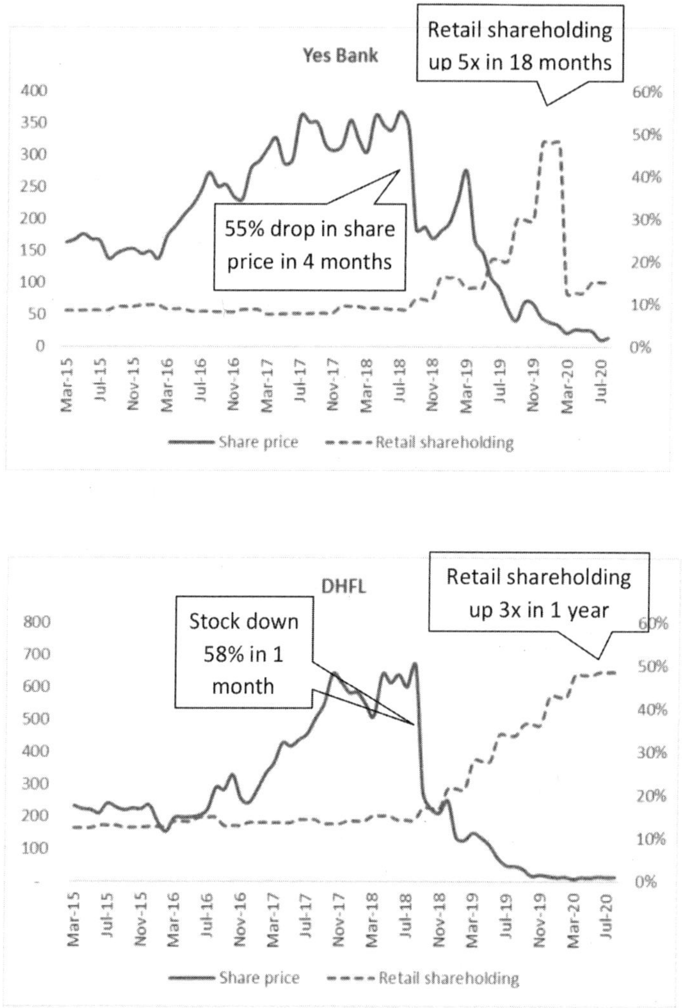

Source: Marcellus Investment Managers, NSE

HOW TO IDENTIFY NAUGHTY FINANCIAL SERVICES COMPANIES

Forensic accounting means the use of accounting skills to investigate a potential fraud. A forensic accounting model uses a combination of financial analysis tools to flag off risks in the reported financial statements of banks and financial services companies. Marcellus has developed a model using a set of eleven accounting ratios specifically for conducting forensic checks on the numbers of financial services companies. These ratios, covering the balance sheet, profit and loss statement and cash flow statements, grade financial services companies based on the quality of their accounting. Some of the key ratios and the rationale for using them are shown in Exhibit 53 below.

Exhibit 53: Some key ratios in Marcellus's forensic accounting framework for financial services companies

Checks	Ratios	Rationale
Income Statement	1. Treasury income as % of net interest income (NII)	To check if treasury income is being booked aggressively
	2. Fee income as % of NII	Higher proportion of fee income vs peers may be because of aggressive lending practices to boost profitability at the cost of asset quality
Balance sheet	3. NPA volatility	Higher NPA volatility may be due to inconsistency in NPA recognition
	4. Provision as % of NPA	A low ratio indicates inadequate provisioning and therefore artificially higher profitability
	5. Contingent liabilities to net worth	Indicative of the extent of off-balance sheet risk
Auditor	6. Growth in auditor remuneration vs total interest income	Faster growth in auditor remuneration vis-à-vis company's operations raises concerns surrounding auditor's objectivity

Source: Marcellus Investment Managers

Our methodology is to evaluate eleven accounting ratios covering income statement (for revenue/earnings manipulation), balance sheet (for incorrect representation of assets/liabilities), NPA recognition and audit-quality checks using at least six years of historical financial statements. The financial services companies are then ranked on each of these eleven ratios individually and slotted into ten deciles, from D1 to D10 (D1 being the best score and D10 the worst). These ranks are then cumulated across parameters to give a final pecking order on accounting quality. We term the top three deciles as the 'Zone of Quality', the next three as the 'Zone of Opacity' and the bottom four as the 'Zone of Thuggery'.

There are several qualitative aspects of accounting and corporate governance which our forensic model may not be able to pick up due to lack of data uniformity across companies, or where there is subjective judgement involved. Such areas can only be evaluated through a deep dive into historical financial statements and through primary data checks around management integrity. Some of the aspects we check to determine these include loan sourcing strategies, underwriting processes, risk management practices, the quality of the board of directors, the nature and significance of related-party transactions and the governance culture within the bank/NBFC.

As illustrated in Exhibit 54 below, companies in the 'Zone of Quality' outperformed companies in the 'Zone of Thuggery' by a massive 33 percentage points per annum over CY2016–20. Investors can improve their portfolio returns simply by avoiding companies with dubious accounting practices.

Exhibit 54: Quality wins big time over the long term (CY16-19) for financial services companies

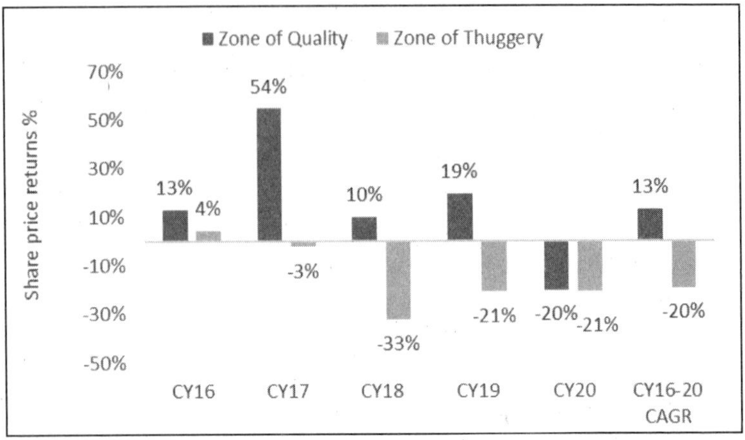

Source: Marcellus Investment Managers; Universe of 95 financial services companies with market capitalization of over Rs 1,000 crore

CASE STUDY—UNRAVELLING DEWAN HOUSING FINANCE LTD BASED ON FY2013–18 ANNUAL REPORTS

Exhibit 55: Dewan Housing Finance's group structure (December 2018)

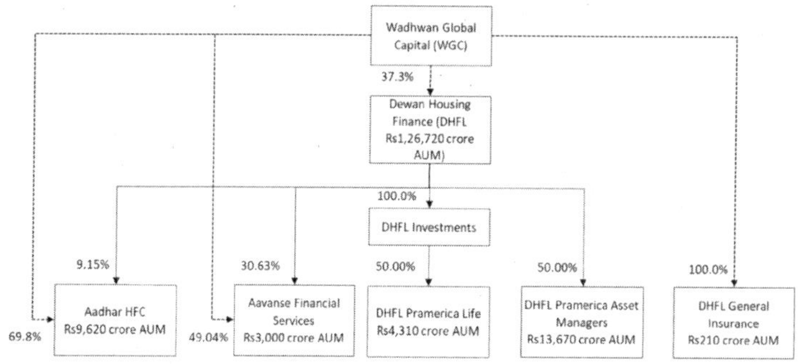

Source: Company disclosures; Marcellus Investment Managers

Dewan Housing Financing Limited (DHFL) is a prominent housing finance company founded in 1984. It had achieved a peak market capitalization of over Rs 20,000 crore in 2018. In the six-year period from FY2013 to FY2018, DHFL's loan book had grown at a CAGR of 22 per cent and its profit after tax at a CAGR of 21 per cent. While a plain reading of these numbers suggests that DHFL was growing its balance sheet and profits at a healthy rate, our proprietary forensic model showed a completely different picture. Based on DHFL's FY2013–FY2018 annual reports, our forensic model ranked DHFL as a D10 company, i.e., it had the worst possible score among peer housing finance companies. So, why did our forensic model throw up red flags well in advance of the eventual admittance of DHFL in the insolvency court?

Exhibit 56: Marcellus's forensic accounting model pointed out multiple red flags in DHFL's accounting well before its collapse in 2019

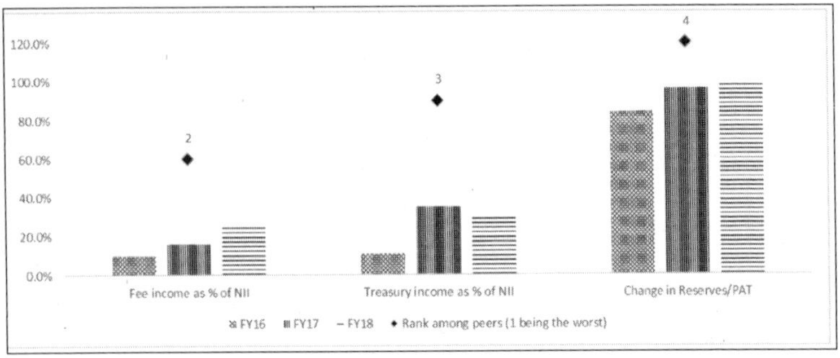

Source: Marcellus Investment Managers

WHAT OUR FORENSIC MODEL ACCOUNTING RATIOS TOLD US ABOUT DHFL

FEE INCOME AS A PERCENTAGE OF NET INTEREST INCOME

Fee income represents all income other than interest, and includes loan processing fees, banking charges, commissions earned on insurance sold, etc. In FY2018, fee income for DHFL was equivalent to a quarter of its net interest income. A high fee income as a proportion of net interest income compared with peers suggests that a lender may be booking a higher upfront fee income to inflate profitability. To take a simple example, a lender who wants to inflate its short-term profitability may lend money to a high-risk borrower because the borrower is willing to pay a large upfront processing fee. Thanks to the upfront fee, the high-risk borrower is able to raise debt and the lender is able to book the fee income upfront, thereby boosting its profitability. This sort of lending practice usually leads to what economists call adverse selection, i.e., in the quest to increase short-term profitability, the lender ends up lending to only those borrowers who are willing to pay a large upfront fee income, and they would naturally be borrowers to whom no other lender wants to lend. This in turn leads to a build-up of risky loans, and while the P&L looks glossy, the risk keeps stacking up on the balance sheet. This ratio raises a clear red flag, but needs to be corroborated with primary data checks and other checks on features such as the lending mix, fee-generating capabilities of the business, and nature of fees being booked. However, post the implementation of Ind-AS for NBFCs (Ind-AS was implemented by DHFL in December 2018), fee income cannot be recognized upfront and must be amortized over the residual loan tenure using the effective interest-rate accounting method.

TREASURY INCOME AS A PERCENTAGE OF NET INTEREST INCOME

Treasury income is the income earned from or generated by the investment portfolio of the lender. In FY2018, treasury income for DHFL was equivalent to 30 per cent of its net interest income. A consistently high treasury income as a percentage of net interest income implies a high portion of revenues being generated from non-core assets. High treasury income might arise due to investments in riskier assets or due to profit booking from sale of investments during lean quarters. Apart from the quantum of treasury income, the volatility of treasury income should also be closely analysed, as a higher volatility implies a larger number of one-off transactions. In this context, the treasury book of DHFL during FY2013–18 made for an interesting read—it consisted of investments in non-convertible debentures of Reliance Home Finance, perpetual bonds of Yes Bank and debt funds of its own joint venture, DHFL Pramerica Asset Management. Even more interestingly, the debt funds of DHFL Pramerica Asset Management in turn held bonds of DHFL itself.

CHANGE IN RESERVES AS A PERCENTAGE OF PROFIT AFTER TAX (PAT)

For any company, the residual profit, after deduction of appropriations such as dividend on equity and preference shares and interim dividends, is added to reserves and surplus on the balance sheet. This usually results in the year-on-year change in reserves and surplus being equal to the transfer from the profit and loss account post appropriations. This in turn implies that the change in reserves as a percentage of PAT is usually 100 per cent. This ratio was not 100 per cent in the case of DHFL because of certain adjustments to its reserves:

- A one-off appropriation of Rs 270 crore in FY2017 for a capital reduction scheme in one of its joint ventures.
- Utilization of securities premium towards premium on redemption of zero-coupon NCDs, which is allowed as per the Companies Act. However, such a move artificially reduces the interest expense, thereby improving net interest margins, profitability and return on equity. Shown below is a disclosure from DHFL's FY2018 annual report for the same:

> In accordance with Section 52 of the Companies Act, 2013, during the year the Company has utilised Securities Premium Account towards premium on redemption of Zero Coupon Secured Redeemable Non-Convertible Debentures

and Securities issue expenses amounting to Rs 9,891 Lakh (Rs 11,465 Lakh) net of tax of Rs 5,235 Lakh (Rs 6,068 Lakh).

In addition to the aforementioned red flags highlighted by our forensic framework, further accounting and corporate governance checks, usually employed by Marcellus's research team during deep diligence on specific stocks, yielded other significant red flags, which are listed below:

FREQUENT CHANGE IN AUDITORS

DHFL's auditors were changed three times between FY2013 and FY2019. In FY2013, the company replaced BM Chaturvedi and Co. with two joint auditors, citing that 'the operations of the company have been growing steadily over the past few years, this has resulted in substantial increase in accounting and financial transactions'.[3] In FY2016, the joint auditors who were appointed in FY2013 did not offer themselves for reappointment, 'in view of their pre-occupation with other work'; and therefore Chaturvedi & Shah were appointed as the sole auditors.[4] In FY2018, Deloitte Haskins & Sells were appointed as the joint auditors. Eventually, in August 2019, both the joint auditors, Deloitte as well as Chaturvedi & Shah, resigned.

RAPID INCREASE IN CHUNKY LOANS

As seen in Exhibit 57 below, the proportion of project loans[5] increased from 5 per cent in FY2013 to 15 per cent in FY2018. When this is correlated with the gradual increase in fee income as a percentage of net interest income, it becomes a very significant red flag.

Exhibit 57: DHFL saw a rapid increase in the share of project loans and loan against property (LAP) over the years

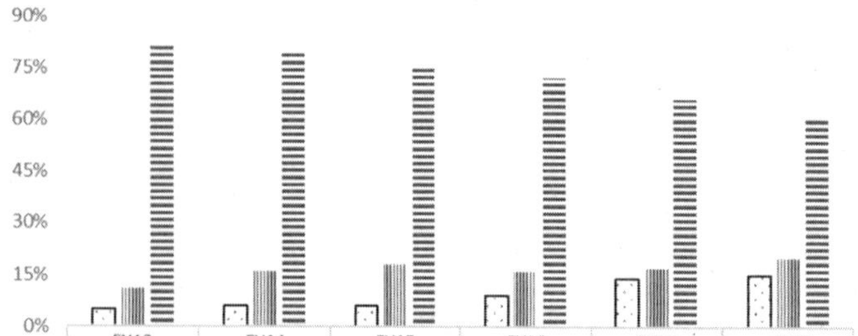

	FY13	FY14	FY15	FY16	FY17	FY18
Project Loans	5%	6%	6%	9%	14%	15%
LAP	11%	16%	18%	16%	17%	20%
Home Loans	81%	79%	75%	72%	66%	61%

Source: Marcellus Investment Managers; company disclosures

LACK OF INDEPENDENCE OF BOARD COMMITTEES

Remarkably, the promoter of DHFL, Kapil Wadhawan, was himself the chairman of the firm's Risk Management Committee as well as of the Finance Committee. It was the responsibility of the Risk Management Committee to ensure that the credit exposure of the company to any single borrower or group of borrowers did not exceed internally set limits. The Finance Committee, among its other powers, had the authority to grant loans above a certain threshold and issue corporate guarantees in favour of any person. Until FY2015, this limit was set at Rs 400 crore. However, that was changed in FY2016, and power was given to the Finance Committee to grant approval for loans above Rs 200 crore. This gave the promoters virtually unlimited freedom to lend to related parties and shell companies without any checks and balances.

RELATED-PARTY TRANSACTIONS WITH MULTIPLE SUBSIDIARIES, JOINT VENTURES AND ASSOCIATES

As shown in Exhibit 55, DHFL had JVs, subsidiaries and associate companies, and shareholding in these companies was held by DHFL as well as its parent company. DHFL also had numerous related-party transactions with these entities.

INCONSISTENCY IN CREATING DEBENTURE REDEMPTION RESERVE

As per the Companies (Share Capital and Debenture) Rules, companies were earlier required to create a debenture redemption reserve of 25 per cent of the amount raised by way of public issue of debentures. DHFL created a debenture redemption reserve that was lower than the required 25 per cent. DHFL was eventually fined by SEBI in 2020 for failing to transfer enough money to the debenture redemption reserve during FY2016–18.

TIE-UPS FOR LOAN DISTRIBUTION WITH OTHER LENDERS WITH POOR ASSET QUALITY

DHFL had entered into tie-ups with Dhanlaxmi Bank, Yes Bank, Central Bank, Punjab & Sind Bank and United Bank of India for loan distribution and syndication. The Gross Non-Performing Assets (GNPA) ratios of these banks in FY2018 were as follows: Dhanlaxmi Bank—7.4 per cent; Yes Bank—1.3 per cent (rising to 17.3 per cent in Q1FY2021); Central Bank—21.5 per cent; Punjab & Sind Bank—11.2 per cent; and United Bank—24.1 per cent. Assets to the tune of Rs 1,650 crore were generated through alliances with these banks.

THE END GAME

On 21 September 2018, DSP Mutual Fund sold 'AAA'-rated DHFL papers worth Rs 300 crore at a yield of 11 per cent. When the 'AAA'-rated paper was sold at a yield much higher than what it used to trade at, it caused panic in the market as investors started to speculate around DHFL's ability to repay, and some believed that DHFL would default on its debt service obligations, just as ILFS did in June 2018. This turmoil in the debt markets spilled over to the equity markets, leading to a sharp share price fall in the DHFL stock. Later, the mutual fund clarified that it had sold the bonds not because they knew about some credit risk but because they wanted to reduce the duration of their portfolio; however the damage had been done by then. This transaction by an influential mutual fund house triggered turmoil in DHFL's equity shares. DHFL's share price crashed by 60 per cent on that day, eroding over Rs 8,000 crore in market capitalization.

In February 2019, credit rating agencies downgraded their ratings on DHFL's various debt instruments by a notch. By May 2019, DHFL had stopped accepting and renewing fixed deposits and had also stopped withdrawals of fixed deposits. On 4 June 2019, DHFL delayed interest payments on its bonds and bond repayments worth Rs 960 crore, leading to ICRA, CRISIL, CARE and Brickworks downgrading DHFL's credit rating to 'D' the next day.

An initial forensic audit of DHFL's books conducted by Grant Thorton has revealed that over Rs 17,000 crore was allegedly siphoned off between 2006 and 2019. During a raid by the Enforcement Directorate (ED) in early 2020, it was further found that DHFL had used customized software to create lakhs of fake accounts to camouflage loan defaults. DHFL had created one lakh such fictitious borrowers to route money into eighty shell companies.[6] DHFL has become the first financial services company to be admitted into the National Company Law Tribunal (NCLT) under the Insolvency and Bankruptcy Code. Its financial creditors have made claims amounting to over Rs 86,000 crore.[7]

KEY TAKEAWAYS

- About 70 per cent of Indian banks and NBFCs have poor quality accounting and have destroyed wealth during CY2016–20. During this period, financial services companies with high quality accounting generated a 13 per cent CAGR return, vs a -20 per cent by financial services companies with poor quality accounting.
- To uncover manipulation of accounts on the part of naughty financial services companies, Marcellus has designed a set of eleven accounting ratios specifically for financial services companies. A combination of these ratios, along with other qualitative indicators from the annual reports of lenders, proves to be a powerful indicator of accounting quality.

* * *

CHAPTER 4

What to Buy—Part 2: Great Franchises

'The ideal business is one that earns very high returns on capital and could keep using lots of capital at those high returns. I mean that becomes a compounding machine.'

—Warren Buffett[1]

Continuing from the quote he made above, Warren Buffett highlighted the rarity of such businesses:

> So if you have your choice, if you could put a hundred million dollars into a business that earns 20 per cent on that capital—say 20 million—ideally, it would be able to earn 20 per cent on 120 million the following year, and 144 million the following year and so on. That you could keep redeploying capital at these same returns over time. But there are very, very, very few businesses like that. The really—unfortunately, the good businesses, you know, take a Coca-Cola or a See's Candy, they don't require much capital. And incremental capital doesn't produce

> anything like the returns that this fundamental return that's produced by some great intangible. So we would love the business that earn—that could keep deploying, in fact, even well beyond the earnings. I mean we'd love to have a business that could earn 20 per cent on a hundred million now. And if we put a billion more in it, it would earn 20 per cent more on that billion. But like I say, those businesses are so rare.

In this chapter we have laid out a framework that helps identify such rare businesses—those that are able to sustain exceptionally high pricing power over several decades and hence deliver healthy returns on capital employed whilst deploying a large part of their free cash flows back into the business.

The key questions that we seek to answer in this chapter are:

- What are the benefits of high pricing power and strong competitive advantages?
- What are the sources of competitive advantages?
- Which companies in India have demonstrated the rare ability to deliver high returns on capital as well as a high rate of capital redeployment?

THE VIRTUOUS CYCLE OF HIGH ROCES AND HIGH REINVESTMENT RATES

Saurabh's twelve-year-old daughter is a budding pastry chef. Early on in her baking foray, she figured that if she wanted to make money from baking, then the recipe for generating cash flow was straightforward. She would have to buy the ingredients required to bake a cake for Rs 100 or less and sell the cake for

Rs 150 or more, thus assuring herself a minimum of Rs 50 of cash flow. Once she had the Rs 50 in hand, she realized that now she had to make some tricky decisions—should she spend this money at the local ice-cream parlour or should she buy the latest books on baking?

At a very basic level, running a company is simply a scaled-up version of what Saurabh's daughter is doing. Operating a firm is about using capital to drive a virtuous circle of resource allocation. A firm uses capital to consume and invest in resources such as raw materials, utilities, R&D, manpower, technology, manufacturing facilities and logistics. Typically, 'resources consumed' relates to the current requirements of a business and is classified as operating expense on the income statement. On the other hand, 'resources invested' relates to the future requirements of a business and is usually classified as fixed capital (capex) or working capital investment on the balance sheet. Consumption and investment of these resources then helps the firm produce products and provide services, which can then be sold to generate capital for the firm. This capital can then be reinvested into the business for further 'consumption and investment', and hence future business growth.

The capital (and hence the resources) available with a firm is limited, and like all resources, has a cost attached to it—the cost of capital for most listed firms in India is around 12–15 per cent. Return on capital employed (RoCE) measures the cash flows generated by a firm per unit of capital employed. If the RoCE earned by a firm is less than its cost of capital, it is unable to pay the capital providers for the use of this limited resource. As a result, the business destroys value for shareholders, since the shareholders would have earned a higher return on their capital had they invested it somewhere else. Similarly, an RoCE substantially higher than the cost of capital adds value for shareholders. However, the higher the RoCE of a firm, the greater the number of competitors it will likely attract. Intense competition tends to reduce an incumbent firm's RoCE down to as low as it can possibly go. This is where the competitive advantages or the moats of the firm come to the rescue. Competitive advantage is what enables a business to outperform its competitors and allows a company to achieve relatively healthy returns for its shareholders. This makes **Competitive Advantage** the second pillar of Marcellus's investment philosophy for identifying Consistent Compounders.

Firms with strong and sustainable competitive advantages can sustain RoCEs substantially higher than cost of capital over long periods of time. This is because the stronger the competitive advantages are, the greater the barriers to entry faced by competition, and hence the greater the pricing power that the firm possesses. For instance, in India's innerwear industry, Page Industries (the master franchisee in India of Jockey and Speedo) has delivered an average pre-tax RoCE of 60 per cent over the last ten years, substantially above its cost of capital (which is likely to be around 12–15 per cent), and has thereby generated substantial free cash flows for its shareholders.

However, operating in the same industry, peers like Rupa and Company, Dollar Industries and VIP Clothing have, over the same period, earned RoCEs of only 23 per cent, 17 per cent and 6 per cent, respectively, generating significantly lower free cash flows than Page. Page's ability to generate and sustain RoCEs substantially higher than its cost of capital is reflective of its being a much stronger business than its peers. Similarly, in India's passenger car industry, Maruti Suzuki has delivered a pre-tax RoCE of 22 per cent over the past ten years, while the corresponding RoCE for Tata Motors is only 13 per cent.

Whilst 'high RoCE' is reflective of strong competitive advantages, it is not sufficient by itself to deliver growth for a business. If all the cash flow generated by a firm with a high RoCE is returned to shareholders, then it is difficult for the firm to grow its revenues over time. Firms that can sustain high RoCEs, along with a high rate of reinvestment of capital into the business, deliver higher and more sustainable earnings growth compared with the firms that have high RoCEs but a low rate of capital reinvestment in their business.

Typically, reinvestment of cash flows into the business can be done in two ways. On the one hand, cash flows can be reinvested towards building tangible assets on the balance sheet, like manufacturing plants, machinery and working capital, thereby increasing the firm's overall capital employed, which helps the firm expand faster than competition.

On the other hand, cash flows can also be reinvested on the income statement to build intangible assets like brands (although brands by themselves, we believe, are not sources of sustainable competitive advantages, as is explained later in this chapter) and patents, which aid business growth in the future. For instance, in India's pressure cooker market, Hawkins and TTK Prestige both possess strong competitive advantages, which are reflected in their average RoCEs over the past ten years, of 69 per cent and 38 per cent, respectively. However, with a capital reinvestment rate of only 26 per cent, Hawkins has delivered revenue CAGR of only 9 per cent over FY2010–20, when its competitor TTK Prestige has delivered revenue CAGR of 14 per cent over the same period, supported by a capital reinvestment rate of 80 per cent.

Hence, to sustain healthy growth in cash flows and earnings over the long term, a firm needs to first establish sustainable competitive advantages and high pricing power, which help generate high RoCEs. Thereafter, it needs to reinvest future cash flows in areas that deliver high RoCEs too.

SOURCES OF COMPETITIVE ADVANTAGES

Where do competitive advantages arise from? What are the sources from which a firm derives and sustains its edge over competition, allowing it to sustainably generate RoCEs higher than its peers? Bruce Greenwald and Judd Kahn, in their book *Competition Demystified*,[2] say that there are three kinds of genuine competitive advantages.

Supply: Strictly cost advantages that allow a company to produce and deliver its products or services more cheaply than its competitors.

Demand: Access to market demand that competitors cannot match.

Economies of scale: If cost per unit declines as volume increases, then even with the same basic technology, an incumbent firm operating at a large scale will enjoy lower costs than its competitors.

Beyond these three basic sources, Greenwald and Kahn point out, government protection or superior access to information could also act as a competitive advantage for a business.

But what are the sources of such competitive advantages that allow the firm to demonstrate high pricing power around either supply/demand/economies of scale?

The business guru who has answered this question most clearly is Sir John Kay. His IBAS framework is detailed in Appendix 2 of the book. Sir John's IBAS framework includes four broad sources of competitive advantages—Innovation, Brand, Architecture and Strategic Assets. Here are some examples of Indian firms who possess competitive advantages across these four categories.

INNOVATION

> 'Innovation is an obvious source of distinctive capability, but it is less often a sustainable or appropriable source because successful innovation quickly attracts imitation. Maintaining an advantage is most easily possible for those few innovations for which patent production is effective. There are others where process secrecy or other characteristics make it difficult for other firms to follow. More often, turning an innovation into a competitive advantage requires the development of a powerful range of supporting strategies. What appears to be competitive advantage derived from innovation is frequently, in fact, the return to a system of organization capable of producing a series of innovations.'
>
> —Sir John Kay[3]

Asian Paints, HDFC Bank and Garware Technical Fibres are great examples of firms repeatedly excelling as the first mover, thinking differently and being several steps ahead of the competition.

Asian Paints: Given the voluminous nature of the Indian paint sector's product, its low margins for dealers, the seasonality of demand and the large number of stock-keeping units (SKUs), innovation in supply chain management is a key differentiator and a critical success factor in the industry. Asian Paints has a track record of running the most efficient supply chain network in India, one that makes three to four deliveries every day to more than 70,000 dealers in over 600 cities. This ensures high inventory turns for a dealer, for whom the thin margins from a voluminous product is a key challenge in earning a reasonable return on capital. Some of the initiatives that Asian Paints has taken to strengthen its supply chain include being the first company to (a) use mainframes in the early 1970s to forecast demand for better inventory management; (b) start branch billing on computers in the late 1970s; (c) import a colour computer in 1979, which helped reduce tinting time from five or six days down to four hours; and (d) use a global positioning system (GPS) for tracking movement of trucks carrying finished goods in the channel (implemented between 2010 and 2015).[4]

HDFC Bank: One of the features that distinguishes HDFC Bank from its competitors is the management's ability to use technology in the broadest sense of the word—including hardware, software systems and processes—to create a unique offering. In the late 1990s and for much of the noughties, ICICI Bank was often the bank to come up with the most stylish of technology-driven banking products (e.g., it was the first to provide internet banking and the first to introduce mobile ATM). However, HDFC Bank's strength rests not so much in the uniqueness of the technologies it uses but in the way that it has lined up technology in a clever process flow that was not envisaged by other banks.

In the mid- and late 1990s, when most banks were opting for Infosys's technology platform, HDFC Bank chose Iflex's Microbanker. This proved to be a masterstroke, as the bank's management had sensed that real-time online banking was the future. Microbanker subsequently allowed HDFC Bank to garner large quantities of low-cost deposits by providing payment solutions to capital market players. Stocks were traded in physical form before dematerialization started in the early 1990s, a trend that gathered steam by 1995-96. These dematerialized shares were transferred electronically after trade, but the movement of fund transfers was still slow and in physical form. This did not match the speed of movement in stocks, as different exchanges used different banks. Stockbrokers had to keep liquid money for their payouts, despite having equal pay-ins from other exchanges, because of a slow and manual process for such pay-ins. This increased the working capital requirements for brokers. For exchanges, the risk was that they were not sure whether stockbrokers had enough money in their accounts to honour payouts. To mitigate this risk, the exchanges had to send data on dues from various brokers to its bank (Canara Bank for the National Stock Exchange [NSE]) at the end of the day to check whether the brokers had enough money to honour their dues.

HDFC Bank pulled in all the players in the supply chain—buyers, sellers, brokers and exchanges—and got them into an automated settlement system. It offered a solution to both brokers and exchanges. If brokers had an account with HDFC Bank, exchanges could see in real time whether brokers had the money to settle pay-outs and, if there was a shortfall, there was enough time before the actual settlement to ask the broker to meet this shortfall. Such reduced settlement risk for exchanges drove all major exchanges to sign up with HDFC Bank. The incentive for brokers to sign up with HDFC Bank was that pay-in money was credited immediately to the broker's account, reducing his working capital requirement. This led all the brokers to open their accounts with HDFC Bank for settlements. Since brokers needed bank guarantees for exchanges, the bank also provided credit lines to these brokers. So the bank not only earned a free float on money kept with it by brokers for their settlement, it also earned fees by providing credit lines to brokers. Starting with the NSE in 1998, the bank became a clearing bank for all major exchanges by FY2000. Eight hundred brokers and most custodians were using HDFC Bank's services by FY2000. The bank had captured 80 per cent of market share in the settlement business by the mid-noughties. Buoyed by the success of its capital markets initiative, HDFC Bank implemented similar initiatives in retail banking. This created the foundation of its formidable low-cost deposits platform.

Garware Technical Fibres: Garware Technical Fibres (earlier known as Garware Wall Ropes) is a leading Indian as well as global player in the field of synthetic cordage and fibres used in fishing nets, aquaculture, sports nets, infrastructure, etc. Coming up with innovative products has been the cornerstone of Garware's success in recent years, particularly in aquaculture. Garware's innovative value-added products have helped its customers substantially reduce their overall cost of operations.

For example, in aquaculture, fouling, where marine organisms settle on the surface of the net and lead to occlusion of mesh openings, is a common problem. This can lead to increased pressure on cage structures and reduced water exchange across nets. The traditional solution was to clean the nets at regular intervals and apply a copper solution on the nets to avoid the accumulation of fouling. However, the drawback of this was frequent cleaning cycles (and hence higher costs of maintenance) and high release of copper, which in turn raises environmental concerns.

Around three years ago, Garware launched innovative nets with in-built anti-fouling technology. Almost at the nano particle level, Garware was able to infuse the melted plastic with copper particles; and the company then made the nets with this material. Use of these nets helps the customer reduce cleaning costs by almost half, and with significantly faster cleaning cycles. Although the product is priced at a premium, significant savings on maintenance costs and longer product life results in a much shorter payback period for the end-users.

Another common problem in the salmon aquaculture industry is that of sea lice infestation. Sea lice are external parasites which feed on their host, in this case the salmon. This prevents the salmon from growing. One of the more recent solutions used for this problem consists of wrapping the salmon cage with 'lice skirts' or 'shields', at depths ranging from 5 metres to 10 metres. The major drawback in using shielding skirts is the blocking of water exchange, which is again detrimental to the health of the salmon. Garware has innovated and patented a special fabric, which not only blocks sea lice but at the same time allows almost hundred times higher water flow than a normal lice skirt. The key enablers for innovation by Garware include a strong understanding of and experience in polymer engineering, proactive investments in R&D and in-house manufacturing capabilities in the areas of extrusion, knitting, wet processing, fabric weaving, etc.[5]

BRAND

> 'Reputations are created in specific markets. A reputation necessarily relates to a product or a group of products. It is bounded geographically too. Many reputations are very local in nature. The good plumber or doctor neither has nor needs a reputation outside a tightly defined area. Retailing reputations are mostly national. But an increasing number of producers of manufactured goods, from Coca-Cola to Sony, have established reputations worldwide, and branding has enabled international reputations to be created and exploited for locally delivered services in industries as diverse as accountancy and car hire.'
>
> —Sir John Kay[6]

A firm's ability to create and sustain strong brand recall requires dealing with challenges around the changing definition of aspirational consumption in every category over time. Hence, the brand recall of category leaders needs to evolve accordingly, in terms of price points, type and mode of branding initiatives, and product characteristics. There have been several instances of brands that were once significantly dominant in India in their respective product categories but saw a reduction in their market share with a dilution in their aspirational value. These brands once had allure, because of which customers desired or aspired to own and use them. Some key examples include brands like Titan in watches (2005–12), VIP Frenchie (1995–2005) in men's innerwear, and Bata in footwear (2000–10). Clearly, this loss of aspirational value is a big risk for any brand. On the other hand, firms such as Page Industries (brand: Jockey) and HDFC Asset Management Company (HDFC AMC) have overcome the challenges of brand dilution successfully over the past twenty-five years.

Page Industries: Page's approach towards advertising has been unique on several fronts. Firstly, its advertising campaigns have consistently been high-impact affairs, like 'Just Jockeying' in FY2010–14 and 'Jockey or Nothing' launched in FY2015. Secondly, Page has placed significant emphasis on in-store advertising, to the extent that Jockey advertisements cover the bulk of in-store advertising space at most multi-brand outlets (MBOs). Thirdly, in a neat play on the world view of Indians, Page has made consistent use of Caucasian models in its advertisements and thus firmly entrenched its brand recall as an international brand. This unique approach in advertising has helped Jockey emerge as the sole aspirational brand in the mid-premium innerwear segment over the past two decades.[7]

HDFC AMC: The HDFC brand has become synonymous with trust and dependability over the years. The HDFC group has been able to monetize this trust and the strength of its brand in its asset management business too, apart from monetizing its brand for its lending and insurance businesses,. When it comes to managing the savings of millions of investors, trust and dependability are bigger decision-making factors for the customer compared to product quality. Hence, HDFC AMC is the most profitable asset manager in India and has the largest number of retail investors—one out of every four retail mutual fund investors in India has an account with HDFC AMC.

In 2020, HDFC AMC demonstrated its focus on saving the dilution of its brand by rescuing investors from Rs 500 crore worth of capital erosion. In one of its fixed maturity products (FMPs), the company had purchased non-convertible debentures (NCD) of ~Rs 500 crore, which had to be written off. To protect the interest of investors in the FMP, HDFC AMC transferred the NCDs of the troubled group from the scheme to its own balance sheet.[8] HDFC AMC in a statement said, 'Such liquidity arrangement is in the larger long-term interest of the company and is being undertaken purely as a measure to provide liquidity to the relevant unitholders.'

This step was unique, coming at a time when many FMPs from the competitors of HDFC AMC were facing several such similar write-offs. As a result, HDFC AMC saw large inflows in its debt and liquid funds following this event. The company added Rs 12,500 crore in AUM[9] to its liquid funds in the next quarter, and this led to a 3 percentage points increase in its market share within a period of ninety days. This wasn't a flash in the pan; over 2015–20, HDFC AMC has grown its AUM at a CAGR of 20 per cent.[10] As a fund manager from a mutual fund house told us, with a hint of envy in his voice, 'HDFC is something that customers ask for, rather than something that needs to be pushed to the customer. By providing HDFC products, a distributor increases his credibility in the eyes of the customer.'

ARCHITECTURE

> 'Architecture is a system of relationships within the firm, or between the firm and its suppliers and customers, or both. Generally, the system is a complex one and the content of the relationship is implicit rather than explicit. The structure relies on continued mutual commitment to monitor and enforce its terms. A firm with distinctive architecture gains strength from the ability to transfer firm product and market specific information within the organization and to its customers and suppliers. It can also respond quickly and flexibly to changing circumstances. It has often been through their greater ability to develop such architecture that Japanese firms have established competitive advantages over their American rivals.'
>
> —Sir John Kay[11]

Tata Consultancy Services (TCS) is a prime example of a 'system of relationships within the firm'. In contrast to what happens at other leading Indian IT Services firms, all TCS CEOs are groomed internally and spend decades working within TCS before rising to the CEO role.

As highlighted in *The Victory Project: Six Steps to Peak Potential*,[12] 'By choosing an internal candidate (usually a veteran team player) as her successor, the outgoing leader sends a message of confidence that the firm itself is a team of leaders.' The fact that leadership changes in TCS are organic allows the firm to retain its largest clients for longer. In fact, TCS's largest clients are larger than those of other Indian IT services firms.

For example, TCS's implementation of a core banking platform for State Bank of India (SBI) in 2003–04 remains the largest such project implemented anywhere in the world . . . Successful implementation of colossal projects such as these has helped TCS become the only Indian IT services firm to consistently rank among the world's three largest IT services firm by revenues, since 2015.

Moreover, employees at TCS are aligned to organizational goals as part of a routine process. Unlike many IT companies that were started by first-generation entrepreneurs, TCS came from the Tata Group, and therefore institution and organization building was in their DNA. Hiring and training practices are institutionalized, ensuring that employees are aligned to common goals. In fact, every year, TCS trains or re-trains 2,00,000 employees. It is highly unlikely that any other firm in India trains even half as many people in a given year.

And thirdly, TCS has standardized processes to a very large extent and captured their application development life cycle in an institutional knowledge base. This gives the firm the ability to have the largest scale of implementation among peers and in a much shorter time frame than others. These processes are the result of collaboration and processes laid down by top managements over the years.

Pidilite Industries, the largest player in adhesives and sealants in India, is a great example of a 'system of relationships between the firm and its suppliers and customers'. No other Indian company has a channel connect like that of Pidilite. The company sells its products through mom-and-pop grocery shops, paan (betel) shops, stationery shops, hardware shops, automotive spare parts shops and wood marts. Most dealers of Pidilite have been associated with the company for over two decades and hence have a strong sense of loyalty to the company. Strong IT systems and robust deliveries make transacting with the company easier than with other companies. Continued innovation in Pidilite's products enhances the addressable opportunity of the channel (without any incremental cost to the channel), which no other adhesive company in India enjoys.[13]

Another big strength of Pidilite is the connect it has across intermediaries. Pidilite is the only company in India which has a direct connect with all the home-building intermediaries—carpenters, masons, electricians and plumbers. Other building material companies have influence only on a specific intermediary; for example, the paint companies influence just painters. This advantage not only helps create brand equity with the intermediaries but also a reverse feedback mechanism, wherein the intermediaries feed ideas into the company, which has led to creation of opportunities.

For example, Pidilite launched variants of Fevicol, like HeatX, SpeedX and Marine, based on feedback from carpenters. These value-added products now account for more than half of the revenues from the Fevicol brand. Pidilite's relationships with carpenters in India started strengthening during the 1980s, when the firm started helping the carpenters enhance their skill-sets. In an *Economic Times* interview in 2010, Mr Madhukar Parekh (part of Pidilite's promoter family) said:

> We have maintained a norm of sending furniture design and books to carpenters every quarter. The idea is to add value to the carpenters' jobs. We knew this was a good way of connecting to carpenters, as they would have a wide variety of designs. This is one strategy the company adopted of identifying with the customer and providing wings to his creative imagination, thereby selling our products. For the carpenter community, we have formed the 'Fevicol Champion Club'. This is an exercise to bring them together, and, more importantly, to add value to their life. We bring these carpenters to our office and demonstrate each product.

> We invite them by rotation. Club members from all over the country come here and are received at the railway station like people from the bridegroom's side. We also organise kite festivals for them. All these are a token of appreciation from our side towards this community, which has helped us grow. . . [On Intermediaries' training] Pidilite continues to train intermediaries to use its products effectively and to educate them about new launches. These programmes also help the company to further strengthen its ties with the intermediaries.[14]

STRATEGIC ASSETS

> 'There can be no greater competitive advantage than the absence of competitors. Profits come not only from distinctive capabilities but from possession of strategic assets—competitive advantages which arise from the structure of the market rather than from the specific attributes of firms within that market.'
>
> —Sir John Kay[15]

The strategic assets of a firm could be around intellectual property (i.e., patents or proprietary knowhow), licences, or other such means of access to resources which are not easy for a competitor to replicate. Some examples from Indian companies include Page Industries' relationship with Jockey International, GMM Pfaudler's access to the R&D capabilities of Pfaudler, or Divi's Laboratories' thirty-year relationship with global pharma giants for their contract research and manufacturing services (CRAMS) business.

The relationship of the Genomals, promoters of **Page Industries**, with Jockey International, USA, is Page's biggest strategic asset. Jockey renewed its licence with Page in 2010 for twenty-one years, instead of for five years, which was the earlier practice. Thus, until 2030, Page will remain Jockey's exclusive franchise in India and the UAE. For Jockey USA, Page Industries is now its biggest franchisee. For the Genomals, India remains a large market, growing in size (more consumers aspiring to buy Jockey products) and expanding in depth (new segments like leggings for women and underwear for children). Accessing Jockey's innovations in the US and bringing them to a steadily growing market like India is a formula that has worked since 1995 for Page, and should continue in the foreseeable future.[16]

GMM Pfaudler started out as an Indian joint venture between Gujarat Machinery Manufacturers (GMM) and Pfaudler Inc. GMM's promoters continue to run the company on a day-to-day basis. Pfaudler Inc. is a 130-year-old multinational giant, founded by the inventor of the process of glass-lining of steel. Glass-lined equipment is a necessity in industries such as such as chemicals, pharmaceuticals and food and beverages, where the production process requires equipment with corrosion resistance or cleanliness properties. As manufacturing processes evolve, glass-lined vessels also have to evolve through significant R&D investments. Over its long history, Pfaudler Inc. has pioneered multiple other innovations in glass-lined vessels, reactors and related equipment, and it is today a global leader in the space. GMM has leveraged Pfaudler Inc.'s capabilities to establish a clear edge in India, and its access to Pfaudler's product development pipeline enables GMM to maintain the technology leadership. GMM has bolstered the technology edge with its manufacturing capabilities, building production capacity that exceeds the aggregate of all other players in the industry.[17]

GMM has also recently acquired the manufacturing facilities of De Dietrich Process and Systems, the other MNC operating in India's glass-lined equipment sector, thus consolidating its market position even further. This was followed by GMM acquiring its parent entity Pfaudler Inc., which makes GMM now the largest glass-lined equipment manufacturer globally.[18] These strategic assets, of technology access and manufacturing scale, combined with its long-standing customer relationships, have proven to be potent, driving healthy RoCEs for the company (five-year average, FY2016-20, of 26.6 per cent).

Divi's Laboratories counts global pharmaceuticals giants like Abbott, Sanofi, Mylan, GSK and Pfizer amongst its clients for their CRAMS business. These business relationships have been developed over decades and are based on two very important parameters—timely supply of quality products and protection of the client's IP.

Since its inception, Divi's worked with a clear strategy of partnering with western big pharma as their outsourced manufacturing business partner whilst ensuring that it neither infringes the client's intellectual property nor competes with its clients in the end-product market (i.e., the market for formulations). This strategy was radically different from the most prevalent business model followed by Indian pharma companies in the 1980s and 1990s, which was to manufacture generic formulations of branded products from the stables of western big pharma companies and then launch those products in developed markets. The non-compete and trust-based approach adopted by Divi's helped it get business from western pharma giants who were wary of IP infringement by their Indian and Asian partners. This strategy received a further boost with India's adoption of intellectual property protection rules under the regulations of GATT/WTO, which helped Divi's get more outsourced business.

Our discussions with industry participants suggest that from its inception in the 1990s to date, Divi's hasn't lost any client on the grounds of intellectual property leakage and that the firm is so obsessed with maintaining the confidentiality of their clients' intellectual property that it sometimes also monitors the calls and personal conversations of staff at its plants and offices. As Divi's delivered on intellectual property confidentiality and maintained the quality of its products, it became a preferred choice for any incremental outsourced manufacturing by clients for whom IP protection is more critical than the cheapest price. The fact that Divi's clients are not price sensitive (but focused on quality and confidentiality) also helps Divi's maintain the healthy pricing of its products.[19]

COMMON FALLACIES ABOUT COMPETITIVE ADVANTAGES—PRICING POWER AND THE IMPORTANCE OF BRANDS

Frameworks like Sir John Kay's IBAS or Michael Porter's Five Forces are well understood by most promoters and management teams (even if they haven't formally been taught these frameworks in a classroom), and several businesses attempt to build their business strengths around these aspects of competitive advantages. However, only a small minority of such businesses successfully create strong competitive advantages. Lack of a clear understanding of the strengths of competitive advantages of a business often leads to several fallacies in investing. Pricing power is one such fallacy.

The standard definition of high pricing power is the ability of a firm to hike product prices without witnessing an attrition in its customer base. However, since most business battles are fought around price cuts (instead of price hikes), we believe that a more complete and more useful definition of pricing power is as follows: If an incumbent firm offers a product to its customers at a certain price (say, Rs 100), and a new competitor decides to offer a similar product to the same customers at a lower price (say, Rs 70)—then can the incumbent retain its Rs 100 product price and also retain its market share? Or will the incumbent need to cut its product prices to defend its dominance? If it is the former, then the incumbent has high pricing power, otherwise it does not.

Almost all large industries are highly competitive, and most firms with dominant market shares in these sectors have weak pricing power. For instance, in India's airlines sector, Interglobe Aviation (Indigo Airlines) has grown its market share over the last decade from ~15 per cent in FY2010 to ~50 per cent in FY2020. However, the bulk of airline passengers make their choices based on ticket prices, i.e., the cheapest price wins. Hence, despite its growing dominance (market share), Interglobe Aviation's 'revenue per passenger' has grown at only 1 per cent CAGR over FY2010–20.[20]

Likewise, India's telecom sector has witnessed a CAGR in excess of 40 per cent in subscriber base addition over the period FY2007–17 (i.e., before Reliance Jio started services). Bharti Airtel retained its market leadership with a market share of ~23 per cent. However, changing a telecom provider in India has historically been decided by customers predominantly on the back of price—the cheapest amongst the top three or four players has always won market share from others. As a result, to retain customers, players like Bharti Airtel have no choice but to reduce their tariffs to match what others are offering. Therefore, despite sustained dominance of market share in the industry, Bharti Airtel's ARPUs (Average Revenue Per Unit customer) **declined** at a CAGR of 8 per cent over these 10 years (FY2007–17). Absence of price hikes, along with weak earnings and RoCE, reflects a clear lack of competitive advantages, even if the firm retains its market share dominance. Bharti Airtel's profits after tax declined at a rate of 2.5 per cent per annum from FY2007 to FY2017.

The importance of brand as a source of competitive advantage is another common fallacy in investing. Building a brand is difficult, as it requires a deep understanding of who the customers are, where they are and how they want to be talked to. Building strong brand recall is also rewarding because it helps accelerate new customer recruitment and creates loyalty amongst existing customers, which incentivizes repeat purchases and reduces the need to shop around. In other words, a strong brand reduces the cost of acquisition of new customers, and for existing customers it increases the costs of switching to competing brands. Brand is also part of Sir John Kay's IBAS framework, discussed earlier in this chapter. However, brand does not create an insurmountable barrier to entry around a firm. Several firms in India have historically built exceptionally strong brands but have not offered much beyond a brand to their customers and stakeholders. Such companies have found it hard to demonstrate their pricing power in the face of fierce competition. Hindustan Unilever Ltd and Colgate Palmolive India Ltd are two such examples from India's FMCG sector.

Whilst Unilever has retained a 50 per cent market share in soaps and detergents, Colgate has retained more than a 50 per cent market share in oral care (toothpastes and toothbrushes) for several decades. Lifebuoy, Lux and Dove from Unilever even dominate market shares in the respective sub-segments of the industry, i.e., economy, mid- and premium segments. Brands like 'Surf' and 'Colgate' are so strong that they have become synonymous with 'detergent' and 'toothpaste' as categories for many customers! 'Colgate' has also ranked amongst the top five in India on Brand Equity's Most Trusted Brands 2020 list.[21] Despite the brand having such strong brand recall, Colgate's market share dominance has come at the cost of profitability in the face of fierce competition. Time and again, these firms have faced price wars from competitors like Patanjali (around five years ago), Nirma (more than twenty years ago), P&G and Dabur. In each such price war, Hindustan Unilever and Colgate reduce their product prices to address the challenge posed by a cheaper product. Hence, while their market share dominance is retained through such price wars, their profitability suffers. As a result, over the past ten years (FY2010–20), Hindustan Unilever has compounded profits at only 12 per cent CAGR and Colgate at only 6 per cent CAGR.[22]

A FRAMEWORK TO IDENTIFY DOMINANT FIRMS IN INDIA THAT HAVE SUSTAINED HIGH PRICING POWER

> 'All happy companies are different: each one earns a monopoly by solving a unique problem. All failed companies are the same: they failed to escape competition.'
>
> —Peter Thiel[23]

Just like it is hard to build pricing power, it is equally hard to sustain pricing power over time. In a dynamic world, the evolution of both demand (i.e., customer behaviour) and supply of a product or service can disrupt monopolies overnight, the way firms like Polaroid, Kodak and Xerox got disrupted, despite being great companies with strong competitive advantages.

In fact, several great firms with high pricing power have systematically slid to mediocrity in India. The Nifty50 Index, the Indian stock market's premier benchmark index, churns by around 50 per cent every decade. Hence, if a stock is in the Nifty50 index today, there is a 50 per cent probability that it will not be in the index ten years from now, and a 75 per cent probability that it will not be in the index twenty years from now. The tendency for large, successful companies to slide down the market-cap spectrum is not confined to those in the Nifty50. In most developed and emerging markets globally, 25–40 per cent of the indices composed of large companies churn every decade.[24]

Some of the reasons for the destruction of great Indian firms include: a) disruption of the product/service due to evolving technology or changing consumer habits; b) disruption of the distribution channel/marketing/supply chains; c) capital misallocation decisions by the company; d) change in the management team or ownership of the firm; and e) drop in focus/rigour of the management team due to complacency or lethargy.

Therefore, a creative monopolist or a dominant company reinvests the monopoly profits to innovate new products, improve existing products and figure out better ways of meeting evolving customer preferences.

Exhibit 58 shows a flowchart of the most common framework adopted by Indian monopolies/dominant firms that have sustained their dominance over decades despite several disruptions and evolutions. They approach a challenging aspect of the industry. Then, instead of resolving the challenge in a manner adopted by the firm's incumbent competitors, the monopolist first deepens the challenge further in order to change the structure of the industry in its own favour. And then it brings out a solution to this challenging construct, which cannot easily be replicated by competitors. Over the long term, these firms keep evolving the challenge and the solution to make it difficult for competitors to catch up.

Exhibit 58: Indian monopolists' business framework

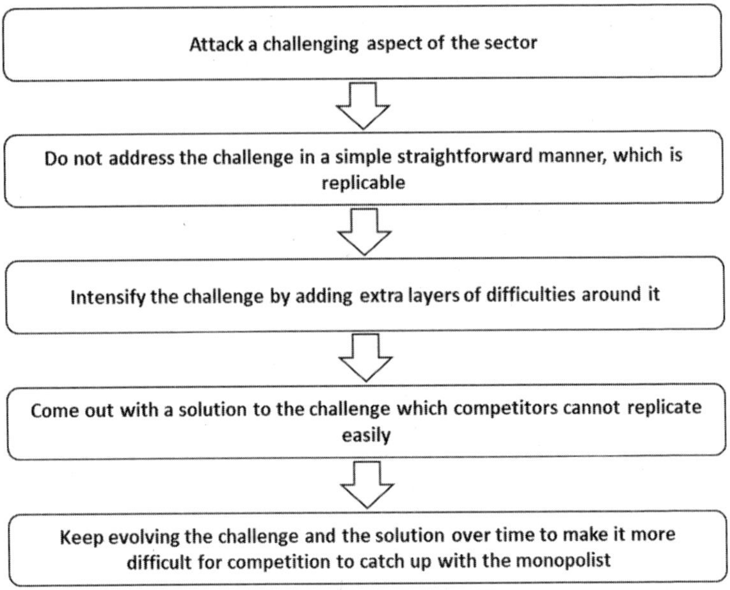

Source: Marcellus Investment Managers

When it comes to disruptions and evolutions, it is difficult to foresee exactly how an industry or business or customer will evolve in the future. However, certain characteristics are common to existing leaders who are likely to disrupt/innovate in their businesses to ensure that their leadership cannot be challenged by a competitor. The most important one includes a single-minded focus on the company's business and its capital allocation without any signs of complacency, lethargy, fatigue or boredom. Warren Buffett highlighted this point in Berkshire Hathaway's 1996 annual letter to shareholders: 'Loss of focus is what most worries Charlie (Munger) and me when we contemplate investing in businesses that in general look outstanding. All too often, we have seen value stagnate in the presence of hubris or of boredom that caused the attention of managers to wander.'

We now give you three case studies of Indian companies which have successfully followed the template shown in Exhibit 58, and by so doing relentlessly deepened their competitive advantages and created enormous wealth for their shareholders.

CASE STUDY: ABBOTT INDIA LIMITED (AIL)

AIL is a leading manufacturer of branded generic drugs, OTC products and nutritional supplements in India. Several of its brands have a dominant market share in their respective therapy areas like metabolics, women's health, vaccines, etc. For example, Abbott's Thyronorm has a market share of around 52 per cent in hypothyroidism management. Abbott's Creon has a market share of around 33 per cent in pancreatic enzyme replacement therapy, and Abbott's Influvac has a market share close to 63 per cent in vaccines for prevention of influenza.[25]

The examples cited here are just a few from the overall portfolio of AIL, where sixteen of its top twenty brands are ranked number 1 or number 2 in their market. Helped by the dominance of its products, between FY2010 and FY2020, Abbott India has been able to grow its revenues at an 18 per cent CAGR, coupled with a 23 per cent CAGR in its profit after taxes. So, how is AIL able to churn out this sort of performance year after year? The answer lies in its ability to create moats around different aspects of its business.

GLOBAL PRODUCT PORTFOLIO AND LOCAL R&D

AIL is a subsidiary of Abbott Laboratories, USA, and benefits from access to the vast product portfolio of its parent comprising over 1,500 products (with several hundred more in development). By accessing this portfolio, AIL is able to introduce multiple new products every year in the Indian market to address various needs in different segments. The local R&D team ensures that the product coming from the overseas portfolio is altered to meet the requirements of the Indian population and Indian regulators. This helps AIL introduce newer products at significantly lower costs compared with its competitors who do not have a global product portfolio.

Further, the R&D and product teams at AIL also work to fill the unmet needs of patient populations in therapy areas and products that are already well established. For example, Abbott had launched Thyronorm in several differential strengths (tablets with dosages starting from as small as 12.5 mg going up all the way to 200mg) when an established and market-leading product, Eltroxin from Galxo, was available only in higher dosage forms. In addition, Abbott India also differentiated Thyronorm by creating combination drugs that added vitamins or supplements—for example, Thyronorm Plus Iodine or Thyronorm with calcium. These versions of Thyronorm addressed deficiencies that often occurred in women with hypothyroidism.

CREATING MARKETS AND CONNECTS WITH PATIENTS AND PRESCRIBERS

Considering the fact that the bulk of AIL's revenues come from the prescription drugs business, where direct advertising to consumers is prohibited, merely introducing newer products does not guarantee success. In order to generate the best possible returns from its products, AIL focuses on building and raising awareness about medical conditions that are addressed by its products. As AIL creates such awareness, it also gets the benefit of gaining a foothold amongst the prescriber community, which it further strengthens by effectively building connect with key opinion leaders (KOLs, i.e., renowned specialists) through focused medico-marketing efforts. Such marketing efforts involve sponsoring conferences for KOLs, dissemination of scientific studies and journals, and shaping guidelines for treatment.[26]

The benefits that AIL derives from such a differentiated marketing approach are clearly visible in Thyronorm's journey to market domination. In FY2010, GSK's Eltroxin was the market-leading drug for treatment of hypothyroidism, with an ~ 50 per cent market share, and Abbott's Thyronorm had about a 40 per cent market share. The market size was around Rs 32 crore. Between 2011 and 2014, the government of India introduced the National List of Essential Medicines 2011 and the Drug Pricing Control Order 2013. Both these regulations led to a substantial decrease in the selling price of Eltroxin and Thyronorm (20–25 per cent reduction in prices). Instead of losing focus on Thyronorm due to decreased margins from the product, Abbott's management doubled down on increasing the market share of Thyronorm.[27]

In 2011, AIL launched its 'Think Thyroid Think Life Campaign' in association with the Indian Thyroid Society. Under this programme, AIL worked on increasing awareness about thyroid disorders, conducted over 5,600 camps for thyroid screening, created brand teams to increase the knowledge base of primary physicians and gynaecologists, and conducted academic programmes—'thyroid update'—which covered 4,000 doctors. It also created a sales team, known as the 'Thyroid Activation Team', which worked with healthcare professionals in rural communities throughout India to test women for hypothyroidism. When the disease was detected, the patient was told how Thyronorm would manage their symptoms and was directed to the local pharmacy to obtain the drug. The endorsement by healthcare professionals, coupled with Thyronorm's low price, reduced the likelihood that the patient would seek alternative treatments. As a result of its focus on the Thyronorm brand, Abbott emerged as the market leader in the hypothyroidism segment, with a market share of ~ 50 per cent in FY2019, a year in which the total market size for the drug in India was around Rs 700 crore.[28]

EMPOWERED LOCAL MANAGEMENT AND GLOBAL SUPPORT

Two issues that plague the Indian operations of several globally successful companies are the lack of focus of global management on the Indian business due to its relatively smaller size, and the staffing of Indian business at the board level with foreign executives who do not understand India well. As a result of these two issues, multinational companies (MNCs) are often not able to flourish in India and end up losing out on the tremendous opportunities provided by the Indian market for their products and services.

For Abbott Laboratories, the Indian business constitutes a significant part of its Established Product Division and hence gets adequate attention from the global management. As a result of this attention, the operations at AIL are highly metricized, with well-defined goals and regular reporting to regional and global headquarters. Although the global management sets the goals and targets for AIL, it gives complete freedom to the local management for charting and implementing strategies for achieving these goals. Further, the top management comprises largely of local talent, who understand the nuances of the domestic market better. This also reduces the risk of the best people leaving the organization for lack of career growth opportunities. So, instead of sending country heads and vertical in-charges from its global headquarters, Abbott sends American managers to Asia, not as expat bosses, but as consultants on short assignments 'with a definite end date'.[29]

Abbott also offers the same career-development opportunities to its Indian managers as to its American managers, including coaching, training, special projects and frequent contact with top executives. This helps Abbott maintain high retention rates for its top talent and, unsurprisingly, Abbott's attrition rates are much lower than the industry's.[30]

Abbott India's unique combination of global strengths and local competitive advantages has created enormous wealth for its shareholders. Re 1 invested in the company on 31 December 2000 would have become Rs 45.5 by 31 December 2020 (excluding dividends), a CAGR of 21 per cent. In contrast, Re 1 invested in the Sensex on the same day would have grown to only Rs 12.0 by 31 March 2020, implying that Abbott India has outperformed the Sensex by almost 3x in the twenty-year time period cited here.

CASE STUDY: DIVI'S LABORATORIES LIMITED (DIVI'S)

Divi's is a leading global manufacturer of generic active pharmaceutical ingredients (API) and a large-scale custom manufacturer of APIs for pharma companies from the US and Europe. It is the world's largest manufacturer for multiple APIs like Naproxen, Dextromethorphan, Iopamidol, Levetiracetam, etc. For Naproxen and Dextromethorphan, Divi's accounts for over 50 per cent of global production.[31] In addition to its generic API business, Divi's has a very large custom manufacturing business, where it counts some of world's biggest pharma companies, like Abbott, Sanofi, GSK and Pfizer, as its clients. Between FY2010 and FY2020, Divi's revenues have grown at a 19 per cent CAGR, its PAT has grown at a 15 per cent CAGR and its ten-year average RoCE (pre-tax) has been 29.6 per cent. Based on its financial performance, Divi's has been one of the most successful listed pharma companies in India in the last decade. This success has come to Divi's because of the differentiated business model it has created and its continuous focus on building sustainable competitive advantages for its business.

INTELLECTUAL PROPERTY (IP) COMPLIANCE DNA

Divi's Laboratories was started by Murali Divi in 1990 as a consultancy firm engaged in engineering new and efficient processes for API manufacturing, which would then be sold to the highest bidder. After a couple of years in the business as consultants, Divi's started adding manufacturing capacity in order to get some outsourced manufacturing work from international pharma companies. Outsourced production for western big pharma companies was not an established or preferred segment for pharma entrepreneurs in India during that period, as Indian generics manufacturers were aggressively trying to enter the developed markets by challenging the patents of innovators. Having seen the reluctance of innovator companies to give their IP to manufacturers in developing countries, Divi's positioned itself as a 100 per cent IP-compliant and non-competing service provider. To date, Divis has not deviated from these two committed principles and has not entered any end-user product segment. As Divi's was one of the early adopters of IP compliance policy, it was amongst the first companies in India to do custom synthesis for global pharma companies. Over the years, as Divi's continued its adherence to IP protection and continued to deliver on quality, it became a preferred partner for global pharma companies looking for outsourced manufacturing in India. Its commitment to not compete with its customers by entering the formulations segments adds to the trust it has built on IP compliance and gives it an edge over peers who carry out both—custom synthesis and formulations business.[32]

CHEMISTRY CAPABILITIES

Cost of production is one of the biggest determinants of success in the API business. But it is not the manpower cost that is the key for achieving the lowest cost of production of APIs. Instead, it is the simplicity of the process used to synthesize and purify the APIs that drives lower costs. Simplicity is achieved by creating manufacturing processes that reduce the number of steps and intermediates involved for producing the final product. Achieving this requires a very high order of capabilities in chemistry, which Divi's possesses. In its early years, to get traction in the API market, Divi's started working on improving production efficiencies in the manufacturing of Naproxen, an anti-inflammatory drug. Divi's core team (which came from Cheminor and comprised organic chemists and pharma engineers), came up with a more cost efficient and less polluting manufacturing process that used enzymes as catalysts instead of chemicals.[33] This substantially reduced costs and improved productivity in the manufacturing of Naproxen. As a result, Divi's garnered significant market share for this API, even after being the twenty-second entrant in the world market.[34]

FOCUS ON LIMITED PRODUCTS

It is very common to find pharma companies that try to be successful in multiple segments and products. Most of the time, chasing growth in multiple segments ends up being a sub-optimal use of capital. This is another area where Divi's has demonstrated tremendous discipline, by not entering any segments or products where its established skill-sets (in re-engineering the process chemistry in the manufacturing of an API) and its production scale do not give it any advantage. Ever since it started API production, Divi's has stuck to the same business segment and has reinvested its profits in increasing the scale of its API business. This it did by adding clusters of reactors and manufacturing equipment, which can manufacture multiple APIs. Even while selecting the APIs for manufacture, Divi's has only chosen those APIs that are off patent and have very high volumes of consumption globally. Over the years, it has added APIs to its product portfolios but has never bet on attempting to be the first mover. Rather, it has focused on cost, quality, and large-scale production in its API portfolio. As a result of this discipline in sticking to its core business, Divi's has avoided capital misallocations and has largely remained debt-free.

REGULATORY COMPLIANCE

Over 90 per cent of Divi's revenues come from exports. Markets with the most stringent regulations—the US and Europe—account for the majority of the export sales that Divi's makes. From its inception in 1990 until 2020, Divi's labs has received FDA observations only twice. It operates in a business segment where non-compliance leads not only to loss of immediate business but also to cancellation of long-term contracts and difficulties in getting future business from big pharma companies. So it is a reflection of Divi's competence in adhering to the standards prescribed by different regulators that it has received so few observations from the FDA. This track record of FDA compliance gives confidence to Divi's customers in APIs and custom synthesis to give more business to the company rather than risk sourcing from non-compliant suppliers, which could lead to their products inviting adverse regulatory actions. This regulatory track record also helps Divi's get better prices for its products and adds to the profitability of the company, as can be inferred from the financial disclosures made by the company.

Divi's Labs' strengths in process chemistry and the reputation it has built with western pharma companies, alongside the firm's discipline in capital allocation, has created enormous wealth for its shareholders. Re 1 invested in the company on 31 December 2003 would have become Rs 48.8 by 31 December 2020 (excluding dividends), a CAGR of 25.7 per cent. In contrast, Re 1 invested in the Sensex on the same day would have grown to only Rs 8.2 by 31 December 2020, implying that Divi's Labs has outperformed the Sensex by almost 5x over the seventeen-year period.

CASE STUDY: ASIAN PAINTS

Asian Paints is a classic case study of how building durable competitive advantages can help the sustenance of pricing power over several decades. The company has disrupted the paints industry in several ways. First, it disrupted the traditional distribution channel in the 1950s and 1960s, by eliminating channel partners like distributors and wholesalers. As a result, today decorative paint is perhaps the only mass market category where the manufacturer directly reaches 70,000+ points of sale (paint dealers), without any channel intermediation.[35]

The second disruption was in the way healthy margins were delivered to dealers. Typically, a paint dealer earns just 3–5 per cent margins, and in order to obtain healthy returns on invested capital (ROI) he requires very high inventory turns. This is the biggest area of differentiation between Asian Paints and its competitors. Asian Paints has built its strengths around demand forecasting using its technology investments. This, as mentioned earlier, helps it deliver a voluminous product (paints are at least 7-10x more voluminous than FMCG products), directly to 70,000+ dealers, three or four times every day.[36]

Thirdly, Asian Paints has kept product price hikes to the bare minimum—its prices have increased by a CAGR of less than 3 per cent over the past two decades! This is because Asian Paints keeps extracting incremental operating efficiencies by investing in technology and in building systems and processes in partnership with leading companies such as Cognizant,[37]

ABB[38] and Sight Machine.[39] Without access to such operating efficiencies, several paint manufacturers have found it difficult to survive in India. These efficiencies have helped Asian Paints consolidate market share very substantially.

As a result, as shown in Exhibit 59 below, Asian Paints has sustained greatness (healthy growth and RoCE) and leadership in the paints industry for over seven decades now. These seven decades have included several events/phases of disruption and evolution in the external and internal environment that Asian Paints has faced—including the exit of Champaklal Choksey in 1997, one of the four founders and, arguably, the biggest contributor towards the DNA of Asian Paints until that point. However, even in the post-Choksey era, Asian Paints continued to strengthen its dominance of the sector as well as its RoCE.

Exhibit 59: Asian Paints has sustained its greatness for seven decades since 1952

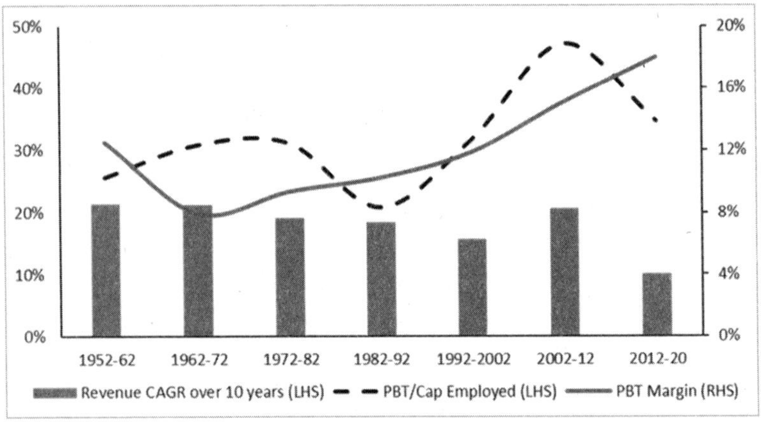

Source: Marcellus Investment Managers; Asian Paints; due to unavailability of data of earlier years, PBT/Capital employed considered as proxy to RoCE

Whilst this was Asian Paints' historical evolution, what is the future of India's decorative paints industry, and within that, what is the future of Asian Paints' leadership in the face of disruptions? Whilst we cannot foresee exactly how the sector will evolve, or get disrupted, over the next three to five years, there are some interesting pointers that could guide us towards an answer to this question. The paints sector in India has undergone a transition over the past few decades.

As mentioned above, Asian Paints has limited product price hikes to a less than 3 per cent CAGR. In a typical house painting project at the retail level, a customer pays for two separate items—the paint (material) and the labour. While paint costs have gone up at a CAGR of less than 3 per cent, labour costs have increased at a much higher rate of 8–10 per cent CAGR. This in turn has meant that today, on average, labour costs make up 65 per cent of the total cost of a painting project. This ratio was ~20 per cent two decades ago. For such high labour costs, customers expect a value-added experience in return. In order to use this new labour cost ratio as a source of disruption and an opportunity to gain market share, Asian Paints has spent more than a decade in establishing value-added labour-oriented offerings, like Asian Paints home solutions, waterproofing solutions and colour consultancies.[40]

More recently, leveraging on the paranoia amongst households around the COVID-19 crisis, Asian Paints launched and aggressively marketed 'Asian Paints Safe Painting Service'—to help accelerate the acceptance of value-added services as a concept in household painting projects. Moreover, the firm has indigenized mechanized solutions (express painting solutions), which are used by the labour workforce to execute painting projects in less than half the time it would otherwise take them via the manual painting processes. The next logical step would be to offer such mechanized solutions in a DIY format to customers directly.[41]

In 2020, Asian Paints launched a separate DIY brand called ezyCR8, in an attempt to kickstart the process of habituating customers around DIY as a concept for household painting and home improvements. DIY, short for Do it Yourself, is when home owners do not engage painters to paint their houses but do it themselves—a concept common in many western countries. None of Asian Paints' competitors are remotely close to Asian Paints in their readiness around these concepts. These concepts could drive the next wave of evolution or present themselves as a solution to a disruption in India's decorative paints industry.

Asian Paints' focus on deepening its competitive advantages has created enormous wealth for its shareholders. Re 1 invested in Asian Paints on 31 December 2000 would have become Rs 150.0 by 31 December 2020 (excluding dividends), a CAGR of 28.5 per cent. In contrast, Re 1 invested in the Sensex on the same day would have grown to only Rs 12.0 by 31 December 2020, implying that Asian Paints has outperformed the Sensex by almost 12x over the intervening twenty-year period.

'LETHARGY TESTS' FOR CONTINUOUS ASSESSMENT OF COMPETITIVE ADVANTAGES AND PRICING POWER

The frameworks discussed in this chapter for assessing the pricing power of a firm can be applied as a one-time exercise by an investor while building his portfolio or when including a new stock in it. However, after a firm has been included in an investor's portfolio, there is a possibility that, as time progresses, the pricing power of the firm gets diluted, either due to management complacency, loss of focus or fatigue in the face of competition. Just like while driving a car on 'cruise control', fatigue and a false sense of security can lead to loss of attention and then an accident.

When it comes to business management, focus on core strengths in a disciplined and sustainable manner over a long period of time sounds simple, but it is one of the hardest characteristics to develop. This is partly because it tends to get monotonous or boring over a period of time, especially when the external environment offers more 'exciting' opportunities. It is like Rahul Dravid waiting patiently for a loose delivery to play an aggressive shot, while at the other end, some other batter, losing patience after a couple of dot balls, risks trying to smash even good deliveries to the fence. As a result, investors in these firms run the risk of their management teams either doing too little to sustain their competitive advantages or doing too much by chasing alternative opportunities aggressively. In both these scenarios, management loses its focus on its core strengths (in cricketing parlance—after a long and successful innings, either the batter gets clean-bowled out of fatigue or gets caught, while hitting in excitement a ball on the up). Therefore, the firms that do well in the long run are the Rahul Dravids of the world, because they never lose their focus on their core strengths and capabilities.

Hence, any investment, even if it is in 'Consistent Compounders', needs to be tested for signs of lethargy/complacency/indiscipline using a framework centred on the aspects discussed below. We call these exercises, very simply, 'Lethargy Tests'.

COMPETITION

Consistent Compounders operate in large industries and generate high returns on capital employed. So they always attract competitors who try to narrow the gap between return on capital and cost of capital for these companies.

Such competitors either attempt to replicate the offerings of these companies, or start a price war, or introduce a new way of catering to the requirements of various stakeholders (customers/channel partners/raw material vendors, etc). For instance, in 2019, JSW Paints entered the paints industry with an 'any colour one price' offering. In 2017–18, Van Heusen (Aditya Birla Fashion and Retail) launched premium innerwear to compete directly with Jockey by offering higher incentives to distribution channel partners. Dr Lal Pathlabs faced a massive price war from competitors like Thyrocare in 2017. Reactive research—of understanding the response of a portfolio company to such competitive action—is important but not sufficient. Marcellus's 'Lethargy Tests' proactively aim to understand how a Consistent Compounder is deepening its competitive advantages, is strengthening ties with various stakeholders and is refreshing its offerings so as to leave no room for a competitor to take away market share through such actions as described above.

DISRUPTIONS

Over the past few years, event-based disruptions like the introduction of GST, demonetization, financial crises (e.g., those at IL&FS, GFC), and the COVID-19 crisis, have become very frequent. On the other hand, there are several disruptions caused by new technologies or new infrastructure (digital or physical) to meet customer requirements. Consistent Compounders typically use such disruptions to consolidate the dominance of their franchise by benefiting from the challenges faced by their competitors through such disruptions. Our Lethargy Tests need to keep a close track of the attempts made by our portfolio companies during periods of disruption.

EVOLUTION

As time progresses, there will be changes in customer preferences, market demographics, scale of operations and in penetration levels of the relevant products and services in existing geographies, etc. Our Lethargy Tests need to measure how alive, awake and adaptive the business models of an investor's portfolio companies are to such evolutionary changes, to ensure that they sustain earnings growth over long periods of time.

RISK OF CAPITAL MISALLOCATION

As Consistent Compounders grow and deepen their competitive advantages, the quantum of free cash flows available for redeployment tends to far exceed the amount that can be reinvested to grow the core business further. Promoters with aspirations of 'empire building', or those who want to add to their business new revenue growth drivers for the longer term, tend to use surplus capital to diversify across geographies or product categories. This could be either organic or inorganic diversification. Many firms prefer the inorganic route towards diversification, acquiring companies in related or unrelated businesses, forging joint ventures with other companies, acquiring minority stakes in other companies, etc. Whilst all this sounds straightforward, many firms with a great core franchise that consistently generates high RoCE have found it difficult to sensibly allocate surplus capital to diversify their business. Hence, our Lethargy Tests need to focus substantially on capital allocation decisions taken by a firm on an ongoing basis.

These Lethargy Tests need to combine secondary data research (annual reports, quarterly management commentaries) with primary data checks (e.g., extensive discussions with channel partners, vendors, customers, IT and HR consultants, former employees, etc.).

KEY TAKEAWAYS

- Firms which can sustain high RoCEs along with a high rate of reinvestment of capital into the business deliver higher and more sustainable earnings growth compared with firms which have high RoCE but low rates of reinvestment.
- The ability of a firm to achieve a combination of high RoCE and high rate of capital reinvestment is an outcome of the competitive advantages it has built around innovation, brands, architecture and strategic assets.
- Strong competitive advantages can help a firm create and sustain a monopolistic control over the profitability of the entire sector.
- As time progresses, such companies and their industries evolve. Hence, an investor's ability to compound wealth through such companies also means regular and rigorous understanding of their pricing power as well as testing of the firms for signs of lethargy/complacency/fatigue/indiscipline.

* * *

CHAPTER 5

What to Buy—Part 3: Masters of Capital Allocation

'Two companies with identical operating results and different approaches to allocating capital will derive two very different long-term outcomes for shareholders. Essentially, capital allocation is investment, and as a result all CEOs are both capital allocators and investors. In fact, this role just might be the most important responsibility any CEO has, and yet despite its importance, there are no courses on capital allocation at the top business schools.'

—William Thorndike Junior[1]

In Chapter 4, we discussed how the gap between RoCE and cost of capital is the key determinant of free cash flow generation for a business. In this chapter, we discuss what a business should do with the free cash flow that it generates. It is crucial that this cash, a source of capital, is invested in avenues where it continues to earn a return higher than the cost of capital. It is such capital allocation decisions that drive future value creation for a business.

The key questions we will address in this chapter include:

- How to review the capital allocation decisions of companies.
- What risks to look out for when analysing capital allocation decisions.

WHAT IS FREE CASH FLOW?

As we have discussed earlier, a business creates value only when it earns more on the total fixed and working capital invested in the business than what it has to pay the providers of this capital. We have also discussed that the difference between the RoCE and the CoC is the free cash flow of the business. But how is the RoCE linked to free cash? A simple way to understand the link between RoCE and free cash flow is to break down the calculations of these metrics into their key components. RoCE is expressed as:

$$Post - tax\ RoCE = \frac{Earnings\ Before\ Interest\ and\ Tax\ - Tax}{Capital\ Employed\ (Net\ Fixed\ Assets + Net\ Current\ Assets)}$$

Earnings before interest and tax (EBIT)[2] is used as the measure of operating profit or return that the business has earned or generated. It is noteworthy that in this instance, we consider EBIT and not EBITDA (earnings before interest, depreciation, amortization and tax), which is a better measure of cash flows. This is because the amount charged to depreciation can be used as a proxy for maintenance capital expenditure—that is, the minimum amount of capex the business needs to undertake simply to maintain the current scale of operations. Effectively, EBIT is the cash profit earned without any growth capex (i.e., from capacity additions). From this cash profit, the business must be able to pay the providers of capital—i.e., the lenders (debt holders) and equity shareholders. And only if the EBIT is higher than the amounts due to the providers of capital will the business generate surplus, or free cash. And only if the business generates surplus cash will it have the ability to invest in capacity expansion and grow revenues and earnings further. The accounting representation of this equation has the same implications, but looks a little different and flows in the manner as shown in Exhibit 60.

Exhibit 60: A simple representation of a company's cash flow waterfall

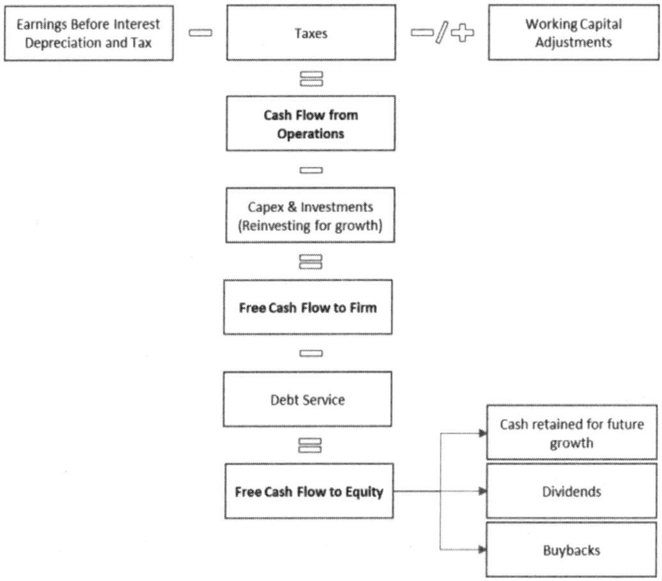

Source: Marcellus Investment Managers

A key responsibility of a company's management is deciding on the best use of the free cash flow the business generates. If a company sees sufficient growth opportunities in its business, it will prioritize the allocation of free cash for reinvesting in the business. Such reinvesting is done both to expand capacity (which drives future growth) as well as to deepen competitive advantages (which helps sustain RoCE higher than CoC). Another way of thinking about the situation is that if a company is consistently reinvesting cash flows at a rate of return higher than the cost of capital, it reflects both the company's competitive advantages and the management's ability to redeploy surplus capital successfully. The objective of the company's management, therefore, must be to keep the cycle going, as shown in Exhibit 61—building strong competitive advantages to earn high RoCEs, which leads to large free cash generation, which in turn is invested in increasing the capital employed and deepening competitive advantages.

Exhibit 61: Cash generation should be a virtuous cycle

Source: Marcellus Investment Managers

It follows that growth that generates an RoCE that is less than the CoC is not a sensible use of free cash. Therefore, the role of the company's management in identifying the right investments and allocating capital towards those projects is critical. However, most businesses, even the ones with deep moats, will be eventually constrained by the size of the market they operate in. Beyond a point, the quantum of free cash flow available for redeployment will far exceed the amount that the business needs to keep growing. In the absence of investment opportunities that cover the cost of capital, it is prudent for the management to return the free cash to shareholders as dividends or through buybacks.

However, smart management teams and Consistent Compounders do not allow themselves to be constrained by the lack of prevailing market opportunities; they expand the business to find growth in newer avenues, without diluting returns or increasing the business risk. For investors, identifying such management teams is crucial for long-term wealth creation; and that makes **Capital Allocation** the third pillar of Marcellus's investment framework.

A FRAMEWORK TO ASSESS ALLOCATION DECISIONS

Business expansion, whether in new markets or in new products (or in both), is a double-edged sword. While there may be lucrative growth opportunities to pursue, all companies start out with very little or no competitive advantage in the new product or market. No matter how strong the strategic rationale for diversification is, successful execution is not always easy. The Kellogg Co., USA, launched its breakfast cereals in India in 1994. A newly liberalized economy with the second-largest population in the world and favourable demographics, India was considered the natural market to enter for a multinational company seeking newer growth opportunities. But after over two decades in India, Kellogg has met with only limited success in becoming a regular part of the Indian breakfast plate.[3] Despite the company's size (it had $6.5 billion in sales globally in 1994)[4] and financial muscle, success in India proved to be elusive.

The struggle to make a dent in newer markets is also clearly visible in the online matrimonial classifieds space in India. Matrimony.com, the undisputed leader in south India, has found it challenging to get a foothold in other markets, while Jeevansathi and Shaadi.com, the key players in the west and north, have failed to make a mark in the southern region.[5]

New products are even more difficult to crack. In 2009, GlaxoSmithkline Consumer Healthcare (GSCH), then the makers of the health drink Horlicks, entered the instant noodles market. More than ten years hence, Horlicks's Foodles remains a marginal player in the category, and possibly eight out of ten people reading this might have not have even heard of the brand. Although this move did not make a financial dent on the company (RoCEs rose in the five-year period from the first launch of noodles, largely due to growth in the core health drinks products of Horlicks and Boost), whatever capital and management bandwidth that was expended in launching instant noodles could have been utilized better elsewhere. Interestingly, in April 2020, GSCH merged with Hindustan Unilever (HUL). Along with the merger, HUL also paid Rs 3,045 crore to acquire the Horlicks brand from GSK.[6]

Tata Motors could not replicate its dominance of the commercial vehicles market in passenger cars. The company reported the first-ever loss in its history in FY2001 as the Indica, launched in late 1998, failed to make a mark. Although the Indica tasted success for a few years after a refurbished model was introduced, it never became a serious competitor to Maruti, Hyundai or Honda's models.[7] After achieving a peak market share of 24.3 per cent in its category in FY2003, the Indica kept losing base over the years, and the model was eventually discontinued from April 2018.

How, then, should investors assess management's capital allocation decisions? The first step is to assess the extent of risk in the new growth strategy. What could be the chances of failure or success? Once you have an assessment of the risk, the next step should be to view the strategy in terms of the quantum of capital the management is seeking to allocate towards the strategy. Is the management trying to bite off more than it can chew? Or, can the balance sheet take the risks of the proposed capital allocation decision going wrong?

To assess the risk of the strategy itself, a useful place to start is the Ansoff Matrix, a tool developed by H. Igor Ansoff in the 1950s. The tool considers the sources of growth as coming either from new products or from new markets. As seen in Exhibit 62, the top-left quadrant is where all companies start—what is commonly termed as the 'core' business. Once market share dominance is achieved or growth opportunities are fully exploited in the core business, the natural progression for a company is to either take its products into newer markets or to expand its product portfolio, while continuing to operate in the same market. This should be followed by achievement of dominance in the new markets or new products, and so on and so forth.

Exhibit 62: The Ansoff Matrix

		PRODUCTS	
		EXISTING	NEW
MARKETS	EXISTING	**Market Penetration Strategy** This is the core business; growth comes from market share gains. E.g. Nirma started out by selling detergent powder door-to-door locally in Ahmedabad	**Product Development Strategy** Growth comes from selling new products to existing customers. E.g. Nirma selling bathing soaps to buyers of its detergents.
	NEW	**Market Development Strategy** Growth comes from selling existing products in new markets. E.g. Nirma expands beyond Ahmedabad to other markets around the country	**Diversification Strategy** Growth from selling new products in new markets. E.g. Nirma enters the business of cement

Source: Marcellus Investment Managers; *Harvard Business Review*

The success of growth strategies depends on how well they are executed. Unfortunately, the success, or lack thereof, of a company in executing a growth strategy is not easy to forecast. Whilst the past track record of the management is the most comforting indicator investors can draw upon, that may not predict success in a new strategy in the future. Therefore, it is important to juxtapose the strategy against the quantum of capital the management is allocating towards it. A calibrated capital commitment would mean the ability to reverse tack in time without doing too much damage to the overall financial health of the company. This would mean test marketing or a limited launch on the company's part to assess consumer feedback before going full throttle.

HDFC Bank, for example, usually tests a new product on a small set of existing customers and then offers it to all eligible existing customers. It is only after this that any product is widely launched to outside customers. This enables the bank to modify its credit processes based on the initial underwriting experience, and then grow the product with much lower risk.[8] Following this calibrated approach over long periods of time has held HDFC Bank in good stead across the multiple credit cycles that India has seen.

Another example is that of Coca Cola India's plans to enter the dairy-based drinks segment. The company launched its 'Vio' brand of flavoured milk in January 2016. In the first phase, Vio was made available only in about 500 Reliance Retail stores across the country. The plan was for Reliance Retail to build awareness about the product through special promotions, sampling the product among its regular consumers as part of its 'loyalty programme', and eventually extending the offer to all consumers.[9] If successful, 'Vio' would have been launched widely across markets and channels. However, the product failed to take off and Coca Cola had to take it off the shelves.[10] The company then introduced 'Vio' Spiced Buttermilk in 2020, again through a limited launch in select cities and towns in just six states.[11] We believe that the future of the product will be decided on the basis of the results of the limited launch.

When assessing capital allocation decisions, investors can always draw comfort if managements take a cautious, incremental path in new markets or products. It was smart thinking on Coca Cola's part to refrain from a big-bang pan-India entry in the dairy segment, where it did not (and arguably, still does not) have any significant competitive advantages, and where the segment is already dominated by national players such as Amul and Britannia, and several regional brands.

INORGANIC PRODUCT OR MARKET EXPANSIONS ARE RISKY

Product or market extensions can be done either organically or inorganically. Organic expansions are those that are undertaken internally, like expansion of manufacturing capacity or increasing the number of retail stores, etc. Inorganic expansions are achieved by mergers, acquisitions and takeovers—say, buying out a manufacturing capacity. In sectors where market shares are fragmented, inorganic expansion becomes a relatively higher contributor to growth. Over time, players with strong competitive advantages in such fragmented industries tend to acquire the weaker players who struggle to cover their cost of capital on a sustainable basis. Smart management teams also use their strong free cash generation to buy out players in adjacent products, thereby gaining an immediate foothold in a new segment, which would have otherwise taken years to build organically.

Market or product extensions are, however, tricky when a company tries to enter an unfamiliar overseas market, and that too by acquiring a local player.

Starting from the mid-2000s, several Indian companies had deployed surplus capital towards international expansions through acquisitions—for example, Godrej Consumer Products Ltd. (GCPL) in Africa, Indonesia and Latin America; Pidilite in Brazil, the US and the Middle East; Marico in the Middle East, Bangladesh and South Africa; Dabur in Africa, the US,

Turkey and Egypt; Havells in Sylvania; Tata Steel in Europe, Asian Paints (Berger International, 2001); and Bharti Airtel in Africa.

Analysis of the RoCEs of some of the overseas acquisitions (RoCE of consolidated entity less RoCE of standalone entity, where the India business is housed) shows how these international acquisitions have fared. Several interesting aspects emerge from this analysis:

A substantial part (more than 100 per cent, in one case) of operating cash flows generated from the standalone business was deployed towards international acquisitions—see the fourth column of Exhibit 63.

The domestic (standalone) businesses of these firms have generated RoCEs substantially higher than cost of capital, many often even higher than 50 per cent (see Exhibit 64). This is reflective of the strong moats built by these firms in India.

The international (non-standalone) business RoCEs of these firms have been sub-par. In several instances, these businesses have generated RoCEs substantially below the cost of capital (see Exhibit 64). This is reflective of the weak moats existing in these international businesses.

Exhibit 63: Capital allocation towards overseas M&A, as percentage of standalone operating cash flows[12]

Company	Overseas acquisitions	Period	% of operating cash flow allocated to overseas acquisitions
Godrej Consumer Products	Tura group, Africa (2010); Darling, Africa (2012); SON, Africa (2017) etc.	FY11-18	112%
Marico	Enaleni Pharma, Africa (2008); Int. Consumer Corp., Vietnam (2011) etc.	FY08-12	46%
Dabur	Redrock, Dubai (2004); Hobi group, Turkey (2011) etc.	FY04-12	41%
Pidilite	Pulvitech, Brazil (2008); Jupiter, Middle East (2006); Bamco group, Thailand (2008); Cyclo, USA (2007) etc.	FY06-09	35%

Source: Marcellus Investment Managers; Ace Equity

Exhibit 64: Implied RoCEs of non-standalone business have been lower than those of the standalone business for some companies[13]

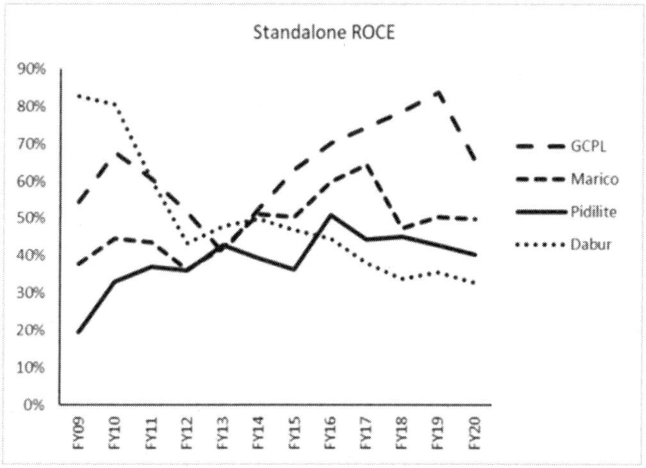

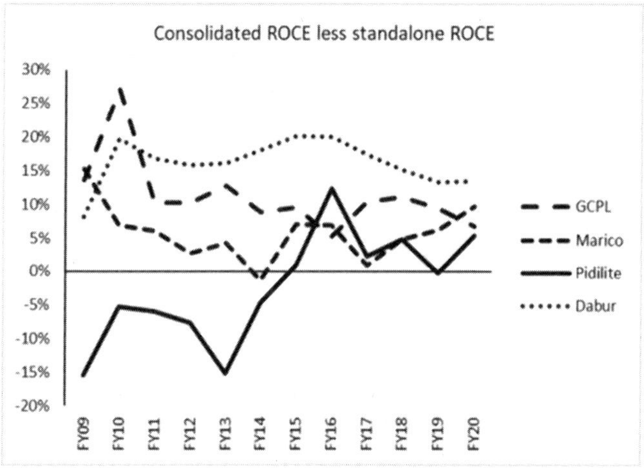

Source: Marcellus Investment Managers; Ace Equity; *GCPL stands for Godrej Consumer Products Ltd

The analysis above highlights the fact that an inorganic growth strategy might not always be the right use of free cash. There might be many reasons for such a strategy to fail. Managing a business in an unknown (or lesser known) overseas geography may require a different organizational structure than what the acquiring company operates with in its home territory. Or the acquisition might stretch management's bandwidth, and the resultant attention deficit could impact the core business's performance.

UNRELATED DIVERSIFICATION POSES THE BIGGEST RISK

It is evident from the Ansoff Matrix that the riskiest strategy is 'new products in new markets', and the one that investors should be most wary about. Such diversification not only requires large capital commitments but also demands a disproportionate share of management bandwidth. As highlighted, the split focus could hurt even the core business, as competitors will exploit the opportunity to weaken the barriers to entry built in that business. Moreover, it is always easier and more cost-effective for an investor to herself diversify her portfolio (by buying the shares of a cement company, for example) rather than have a company she is invested in do it for her (e.g., Nirma entering the cement business).

In pursuing an unrelated diversification, a company starts off with what we can call a double handicap—it lacks competitive advantages in the new product as well as in the new market. More often than not, it is difficult to build sustainable advantages that can allow the company to earn justifiable returns in the new areas of business. And even if it is not complex to build a new business (in the sense that it is not rocket science to build a competitive advantage), it can take several years to do so. A comparison of conglomerates with companies focused on a single product/market and/or its adjacencies clearly drives home this point.

Exhibit 65: Comparable RoCEs of conglomerates with companies focused on core business

Conglomerates		**Single-sector focused companies**	
Company	**Avg 10-year RoCE (FY11–20)**	**Company**	**Avg 10-year RoCE (FY11–20)**
Grasim Industries Ltd. *Natural fibres, cement, financial services*	15.1%	Shree Cement *Cement*	18.3%
Mahindra & Mahindra Ltd. *Automobiles, financial services, logistics, IT services, timeshare holidays etc.*	14.2%	Maruti Suzuki Ltd. *Passenger vehicles*	21.6%
Larsen & Toubro Ltd. *Construction and Engineering, financial services, IT services, infrastructure assets*	13.0%	Pidilite Industries Ltd. *Adhesives & related*	35.4%
Reliance Industries Ltd. *Petroleum refining, retail, telecom services, digital services*	11.0%	Asian Paints Ltd. *Paints & related*	44.6%

Source: Marcellus Investment Managers; Ace Equity

The conglomerates cited in Exhibit 65 are actually among the better-managed instances of unrelated diversification. Although these conglomerates have recorded relatively lower RoCEs, their business expansions have not had disastrous effects on the entire group. Contrast this with cases in Exhibit 66, where the companies, including a very long list of group companies which we have not mentioned here in the interest of space, have either ceased to exist or the original promoters have had to sell the business to new owners.

Exhibit 66: Conglomerates with disastrous outcomes for shareholders

Company	Core/Original business	Unrelated diversifications	Outcome
Videocon Industries	Home appliances	Telecom, Oil, Media	Taken to NCLT under the Indian Bankruptcy Code
UB Group	Liquor	Airlines	Airline business under liquidation
Jaiprakash Associates	Construction	Cement, hydropower plants, BOT roads, real estate, hotels	Taken to NCLT under the Indian Bankruptcy Code
Alok Industries	Textiles	Retail, real estate	Taken to NCLT under the Indian Bankruptcy Code
Lanco Infratech	Construction	Power generation, BOT roads, real estate	Under liquidation

Source: Marcellus Investment Managers; *www.ibbi.gov.in*

We now look at three different case studies to understand how investors can assess the capital allocation decisions of listed companies. These case studies, although analysed with the benefit of hindsight, provide a useful framework for putting the opportunities of expansion strategies in the right perspective of risks and rewards.

CASE STUDY: TATA STEEL

Tata Steel is the oldest and one of the largest steel manufacturers in India. The company, for most of its long history, was an integrated steel maker. That is, it mined the ore and also made the metal. The company has mining rights to iron ore and coal, the key raw materials.

In its quest for growth, Tata Steel embarked on an overseas expansion drive with the acquisition of NatSteel, a Singapore-based steel maker with plants in Malaysia and Vietnam, in 2004. They followed this up with the acquisition of Millennium Steel, Thailand, in 2005. And then, in 2007, Tata Steel acquired Corus, a European steel maker. In a matter of three years, Tata Steel went from about 5 million tons of steel capacity in India to around 28 million tons of steel capacity across Asia and Europe.[14]

Let us analyse these acquisitions in the context of capital allocation. While we have the benefit of hindsight in analysing this, the Tata Steel case provides a good framework to investors for considering what risks to evaluate in the capital allocation decisions of companies.

NEW MARKETS

According to the World Steel Association,[15] on a per capita basis in 2004, India consumed 35 kgs of steel, whereas China consumed 217 kgs, Brazil 111 kgs, the USA 437 kgs and South Korea 1,013 kgs. A simple comparative analysis back in 2004 would have been indicative of the long-term growth potential for Indian steel consumption. And, sure enough, over the following ten years up to 2014,[16] India was the second fastest growing large steel market (countries with over 10 million tons of annual consumption), with a 7 per cent CAGR, next only to China's 8 per cent. Compared to this, most European markets saw significantly weaker growth over the period 2004–14, including Germany (0.9 per cent), Italy (-3.4 per cent), France (-2.1 per cent) and the UK (-2.7 per cent). This implies that India should have been the market of choice for deploying any surplus capital Tata Steel had, rather than Europe where it spent its money acquiring plants.

NEW PRODUCTS

One of the reasons for the Corus acquisition, as highlighted in Tata Steel's 2006-07 annual report, was to obtain access to domain expertise in the automotive, packaging and construction sectors, which would enable Tata Steel to supply high-value, sophisticated finished products in India. This could have been a justified strategic move, especially considering that a developing country like India was likely to see increased use of high-value steel products. In that sense, product development scores over market development, as far as the Corus acquisition goes.

QUANTUM OF CAPITAL ALLOCATION

To be fair, the long-term outcomes of the product and market extension strategies could not have been predicted with certainty back in 2005–07, when Tata Steel made acquisitions in south east Asia and Europe. However, as discussed earlier, it is important to juxtapose any expansion strategy with the quantum of capital the management is allocating towards it. Between the three overseas acquisitions, Tata Steel spent approximately Rs 58,000 crore over FY2005–08, when its net worth as of March 2004 was about Rs 4,500 crore and its market capitalization Rs 14,100 crore. Regardless of what strategic benefits could have been derived from the acquisitions, the quantum of capital allocation alone signifies a high degree of risk. Moreover, the acquisition was not funded from Tata Steel's free cash flows, but by borrowed money. A leveraged acquisition raises the risks even higher.

Exhibit 67: Tata Steel consolidated RoCE FY03–20

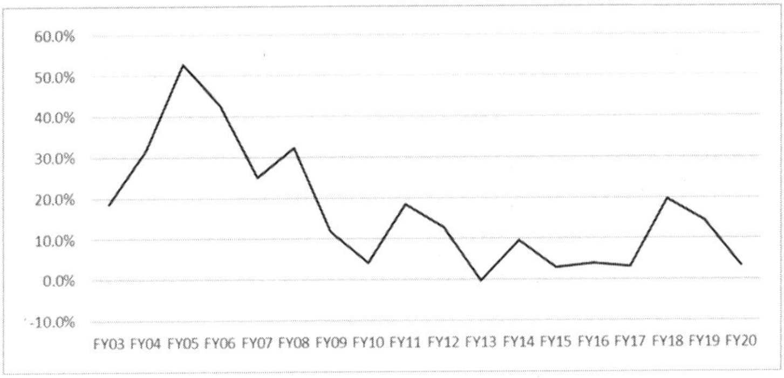

Source: Marcellus Investment Managers; Ace Equity

In conclusion, there were pointers for investors, which would have given them an inkling of the potentially large risks in the decision of Tata Steel's management to allocate capital towards these acquisitions. And, as it turned out, there has been a structural decline in the company's RoCE since FY2008, the year of the Corus acquisition, as seen in Exhibit 67.[17] For investors, the key lesson to take home here is to evaluate upsides from a growth strategy in the context of risks involved in pursuing that strategy, especially if it is a debt-fuelled, inorganic product or overseas market expansion.

Tata Steel's capital allocation missteps have impacted its ability to deliver shareholder value. Re 1 invested in the company on 31 December 2000 would have become just Rs 8.7 by 31 December 2020 (excluding dividends), a CAGR of 11.4 per cent. In contrast, Re 1 invested in the Sensex on the same day would have grown to Rs 12 by 31 December 2020, implying that Tata Steel underperformed the Sensex by 1.8 percentage points.

Let us look at another company to highlight the criticality of prudent capital allocation to long-term wealth compounding. This company also tried to foray into the international markets through the acquisition route. But the quantum of free cash deployed for acquisitions was modest, and hence, when the acquisitions failed to deliver returns, it was relatively easy for the management to take remedial measures.

CASE STUDY: PIDILITE

Pidilite spent the first nearly four decades of its existence (1959–2000) establishing dominance in white glue adhesives in the Indian market through its brand Fevicol. Subsequently, the company has regularly expanded its markets as well as products, organically as well as inorganically through acquisitions.

Over the years 1999–2005, Pidilite made several acquisitions in the domestic market to add to its product portfolio and to extend the firm's channel presence and intermediary influence. These included:

a) Ranipal, a fabric whitener brand, acquired in 1999 for Rs 4 crore
b) M-Seal and Dr Fixit in the sealants and waterproofing segments, respectively, acquired in 2000 for Rs 32 crore
c) Steelgrip, an insulation tapes brand, acquired in 2002 for Rs 10 crore, and
d) Roff, a tiling and flooring adhesives brand, acquired in 2005 for an undisclosed amount.

Pidilite spent 11 per cent of the total operating cash flows (no debt) generated by the firm on these acquisitions over this period. Most of these acquisitions have become dominant brands in their respective categories by now and have delivered RoCEs substantially higher than the cost of capital for Pidilite. Thanks to this phase of expansion, Pidilite has one of the most diversified distribution networks of any Indian company, with its products reaching the customer through multiple channels, including convenience stores (kiranas), hardware stores, paint shops, modern retail outlets, e-commerce, paan-wallahs and stationery shops.[18]

From 2006 onwards, Pidilite tried venturing into markets outside India, deploying approximately Rs 685 crore in international acquisitions (26 per cent of operating cash flows over a nine-year period) in Brazil, the Middle East and the USA, and also an elastomer manufacturing plant in France. Pidilite bought small companies, some of which were operating in unrelated industries without any market leadership. In countries like Brazil, the acquisitions were faced with an economic collapse in the country and issues with the legacy management team of the company. Over 2011–2020, Pidilite has written off ~Rs 180 crore worth of its investments in subsidiaries in Brazil and the Middle East, and ~Rs 300 crore of its investments in the elastomer project. The acquisition made in the USA (Cyclo) was sold off in 2017 for ~Rs 45 crore.[19]

Having learnt from the mistakes it made in its international acquisitions, Pidilite shifted its focus back to the domestic market and to its core adhesives business. The company acquired many smaller players in the Indian market to consolidate its market position in a wide range of adhesives. These acquisitions include textile chemical and adhesives company Bluecoat for ~Rs 260 crore, and the adhesive brands of Suparshva for an undisclosed consideration. These relatively small domestic acquisitions have turned out to be substantially RoCE-accretive for Pidilite.

Pidilite also deployed ~Rs 300 crore over FY2014–19 (~7 per cent of operating cash flows and ~2–3 per cent of capital employed over this period) to acquire businesses in adjacent categories (CIPY—floor coatings; Nina and Percept—waterproofing contractors) and has formed JVs with MNCs like ICA for niche products like wood finishes. These businesses have shown significant improvement in financial performance post-acquisition. In addition to disciplined capital allocation towards M&A in this phase, Pidilite also completed a share buyback of Rs 500 crore in FY2018 at Rs 1,000 per share, which was at a 12–13 per cent premium to the prevailing market price of the time. This share buyback amounted to 14 per cent of capital employed and 63 per cent of Pidilite's operating cash flows in FY2018. Between FY2010 and FY2020, Pidilite's RoCE rose from 26 per cent to 32 per cent.

In FY21, during the COVID-19 pandemic, when several firms in India were finding it difficult to deal with the uncertainty in the external environment, Pidilite went ahead and acquired one of the Indian subsidiaries of Huntsman Corporation (USA), which manufactures and sells adhesives, sealants and other products under well-known brands such as Araldite, Araldite Karpenter and Araseal.[20] Before this acquisition, epoxy adhesives were the only large category in Indian adhesives industry where Pidilite had failed to establish a leadership presence, because of the strength of Huntsman's Araldite brand. Pidilite made this acquisition at only fifteen times its 2019 EBITDA, when the entity had generated 35 per cent EBITDA margin that year.[21] Pidilite funded this acquisition entirely from the surplus accumulated cash available on its balance sheet. Hence, this acquisition did not weaken the balance sheet of Pidilite; instead, it gave it an opportunity to further dominate the adhesives industry whilst also deriving synergies when Pidilite was already the number 2 player in epoxy adhesives.

Pidilite's journey is a testimony to the benefits of focused capital allocation in the core business and/or adjacencies. It also shows that it is possible to contain damage done by expansion strategies that go wrong, provided the capital allocated to the strategies is calibrated and the management does not bet the proverbial house on it.

Pidilite management's stellar capital allocation has created enormous wealth for its shareholders. Re 1 invested in the company on 31 December 2000 would have become Rs 142.7 by 31 December 2020 (excluding dividends), a CAGR of 28.2 per cent. In contrast, Re 1 invested in the Sensex on the same day would have grown to only Rs 12.0 by 31 December 2020, implying that Pidlite has outperformed the Sensex by almost 11x over the intervening twenty years.

CASE STUDY: KOTAK MAHINDRA BANK

Kotak Mahindra Bank, set up by Uday Kotak in 1985, started life as a non-banking financial company (NBFC). In February 2003, Kotak Mahindra Finance Ltd, the NBFC, received a banking licence from the Reserve Bank of India, and Kotak Mahindra Bank came into being. In the sixteen years of its existence as a bank, KMB has grown earnings per share at a CAGR of 28.6 per cent. At the end of FY2020, KMB had a loan book of Rs 2,20,000 crore.

There are important lessons in capital allocation to be drawn from tracing the journey of Kotak Mahindra Bank (KMB). Some important takeaways are:

THE MERGER THAT PROPELLED KMB INTO THE BIG LEAGUE

In 2015, KMB acquired ING Vysya Bank in what was then the largest merger in India's banking history. This capital allocation decision gave KMB access to markets and products where they had a relatively smaller presence—the region of south India and the SME segment, respectively. However, given the size of the deal, any misjudgement would have cost the bank dearly in the future. To mitigate this risk, KMB structured the deal as a share-swap deal, not having to pay any cash. Moreover, with the valuation differential between KMB (~4.5x P/B) and ING Vysya (~2.2x P/B), the equity dilution was limited to just 15 per cent.

MASTERING THE VIRTUOUS CYCLE OF GENERATING AND REDEPLOYING PROFITS

Capital is the raw material of a bank, and KMB has prioritized redeployment of capital in the form of surplus profits in growing the business. Over the ten-year period from FY2011 to FY2020, KMB paid total dividends of only Rs 908 crore (including dividend distribution tax) out of its profits of over Rs 41,500 crore. That is because the bank consistently found opportunities to use its cash flows to invest capital back in the business while maintaining RoE at about 14.5 per cent.

As a result, KMB's EPS has grown at a ~17 per cent CAGR over FY2010–20. This EPS growth has played a key role in KMB's share price growing at a CAGR of ~21 per cent over FY2011–2020.

MANAGING JOINT VENTURES

For any foray in a new line of lending or financial services beyond banking, KMB has preferred to do it by forming joint ventures (JVs) with global leaders rather than committing resources on its own. KMB's JVs with Goldman Sachs and Ford in 1996 helped it understand global best practices in broking, investment banking and automobile lending. Similarly, KMB entered into a 76:24 joint venture with Old Mutual when it wanted to enter the life insurance business in 2001. Not only did KMB learn from such global players, but it was also able to end those JVs amicably while retaining those businesses. In an era when being acquired by foreign JV partners was the norm (just three months prior to Goldman's exit from Kotak Securities, Merrill Lynch had bought out Hemendra Kothari's 50 per cent stake in DSP Merrill Lynch), KMB not only bought out the stakes of Ford, Goldman and Old Mutual but also ended the joint ventures amicably by paying a fair price to all JV partners. Old Mutual earned a 15 per cent CAGR return on its original investment of Rs 185 crore when its 26 per cent stake was bought out in 2017. Similarly, Goldman earned a 13 per cent CAGR on its Rs 100 crore investment in Kotak Mahindra Capital and Kotak Securities when it was offered Rs 330 crore for its 25 per cent stakes in each of the entities. By the time KMB offered an exit to its JV partners, not only had the bank capitalized on the intangibles of imbibing global best practices but had also become India's number 1 investment bank, brokerage company and automobile lender, and the country's sixth largest life insurer. KMB is now the only large Indian bank which owns 100 per cent of all its subsidiaries, whether in broking, investment banking, insurance or asset management.

TIMING EQUITY CAPITAL RAISES SENSIBLY

Smart capital raising is also, in a way, smart capital allocation. Typically, fast-growing lenders need to raise capital every three years or so, since a growth rate higher than RoE puts pressure on regulatory capital. KMB has also raised capital at intervals of three to four years, but what has set this bank apart from its peers is its ability to raise money from the capital markets while restricting the extent of equity dilution. KMB has raised equity capital through the qualified institutional placement (QIP) route twice—in 2007 and 2017—and on both occasions, at or near the market peak, which meant lower equity dilution and the resultant impact on RoE.

KMB's remarkably effective capital allocation has created enormous wealth for its shareholders. Re 1 invested in the company on 31 December 2000 would have become Rs 532.2 by 31 December 2020 (excluding dividends), a CAGR of 36.9 per cent. In contrast, Re 1 invested in the Sensex on the same day would have grown to only Rs 12.0 by 31 December 2020, implying that KMB has outperformed the Sensex by nearly 43x over the intervening twenty years.

THE DARK SIDE OF CAPITAL ALLOCATION

So far, we have discussed capital allocation decisions taken by the managements of companies. In some cases, it is also very important to assess capital allocation decisions made by the promoters of companies—that is, the way they decide to deploy funds between the different businesses they own. When promoters control more than one business, there could be a risk of them trying to 'allocate' capital from a business that is doing well and generating cash flows to another business that needs funds. Such transfer of funds, even if done transparently, is seldom in the interests of minority shareholders. Usually, the board of directors would object to and block such support to other businesses of the promoter. But a desperate promoter could find means of bypassing the board too. Therefore, it makes sense for investors in any company to be cautious when the promoter has multiple businesses housed in different companies; more so if the promoters' shareholding varies from company to company and there is an incentive for them to favour a company where their shareholding is higher relative to others.

An example of the above, which we have discussed earlier too, is Satyam Computers. In January 2009, Ramalinga Raju, the promoter and CEO of Satyam Computers Ltd, in a letter to the company's board, admitted to a large-scale falsification of the company's financial results, including the inflating of revenues, understating of liabilities and inflating of cash and bank balances.[22] Using many different means, including creation of fake employees and paying them salaries, Raju siphoned cash out from Satyam to ostensibly buy land and properties in his personal name. At one point, when it became difficult to manage and supress the widening gap between actual and reported cash balances, Raju sought to merge two of his family-owned entities, Maytas Properties and Maytas Infrastructure, with Satyam. The plan was to pay for the acquisitions using the fictitious cash on Satyam's books. Since the cash was to be paid to Raju and his family, it did not matter whether any actual payments were made. In return, the assets of the Maytas companies could be used to clean up the fraud.[23] The promoter family owned just 8.61 per cent of Satyam while owning 100 per cent of the Maytas companies. Their financial interests were therefore not at all aligned with the interest of the minority shareholders of Satyam—and, in tough times, it was obvious where the loyalties of the promoters would lie.

While, admittedly, the Satyam case is a rare example of capital allocation gone wrong, it is a pointer to the extreme extent promoters could go to for protecting their personal interests. When evaluating capital allocation decisions, investors should therefore take into consideration the allocations made at the promoter level as well as at the company level.

HUMAN CAPITAL—THE MOST CRITICAL ALLOCATION DECISION

'A leader's lasting value is measured by succession.'

—John C. Maxwell[24]

Human capital is the most precious capital of a Consistent Compounder, since it helps the firm nurture a DNA of deepening competitive advantages over the long term. However, as time progresses, individuals who are part of a firm's human capital could retire, resign or get supplemented by a widening team that shares key responsibilities. Hence, a Consistent Compounder needs succession planning to help sustain its competitive advantages. However, succession planning is not an event. It is a process that must be embedded in the DNA of an organization.

Implementation of a succession plan is challenging at multiple levels for most organizations. When a business is small, it might be run by a leader (the promoter, CEO or MD) who is omnipotent—someone who can do anything and can solve all problems. As such organizations grow bigger in size, the 'omnipotent' leader might feel insecure about letting go of control, which becomes particularly difficult when the firm has built strong competitive advantages under the same leader. Moreover, if the leader builds a layer of CXOs and trains them as potential successors, then there is a risk that the trained CXOs who don't get the top job will leave the firm to assume leadership roles in other organizations. Such exits can then leave a massive void in the organization. Optimal timing for identifying a successor is also important. If the successor is identified too soon, then there is the risk of an increase in attrition amongst other capable CXOs as they see themselves having hit a ceiling in their career progression. If the successor is identified too late, then she might be underprepared for the role and other senior managers in the team might not have built enough trust in her leadership capabilities. Many businesses in India are run by promoter families. Such promoters might tend to think about their sons and daughters as the natural successors to head the business. Unlike some professionals who might have worked in the organization for twenty or thirty years, successors from the next generation of the promoter family might not have spent enough time at the ground level to learn about the strengths and weaknesses of the business and may not have built trust and relationships with various stakeholders. Furthermore, there might also be more than one candidate from the next generation of the promoter family, and this could create friction amongst family members.

Such challenges, if not addressed properly by means of an institutionalized and meritocratic succession planning process, can lead to strategic mistakes, deterioration in employee culture or lethargy and complacency in ground-level execution and capital allocation.

An investor's understanding of the quality of succession planning in a Consistent Compounder has to include the following four components:

1. Evidence of decentralization of power and authority—both in day-to-day business execution as well as in implementing capital allocation decisions;
2. Quality and tenure of CXOs in the organization;
3. Involvement and independence of board of directors—both for decentralizing capital allocation decision making, as well as for recruitment of CXOs in the firm; and
4. Historical evidence of execution of succession at the CXO level without adverse impact on the organization.

Asian Paints is one the best examples of a company that covers all aspects of our succession planning framework reasonably well. For more than a decade now, execution of operations has been totally controlled by empowered professionals from the CEO level down to the middle management level in the firm's hierarchy. Over the last fifty years, the firm has been hiring talent from the best universities as management trainees and has had an outstanding track record of training and retaining this talent pool for more than twenty to twenty-five years. As a result, most of its CXOs and key management personnel have spent more than twenty years at Asian Paints across several functions. Tech investments and data analytics, which also drive decentralization of execution of operations, are a large part of Asian Paints' competitive advantage. All seven independent directors on the board of Asian Paints have highly reputed and relevant professional backgrounds.[25] And last but not least, the firm's historical track record has been healthy and consistent despite: a) three instances of professional CEO changes over the last fifteen years, b) three generations of Asian Paints' promoter families having come and gone in the last seventy years, c) one of the founding promoter families having exited in 1997, and d) several CXOs having changed hands regularly.

Another firm, **HDFC Bank,** is one whose current competitive advantages are perhaps as robust as that of Asian Paints. However, HDFC Bank's succession planning might not come across to be as strong as that of Asian Paints on the framework highlighted above. When it comes to execution of its day-to-day business, HDFC Bank has one of the best systems and processes across India's banking industry and has an army of professionals who have spent more than fifteen years with the bank across various functions. Our interactions with various people who have worked at HDFC Bank for a long period of time suggest that the bank's focus on systems and processes has made manual intervention redundant across most of its routine functions. We believe the strengths of well-established SOPs, robust credit underwriting and a resilient balance sheet will hold HDFC Bank in good stead for the next few years as the company goes through a leadership transition. However, over the past few years, CXO-level attrition has increased substantially, and some of the CXO-level roles are currently managed by individuals who have been external hires and have hence worked for less than five years in the bank. Whilst the quality of its board of directors is good,[26] with relevant experts from diverse backgrounds, the recent retirement of Aditya Puri from the post of managing director (in October 2020) and the succession process that appeared to have been followed did not convey a sense that the candidature and training of potential successors was as well planned as at Asian Paints (which also underwent a transition in its leadership, from KBS Anand to Amit Syngle as CEO, in April 2020).

KEY TAKEAWAYS

- Prudent use of free cash flows is a key driver of shareholder value, and hence investors need to assess risks in capital allocation decisions.
- Growth outside core products and markets must be evaluated in the context of the quantum of capital being allocated. Incremental steps towards market and/or product development are less likely to destroy shareholder value relative to large capital commitments towards diversification.
- Promoters with multiple business interests call for special attention when evaluating the capital allocation decisions of any entity within a group.
- A robust succession planning process and framework is the key to extracting the best returns from the most critical source of capital—human resources.

* * *

CHAPTER 6

When to Buy?

'The idea that a bell rings to signal when investors should get into or out of the market is simply not credible. After nearly 50 years in this business, I do not know of anybody who has done it successfully and consistently. I don't even know anybody who knows anybody who has done it successfully and consistently.'

—John Bogle[1]

'Over the long term, it's hard for a stock to earn a much better return that the business which underlies it earns. If the business earns six percent on capital over forty years and you hold it for that forty years, you're not going to make much different than a six percent return—even if you originally buy it at a huge discount. Conversely, if a business earns eighteen percent on capital over twenty or thirty years, even if you pay an expensive looking price, you'll end up with one hell of a result.'

—Charlie Munger[2]

Once you know what stocks to buy, the next big question investors face is—when to buy? This question manifests both in the timing of the buying (or selling, for that matter) as well as in the waiting for the right price at which to buy. Often, both these factors are redundant. Once you buy clean companies that can grow earnings consistently via their competitive advantages and smart capital allocation, the timing and pricing are really taken out of the equation.

The key questions addressed in this chapter include:

- Is there any merit in trying to time the market for buying and selling stocks?
- What does a relative valuation multiple tell you about the intrinsic value of a business? And,
- To what extent, and in what cases, can you rely on PE multiples to drive your buying and selling of stocks?

In this book so far, we have discussed the question of what stocks to buy. The Marcellus framework of identifying companies with clean accounts, a track record of prudent capital allocation and presence of strong and sustainable competitive advantages are helpful guides to answer this question. Once you know what you need to buy, one common question investors have is—when to buy? As soon as investors come to this juncture, they tend to get mentally submerged in a sea of questions, like:

- 'There are elections in the US this year. Should I wait until we know who the next US President is going to be, before buying this pharma company that gets 80 per cent of its revenues from the US?'

- 'This bank reported good results for this quarter and the stock price has gone up by 10 per cent. Should I wait for it to correct before buying?'
- 'This consumer goods stock is trading at a PE multiple of 30x, while its competitor is trading at a multiple of 20x. Should I sell the 'expensive' stock and buy the 'cheaper' one?'

Such questions broadly cover two aspects of when to buy or sell a stock. The time and the price. In this chapter we try to answer these questions.

TIMING THE MARKET

Between January and March of 2020, as the COVID-19 pandemic began spreading across India and local authorities in some cities began limiting economic activity, the Sensex index fell from its then lifetime high of 41,953 on 14 January 2020 to 25,891 on 23 March 2020—a decline of 38 per cent in just a little over two months. Then came the announcement of a twenty-one-day nation-wide lockdown starting 24 March 2020. A few investors in Marcellus's PMS portfolios expressed worry about the economic impact of the lockdown on nearly all economic activities across the country, and a desire to redeem their investments and shift out of equity to perceived safer investment avenues. At that point in time, amid an unprecedented crisis, it would have been natural to expect the markets to decline further, causing greater wealth erosion, right? No. 23 March 2020 turned out to be the bottom of the Index. It took forty-nine trading sessions for the 38 per cent fall from peak to bottom, and in the following forty-nine sessions, the Sensex had already recovered by 32 per cent. And, by the end of 2020, the Sensex had scaled a new all-time high.

The above example is indicative of how the market typically behaves, and not just during periods of crisis but in normal times as well. The example is also indicative of how most investors react to market behaviour, and in panic tend to sell at the worst possible time. The futility of trying to time the market has been proven time and again, in scores of studies. Identifying the lowest point of a stock for executing your buys and identifying the highest point to sell them is practically impossible. It would be nothing but just incredible luck for anyone to achieve this on a consistent basis.

In his book *A Wealth of Common Sense*, Ben Carlson, fund manager at Ritholtz Wealth Management, lists thirteen 'myths' of investing. The very first myth he lists is, 'You have to time the market to earn respectable returns.' Carlson cites a study in the US, done by legendary Fidelity Investments fund manager Peter Lynch, which looked at the thirty-year period from 1965 to 1995. The study found that if during this period one invested every single year in the market at its annual low, one would have earned a return of 11.7 per cent annually.[3]

If, instead, you ended up buying at the annual high of the market every single year, your returns at the end of thirty years would be 10.6 per cent. And if you simply invested on the first day of the year, not worrying about the price, your returns would have been 11 per cent. Thirty years of expending time and effort in identifying the lowest point of the market each year amounted to just 0.7 percentage points more in returns than from the dull practice of consistent investing on a chosen date. Carlson says, 'The odds of consistently picking the best and worst days are minimal, but putting money into markets on a periodic basis is something every investor can do. So much time and energy is put into trying to figure out the best time to invest when a simple dollar cost averaging (DCA) plan with a long-term horizon is much less stressful and easier to implement.'

We see a similar trend playing out in India too. Let us assume someone started investing in the Sensex from 1991 (i.e., from January 1991) and invested an equal sum each year on the exact date when the Sensex was at its fifty-two-week low. And this investor continues doing so for a period of thirty years, up to December 2020, each year deploying funds at the index's fifty-two-week low. This exercise would have yielded a compounded annualized return of 13.1 per cent over the thirty-year investment period. On the other hand, by just investing each year at the beginning of the year (1 January), the returns would have been 12.1 per cent. Picking the perfect date to invest in the market year after year for thirty years would get you just 0.9 percentage point in excess returns.

An interesting inference emerges when we consider the above exercise for time periods shorter than thirty years. As seen in Exhibit 68, for a twenty-year investment cycle, the excess return for timing the market is 2.1 percentage points and for a ten-year period it is 2.9 percentage points. These numbers have two implications. Firstly, timing the market does not make a material difference to the returns you earn, provided you have a reasonably long investment horizon (we recommended at least ten years). Secondly, the longer the time horizon an investor has, the lesser is the impact of timing. In summary, the popular investment adage of, 'time in the market is more important than timing the market', works as much in India as in the US, and investors would gain from keeping this in mind.

Exhibit 68: Long-term steady and consistent investing makes timing redundant*

Period	Buy at 52-week low	Buy on 1st January each year	Excess returns
1990-2020 (30 years)	13.1%	12.1%	0.9%
2000-2020 (20 years)	15.3%	13.2%	2.1%
2010-2020 (10 years)	14.6%	11.7%	2.9%

Source: Marcellus Investment Managers; Ace Equity; * returns are for the Sensex

It is now amply clear that timing the overall market is not worth the effort and surely not worth testing your luck in getting each buy and sell timing right. Meaning, neither skill nor luck get you much farther than a dumb 'invest regularly' strategy. But what about individual stocks? A stock market index is an 'average' indicator and dilutes the impact of extreme stock performances. If there is greater volatility in prices of individual stocks, does it mean that there could be greater opportunities to time buys and sells in specific stocks and make a difference to one's overall portfolio?

DOES TIMING MATTER FOR SPECIFIC STOCKS?

The Efficient Market Hypothesis (EMH) states that market prices reflect all information known about a stock at any point in time (see Chapter 1 for details). If and when new information comes into the market, that too is immediately reflected in the stock price. This means that it is not possible for an investor to generate returns better than a portfolio of randomly selected stocks, including the index. And if you cannot beat the market, there is really no point in timing the buying or selling of individual stocks that make up the market. One can, of course, keep staring at the stock price, try and react at lightning speed as new information comes in, and maybe get lucky. But with just one pair of eyes, you are not really going to make any money.

The EMH has considerable empirical support. In the US, separate studies by Morningstar, John Bogle and Rob Arnott (of Research Affiliates) have found that over a thirty-year period, 75–90 per cent of US mutual funds underperform the market. In India, over a ten-year period ending December 2019, 65 per cent of large-cap equity mutual funds underperformed the S&P BSE 100 index. The average return of these mutual funds for the ten-year period was 10.42 per cent, while the BSE 100 returned 10.15 per cent, giving credence to the EMH.[4]

Does this mean investors have no hope for making better returns than what the average market does? Not necessarily. In the study of Indian mutual funds cited above, 35 per cent of large-cap equity funds did outperform the market over a ten-year period, which is a sufficiently long period to doubt the EMH. Also, if you consider any three-year period over the past decade, only three leading mutual funds in India have managed to consistently stay in the top quartile of performance. The remaining ninety-seven have either been outside the top quartile for the entire decade or have sporadically entered the top quartile—suggesting that luck, as much as skill, is responsible for their performance.[5]

Legendary investors such as Warren Buffett have also found serious flaws with the EMH. According to Buffett, there are many examples of investors consistently beating the market for many years at a stretch. That clearly goes against the theoretical foundations of the EMH. These investors, whom he calls 'Graham & Dodd investors', instead 'search for discrepancies between the value of a business and the price of small pieces of that business in the market'.[6]

Buffett has also been critical of many other theoretical concepts that have become part of investment academics. He says, 'Our Graham & Dodd investors, needless to say, do not discuss beta, the capital asset pricing model, or covariance in returns among securities. These are not subjects of any interest to them. In fact, most of them would have difficulty defining those terms. The investors simply focus on two variables: price and value.'

Finding the current market price of a stock is the easy part. What then is its 'value'? Buffett's approach to what is 'value' has evolved over the years, from investing in stocks that are cheap or have low valuation multiples, to investing in strong franchises that have sustainable long-term competitive advantages. His long-time associate, Charlie Munger says, 'It's obvious that if a company generates high returns on capital and reinvests at high returns, it will do well.'

As discussed in earlier chapters, we at Marcellus are also advocates of investing in companies with strong and sustainable competitive advantages, which enable them to earn high returns on capital as well as reinvest at high returns. Such an approach to investing not only allows investors to generate returns better than the market, but also makes the timing of buys and sells redundant. How, you might ask. An example would help put things in perspective and demonstrate the role (rather, the lack of it) of timing in investment returns.

Assume that we have two investors, each with Rs 10,000 to invest in stocks each year. And they both chose to invest it in shares of Nestlé India. The first investor has a gift—he can perfectly time the market, and each year for ten years in a row, he buys Rs 10,000' worth of Nestlé India shares at the stock's lowest price point for that year. Something most of us can only aspire to do! Let us call him Mr Gifted. The second investor, a mere mortal, believes he does not have the skills to time share price movements. As a result, he decides to buy Rs 10,000' worth of Nestlé India shares on a chosen date each year, regardless of the prevailing share price. For the sake of simplicity, he chooses to do so on the first day of each calendar year (1 January).

Mr Gifted and Mr Mortal start investing in Nestlé India from January 2011 and continue for a period of ten years, with the last investments made by them in the year 2020.

In their first year of investing, Mr Mortal invests Rs 10,000 at Rs 3,829 per share on the first trading day of 2011, which is on 3 January 2011. Mr Gifted, on the other hand, using his timing skills, invests his Rs 10,000 at Rs 3,209 per share on 10 February 2011, when the stock price is at its lowest during the year

(January–December 2011). Both our investors repeat this exercise annually for a period of ten years, investing a total of Rs 1,00,000 over this period. During this period, their purchase prices differ from each other in the range of three per cent to sixteen per cent.

At the end of their ten-year investing cycle, the two investors compare their portfolio values and the compounded return they have earned (using the XIRR function in Microsoft Excel). What do they find?

As of 31 December 2020, Mr Gifted's portfolio is worth Rs 3,45,818, implying compounding at a rate of 22.5 per cent over the ten-year period. And Mr Mortal's portfolio is worth Rs 3,08,980, having compounded at a rate of 19.9 per cent. The gifted investor earned a mere 2.6 percentage points more than the ordinary investor! And for ten years of timing the stock purchases to perfection, the portfolio value of Mr Gifted was just 11.9 per cent higher than that of Mr Mortal.

Exhibit 69: Portfolio values of Mr Gifted and Mr Mortal for investment in Nestlé India (2011–20)

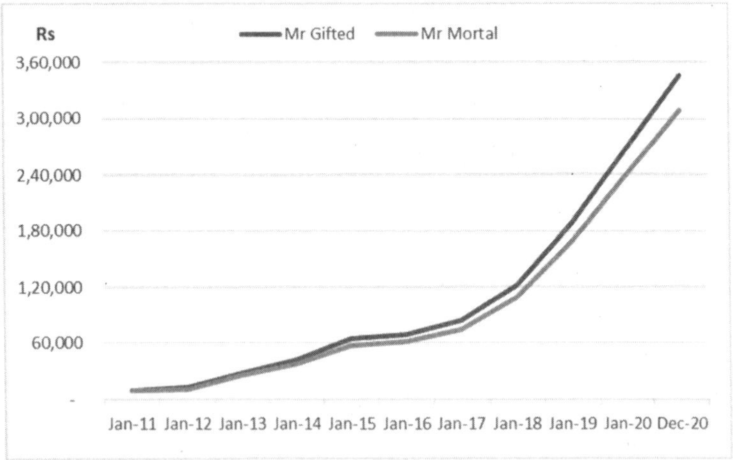

Source: Marcellus Investment Managers; Ace Equity; note: portfolio values do not include dividends—they are based on only share price movements

Even if you consider a longer time horizon of twenty years, from January 2001 to December 2020, the results do not change much. The twenty-year cycle yields a compounded annual return of 22.5 per cent for Mr Gifted and 21.2 per cent for Mr Mortal. Mr Gifted does better by a mere 1.3 percentage points over Mr Mortal. You can even take a shorter horizon of five years and see similar results. The five-year cycle from January 2016 to December 2020 yields just a 10.5 per cent higher absolute return for Mr Mortal over Mr Gifted—surely not enough for getting the timing of each buy right for five years in a row.

We can also look at the performance of the two investors in multiple ten-year cycles over the last twenty years, as shown in Exhibit 70. While Mr Gifted obviously does better than Mr Mortal, the best he does is 4.2 percentage points better, in the compounded return for the period 2004–13. Mr Gifted's average compounded return over the ten cycles is just three percentage points better. With all the time and effort expended in identifying the exact bottom of a stock year after year for five, ten or twenty years, Mr Gifted's returns over Mr Mortal's are nothing to write home about. His timing skills in no way justify his name!

Exhibit 70: Portfolio returns of Mr Gifted and Mr Mortal for various investment periods in Nestlé India

	Portfolio value after 10 years (Rs lakhs)		XIRR		Mortal as a % of Gifted (B/A)
	Mr Gifted (A)	Mr Mortal (B)	Mr Gifted	Mr Mortal	
1 Jan 02 – 31 Dec 11	5.1	4.6	30.2%	26.7%	89%
1 Jan 03 – 31 Dec 12	5.3	4.6	30.4%	26.8%	88%
1 Jan 04 – 31 Dec 13	4.7	4.0	28.5%	24.3%	85%
1 Jan 05 – 31 Dec 14	4.5	4.0	27.5%	24.4%	89%
1 Jan 06 – 31 Dec 15	3.2	2.8	21.3%	18.0%	88%
1 Jan 07 – 31 Dec 16	2.7	2.3	18.1%	14.9%	87%
1 Jan 08 – 31 Dec 17	2.7	2.5	18.5%	16.0%	91%
1 Jan 09 – 31 Dec 18	3.1	2.9	20.6%	18.7%	92%
1 Jan 10 – 31 Dec 19	3.3	3.0	21.3%	19.1%	91%
1 Jan 11 – 31 Dec 20	3.5	3.1	22.5%	19.9%	89%
Average			**23.9%**	**20.9%**	**89%**

Source: Marcellus Investment Managers; Ace Equity

A similar analysis for some of the other Consistent Compounders shows the same results. In the case of Pidilite Industries, Asian Paints, Abbott India and HDFC Bank, shown in Exhibit 71, the excess returns Mr Gifted (vs Mr Mortal) manages range from 1.2 percentage points to 3 percentage points, depending on the time-period for which a steady investment is made.

Exhibit 71: Comparative IRRs for annual investment of Rs 10,000 in 'Consistent Compounders'

	10-year period 1 January 2011–31 December 2020			20-year period 1 January 2001–31 December 2020		
Company	**Mr Mortal**	**Mr Gifted**	**Excess Returns (percentage points)**	**Mr Mortal**	**Mr Gifted**	**Excess Returns (percentage points)**
Asian Paints	27.5%	29.9%	2.4%	29.9%	31.0%	1.2%
Pidilite Industries	29.0%	30.8%	1.9%	30.5%	32.9%	2.4%
HDFC Bank	21.2%	23.5%	2.4%	23.6%	25.6%	1.9%
Abbott India	31.1%	34.1%	3.0%	24.8%	27.0%	2.2%

Source: Marcellus Investment Managers; Ace Equity

The results are, however, not the same for all types of companies. In the case of companies where return on capital is not always above the cost of capital, either because of the cyclicality of the business or due to a lack of sustainable competitive advantages, the results of the above exercise are starkly different. As seen in Exhibit 72, in a ten-year investment cycle, the excess returns made by Mr Gifted over Mr Mortal in case of such companies are more than twice the excess returns made by Mr Gifted in the case of the Consistent Compounders (Exhibit 71). Which again drives home the point that investing in Consistent Compounders takes the timing of stock purchases and sales out of the equation.

This higher return differential than in the case of companies highlighted in Exhibit 71 will be seen as even more valuable by the investor if the absolute value of Mr Mortal's IRR is brought into context. If Mr Mortal generates 20 per cent+ IRRs (which is the case with Consistent Compounders—highlighted in Exhibit 70 and Exhibit 71) and Mr Gifted generates a 1 percentage point higher return, the additional returns would be an insignificant contributor to the outcome. However, if Mr Mortal generates an IRR of only 5–10 per cent (which is the case with most companies that are not Consistent Compounders—see Exhibit 72), then the differential of about 3 percentage points between his and Mr Gifted's returns becomes a significant contributor to the outcome!

Exhibit 72: Comparative IRRs for some 'non-Consistent Compounders'

	10-year period 1 January 2011–31 December 2020			20-year period 1 January 2001–31 December 2020		
Company	**Mr Mortal**	**Mr Gifted**	**Excess Returns (percentage points)**	**Mr Mortal**	**Mr Gifted**	**Excess Returns (percentage points)**
Ambuja Cements	4.3%	8.3%	4.0%	10.7%	12.6%	1.9%
Maruti Suzuki	20.0%	25.0%	5.0%	19.0%	21.6%	2.6%*
Airtel	7.7%	11.9%	4.2%	17.3%	20.1%	2.7%**
Hindalco	8.2%	17.0%	8.7%	6.9%	10.6%	3.8%
Tata Steel	7.9%	16.1%	8.2%	9.3%	12.7%	3.3%

Source: Marcellus Investment Managers; Ace Equity; *returns are for 2004–20; **returns are for 2003–20

WHY IS TIMING NOT RELEVANT FOR CONSISTENT COMPOUNDERS?

Stock prices should ideally reflect the present value of the underlying cash flows of the business, and in the long term they tend to do so. However, in the short term, stock prices fluctuate depending on market participants' assessment of multiple factors, most of them external to the company. For example, stock prices of export-oriented companies might react to every small change in the exchange rate up or down, even though over the long-term it might depreciate steadily. As a result, provided the underlying asset (company or an index) delivers a modest or healthy growth in earnings and cash flows, it does not matter how the near-term stock price moves. And in turn, this means that for such stocks it does not matter whether the entry point of one investor was 20 per cent higher or lower than another's.

In the case of companies in cyclical businesses, earnings tend to be volatile over a period, with a few years of strong growth followed by a few years of weak or even negative growth. As a result, for such stocks it matters when they are bought or sold. The challenge with these stocks, however, is in knowing what the right time to buy or sell them would be. Since the volatility in earnings is driven more by external factors, including macroeconomic variables, and less by the fundamental strength or weakness of a company, it becomes that much more difficult to time the cycle exactly right. For example, the earnings of a metals company depend not just on the efficiency of the producer but also on the price of metals in international markets, which is determined by multiple global demand-supply factors. Let's say there is a temporary supply disruption in a mine in, say, Chile (the largest producer of copper in the world), which increases the short-term prices of copper in the international markets. An individual investor has no means of tracking such events or even getting information about it in time to take advantage of the domestic stock price movement of a copper producer following the change in the metal price.

In any case, as seen in Exhibit 72, even though Mr Gifted is able to do much better on a relative basis than Mr Mortal in the case of companies where return on capital does not consistently stay above cost of capital, his absolute total returns are substantially lower than those generated by the Consistent Compounders (Exhibit 71). It follows therefore that companies where RoCE exceeds the cost of capital consistently—the Consistent Compounders—short-, or medium-term stock price movements are not very relevant, and therefore timing does not add any material value. In fact, in our earlier example of Nestlé India, let us consider one more investor—Mr Unlucky. He is the polar opposite of Mr Gifted and ends up buying the stock of Nestlé India each year for ten years at its **fifty-two-week high**. If Mr Unlucky started this exercise from January 2011, what would have been his compounded annual return as of December 2020? A healthy 18.6 per cent! To reiterate the point we've made earlier, investing in consistent compounders takes the question of 'when to buy' completely out of the equation.

In this context, we draw the reader's attention back to Chapter 1, to the 'ABC framework'. We reiterate that for investors looking to compound their wealth over the long term, the low-risk route is to rely on the Consistent Compounders, whose earnings and cash flows grow at a steady and consistent pace. These Type C companies achieve this through the three foundational pillars of clean accounts, prudent capital allocation and strong competitive advantages.

To round off the discussion on timing, we leave you with one more set of data, which should reinforce the points discussed so far in this chapter on the redundancy of timing Consistent Compounders. Let us say you identified five consistent compounders at the beginning of the year 2001—Asian Paints, HDFC Bank, Pidilite Industries, Abbott India and Nestlé India. You put in an equal amount of money in each of these five stocks every year. But in this exercise you invest the money each year when the market is at its *52-week high*.

After twenty years, your portfolio would have earned a healthy IRR of 27.4 per cent. The same exercise, if done with the Sensex, would have yielded an 12.6 per cent IRR. These numbers convey two crucial facets of investing—first, that it is possible to do better than the broader market by investing in Consistent Compounders; and second, that time spent remaining invested is always more important than timing the market.

DO P/E VALUATIONS MATTER?

The other aspect of when to buy (or sell) a stock is centred on its pricing or valuation. Should you buy a stock if its price, or earnings multiple, is 'low' or 'cheap' compared with peers or the broader market? And should you sell a stock that has an earnings multiple higher than its peers or its sector average?

As noted earlier, the intrinsic value of a stock reflects the present value of the company's cash flows. However, investors more intuitively use relative measures, such as price-to-earnings (PE) multiple or price-to-book value (P/BV) multiple, to assess the stock's value. A company trading at a relatively lower PE than its peers is, as a rule of thumb, considered to be more attractively valued. The comparison, however, ignores a number of factors that drive the value of a business—the return on capital and the reinvestment rate being the chief amongst them. It is like saying my plot of land should be valued at a certain price per acre, because my neighbouring plot of the same size was acquired by someone at the same price. What if the neighbouring plot had fruiting trees or an oil well while mine does not?

Calculating a company's intrinsic value from its underlying cash flows requires use of the discounted cash flow methodology. The calculation is reflected in the equation below—the free cash to equity (FCFE)[7] for each year in the future (to infinity) is discounted back to the present, using the appropriate discount rate (i.e., the cost of capital which is represented in the equation below by 'r').

$$Value = \sum_{t=1}^{t=\infty} \frac{Free\ Cash\ Flow\ to\ Equity\ (FCFE)}{(1+r)^t}$$

In practice, however, it is difficult to forecast the cash flow for each year into the future, especially for periods in the distant future. As a result, what most practitioners do is to forecast cash flows for the foreseeable future of the next five, seven or ten years, and then assign a terminal value to the remainder cash flows. The terminal value is the present value of all cash flows beyond the first five, seven or ten years, as the case may be. While calculating the terminal value, the cash flows of a business are assumed to keep growing at a constant rate for perpetuity (represented in the equation below as 'g'). The terminal value (TV) is expressed with the formula:

$$\mathrm{TV} = \frac{Free\ Cash\ Flow\ to\ Equity\ in\ terminal\ year * (1+g)}{r-g}$$

Here, g = the stable long-term growth rate and r = the cost of capital.

The TV formula implies that a company *cannot* grow perpetually at a rate that is higher than its cost of capital (since that would make the '*r less g*' in the denominator negative, giving a negative TV!). The theoretical underpinnings of this lie in the assumption that when a business earns a return on capital higher than its cost of capital, it attracts competition, which gradually eats away the excess profits, leaving the business to earn a return that is equal to or just marginally above its cost of capital. As the difference between the return on capital and cost of capital narrows, so does the free cash generation and, in turn, the company's ability to reinvest in the business to grow at the same pace as it used to earlier. Hence, the stable long-term growth is assumed to be lower than the cost of capital. Most practitioners in India typically use a 5 per cent terminal growth rate.

However, as we have seen in earlier chapters, there are a few companies in India that defy this conventional application of economic theory. When we try to value such companies using the DCF methodology, we cannot use a five/seven/ten-year DCF plus a TV formula. This is because these companies' growth will continue for a much longer time than five/seven/ten years before they enter a stable growth period.

Let us time-travel a little bit to understand this better. Say you are sitting in March 1996 and are trying to value Asian Paints. You make certain forecasts of the growth in FCFE for the next ten years (FY1997–FY2006), assume a terminal growth rate of 5 per cent and calculate the discounted cash flow value of the company. Also assume that your cash flow forecasts are exactly what they eventually turned out to be—that is, a 20.9 per cent CAGR over FY1997–FY2006. Assuming a cost of capital of 15 per cent back then, and a stable terminal growth rate of 5 per cent from FY2007, the DCF methodology would have yielded a value of approximately Rs 535 crore for the company. However, Asian Paints' market capitalization in March 1996, when you did the DCF valuation, was about Rs 1,374 crore. Would you say that market was overvaluing Asian Paints by more than twice?

Now travel forward to March 2021, when fifteen years have passed since the last year (FY2006) of your DCF period and you are in what was assumed back in March 1996 to be Asian Paints' 5 per cent stable growth period. How would have the company's free cash flow growth been in this period against your assumption? More than 5 times higher! From FY2007 to FY2021, Asian Paints achieved a 25.7 per cent CAGR in FCFE! Now go back to March 1996 and do a twenty-five-year DCF instead of the ten-year one you did earlier. Plug in the actual free cash flow numbers reported by Asian Paints over the next twenty-five years (FY1996–FY2021; 23.8 per cent), apply a TV in FY2021 and calculate the intrinsic value of the company. You'll see that the DCF value jumps nearly 4x, from Rs 535 crore to Rs 2,001 crore. In other words, by restricting your forecast period to just ten years, you undervalued the company by a massive 73 per cent! And the market undervalued it by over 30 per cent! This is because Asian Paints defies the conventional thinking that a firm cannot enjoy competitive advantages for a long period of time and therefore it is futile to forecast its cash flows beyond a reasonable period into the future. The conventional intrinsic-value DCF methodology grossly undervalues the longevity of a franchise. If you conduct a similar exercise for other consistent compounders you will see similar results.

Exhibit 73: Some companies maintain a high growth rate in FCFE for years together

Company	Starting year	10-year	15-year	20-year
Nestlé India	CY1995	13.6%	14.4%	13.2%
Asian Paints	FY1995	20.5%	27.2%	24.5%
Pidilite	FY2002	24.9%	30.3%	26.0%
TCS	FY2006	28.9%	26.1%	NA

Source: Ace Equity; Marcellus Investment Managers

It is natural that the undervaluation using the DCF methodology would manifest even when using relative valuation methods. In March 1996, Asian Paints' market price implied a price-to-earnings multiple of about 26x—the corresponding PE for the Sensex was about 13x. If Asian Paints was quoting at a premium of 100 per cent to the market, was it 'expensive' on a relative-valuation basis? Many investors would have thought so and avoided buying the stock. But as shown above, based on the company's intrinsic value, it was in fact quoting at a huge discount of over 30 per cent. In other words, the stock should have quoted at a PE of almost 38x! And those who might have bought the stock even at a 38x PE in March 1996 would have earned an IRR of 16.3 per cent over the next ten years, 21.1 per cent over the next fifteen years, 22.8 per cent over the next twenty years, and 23 per cent over the next 25[8] years.

Conviction in the ability of a firm with strong and sustainable competitive advantages to deliver sustainable RoCEs as well as growth (which requires capital reinvestment) is often underappreciated in most commonly used valuations tools, including the P/E and other multiple-based valuation methodologies. Like in the Asian Paints example, a PE multiple that is large in the absolute sense is not necessarily expensive. And conversely, what might appear to be a 'low' PE stock might actually be expensive compared to its intrinsic value, if the business cannot support a return on capital higher than the cost of capital for a long period of time. It follows from the above discussion that trying to invest or time your buys and sells based on just the PE of a stock is a futile exercise.

THE EMPIRICAL EVIDENCE

Let us look at how the long-term prices of a broader set of stocks have behaved with respect to the free cash flow generation of the underlying business. We consider a ten-year period (FY2010–FY2020) for this analysis and take the free cash flow to equity (FCFE) of stocks in the BSE100 index.

In order to smoothen the impact of capital expenditure and changes in leverage (i.e., the amount of debt taken on by companies), we take the average FCFE for FY2008–10 and FY2018–20. Next, we consider the correlation between the CAGR in FCFE (average of FY2018–20 over FY2008–10) and the ten-year stock price returns. The correlation coefficient we get is just 37.3 per cent, which would suggest that the growth in stock prices is not adequately explained by free cash flow generation. This conclusion seems quite counterintuitive, but is due to the composition of the underlying data.

Of the stock universe of seventy-four companies in the BSE100 (we are excluding the twenty-one financial services companies here, as the FCFE metric is irrelevant for them, and we are also excluding five stocks which were not listed for the entire year-period), only forty-eight have a positive FCFE (average of FY2008–10 and average of FY2018–20) in the starting and ending years of the ten-year period. While forty-eight companies form a reasonable sample size, the stock price results are impacted by the variability in the cash flows in the intervening years. For example, only nineteen of seventy-four non-financial services companies in the BSE100 generated free cash flow in each of the ten years under consideration. And seventeen companies generated positive FCFE in a maximum of just five out of the ten years during FY2010–20. Such companies would naturally see weak share price performance, even if they had positive FCFE in the first and last years of the period. The fact that only about 26 per cent of non-financial companies in a broad index like the BSE100 generate consistent free cash flows is a pointer to the difficulties faced by many companies in building and sustaining competitive advantages that tide over business and market cycles over the long term.

What happens when we consider a larger index like the BSE500, in the hope of increasing the sample size? The results get obfuscated even more, since the BSE500 is a more heterogeneous sample set relative to the BSE100. Out of the BSE500 constituents, we are left with just 161 names (excluding financial services and companies not listed throughout during the previous ten years), which have positive FCFE in the starting period (average of FY2008–10) as well as in the ending period (average of FY2018–20). The correlation coefficient in this case between the CAGR in FCFE (average of FY2018–20 over FY2008–10) and the ten-year stock price returns is just 23.5 per cent, again mainly because of the fact that many companies end up with negative free cash flows in the intervening years, even if the FY2010 and FY2020 free cash is positive.

Given the constraints in looking at a direct statistical correlation, another way to understand the significance of free cash flow generation to the share price is through an analysis of the number of years (out of a ten-year sample period) a company generates positive free cash flows and comparing the share price return over that period. For the BSE500 as a whole, the results are in Exhibit 74. The inference is stark—a higher number of years of free cash generation corresponds to a higher share price return.

Exhibit 74: Frequency distribution of positive FCFE for BSE 500 stocks

No. of years of positive FCFE	No. of stocks	Average returns
Best (7-10)	163	15.3%
Mid (4-6)	114	9.2%
Worst (0-3)	47	4.7%
Total	**324**	**9.7%**

Source: Marcellus Investment Managers; Ace Equity; only non-financial stocks considered; returns on CAGR basis from April 2010 to June 2020

As we make our sample more homogenous, the results get even clearer. For example, consider consumer stocks that are part of the BSE500, as shown in Exhibit 75. Of the total thirty-one stocks in the sector, 77 per cent generated positive FCFE in seven years or more out of the ten-year period of FY2010–20, and these companies generated, on an average, a 23.4 per cent compounding of their share price. And companies that generated positive FCFE in four to six years out of ten compounded their share price at a relatively lower 22.0 per cent CAGR. A similar trend plays out in the case of capital goods, pharma and durables stocks also.

Exhibit 75: Sector-wise frequency distribution of positive FCFE generation by stocks in the BSE500

	Consumer		Capital Goods		Pharma		Durables	
No. of years of positive FCFE	**No. of stocks**	**Average returns**	**No. of stocks**	**Average returns**	**No. of stocks**	**Average returns**	**No. of stocks**	**Average returns**
Best (7-10)	24	23.4%	12	11.4%	16	19.0%	6	23.7%
Mid (4-6)	7	22.0%	4	-3.6%	10	18.4%	4	11.8%
Worst (0-3)	-	-	1	-16.1%	3	14.1%	-	-
Total	**31**	**22.7%**	**17**	**-2.8%**	**29**	**17.1%**	**10**	**17.7%**

Source: Marcellus Investment Managers; Ace Equity

Auto and IT companies show results that are at variance. In the case of IT companies within the BSE500, the highest share price compounding is in the case of companies in the worst FCFE bucket of 0–3 years—that is, these companies have generated positive FCFE in a maximum of just three years out of a ten-year period. This anomaly is the result of a single company—Vakrangee Ltd—which generated a 38.7 per cent

CAGR over FY2010–20 in spite of having positive FCFE only in three years out of ten. The stock subsequently plummeted by close to 95 per cent from its peak in February 2018.

Exhibit 76: Sector-wise frequency distribution of positive FCFE generation by stocks in the BSE500

	Auto		IT	
No. of years of positive FCFE	**No. of stocks**	**Average Returns**	**No. of stocks**	**Average returns**
Best (7-10)	22	11.9%	16	14.0%
Mid (4-6)	10	14.2%	2	8.4%
Worst (0-3)	1	38.7%	1	22.3%
Total	**33**	**21.6%**	**19**	**14.9%**

Source: Marcellus Investment Managers; Ace Equity

The exception of the auto sector can be explained by the fact that it remains largely a cyclical business, and hence the bulk of the share price gains tend to occur in a few years of a favourable cycle, when FCFE generation is also boosted. For a lay investor however, there is no way of knowing which are the years in which the auto cycle will turn positive and drive positive FCFE generation, and then of timing the purchase of stocks in the sector. The same problem would arise when it comes to knowing when to sell, and timing the downcycle equally well.

This brings us back to the point we have made earlier in this chapter and multiple times in the book so far. The most assured way of consistent compounding is to focus on consistent free cash generation. Doing this frees the investor from the trap of trying to time the market. And how does one figure out the ability of a company to consistently generate free cash flows? Invest in companies with clean accounts, a track record of prudent capital allocation and possession of sustainable competitive advantages.

KEY TAKEAWAYS

- Remaining invested for the long-term is the key to steady and healthy stock price returns. It is practically impossible, and not worth the time and effort it takes, to time short-term buys and sells and hope of making consistent returns.
- The value of a stock is driven by two key elements of its underlying cash flows—growth in these cash flows and, more importantly, the longevity of the cash flows.
- Most valuation methodologies, including absolute methods like the discounted cash flow, as well as relative methods like P/E, EV/EBITDA, etc., ignore or undervalue the longevity of cash flows. This makes investors overlook stocks that appear 'expensively valued', but which could actually be priced much below their intrinsic value.
- Investing in Consistent Compounders addresses the two key aspects of an investor's dilemma about when to invest—the timing and the pricing.

* * *

CHAPTER 7

Preparing an Investment Plan

THE WAY FORWARD FOR DEVIKA

In Chapter 1 of the book, we met Devika Patel, who believes that the system is rigged against her because despite her hard work, diligent saving and proactive investment over the past twenty years, she has not been able to compound her wealth in a meaningful way.

Devika was acutely aware that time was running out for her. Her net worth, excluding the property in which she resided, was Rs 9 crore. This consisted of real estate (i.e., residential apartments in south Mumbai) worth Rs 6 crore, physical gold valued at Rs 2 crore and fixed deposits of Rs 1 crore. To maintain her lifestyle post-retirement, a decade hence, Devika will need at least Rs 20 crore. This means her current wealth of Rs 9 crore would have to compound at an annual post-tax rate of return of 9 per cent over the next ten tears.

In desperation, Devika finally visited the SEBI website and found the section that contains the names and contact details of all SEBI-Registered Investor Advisors (RIA).[1] She found the details of an RIA, Vishnu Krishnamurthy, who lived closed to her residence in Mumbai. After spending a couple of hours with Vishnu, Devika realized that over the next decade she had to put her net worth into two buckets.

The first bucket consisted of a 'rainy day' pot that Devika would create for her mother and for herself, in case she lost her job or in case either she or her mother had a critical illness that required Devika to quit her job and pay for the medical expenses. After much deliberation, Devika put Rs 4 crore into this pot, and Vishnu advised her to invest these monies in Government of India tax-free bonds, which yield around 6 per cent per annum.

The second bucket consisted of the remaining Rs 5 crore. Vishnu advised her to invest these monies in Marcellus's Consistent Compounders PMS Portfolio (CCP). Devika's hackles immediately went up, as she had heard from her friends that the stock market is a very difficult place in which to make money. Vishnu first requested Devika to watch a video available on the Marcellus website about how the CCP aims to deliver relatively healthy returns in the high teens, and with low volatility (typically, less than half that of the Nifty50 basis back-testing data for the last twenty years).[2]

After watching the video, Devika had a reasonable idea of how Marcellus invested their clients' monies. However, she was still not convinced that firms like Asian Paints could consistently compound her wealth. After all, she had seen many people in her social circle lose vast sums of money on dozens of Indian stocks over the past twenty years. In response, Vishnu showed Devika some of the charts from Saurabh's 2020 book *The Victory Project: Six Steps to Peak Potential.*

Vishnu began with a histogram of the Sensex, which showed that in twenty-one of the last thirty-two years (i.e., in 66 per cent of the years), the Sensex has delivered positive returns. In these twenty-one years of positive returns, in the majority of the years (thirteen), the Sensex had given returns between 0 per cent and 30 per cent per annum.

Exhibit 77: BSE Sensex—distribution of annual returns

NEGATIVE RETURNS				**POSITIVE RETURNS**			
< -30%	**-20% to -30%**	**-10% to -20%**	**0% to -10%**	**0% to +10%**	**+10% to +20%**	**+20% to +30%**	**> +30%**
FY93	FY01	FY95	FY97	FY96	FY98	FY08	FY91
FY09	FY20	FY03	FY99	FY13	FY05	FY15	FY92
		FY12	FY02	FY90	FY07		FY94
			FY16		FY11		FY00
					FY14		FY04
					FY17		FY06
					FY18		FY10
					FY19		FY89

Source: Marcellus Investment Managers; Ace Equity

Then Vishnu showed Devika the corresponding histograms for Asian Paints and HDFC Bank, two stocks which are part of Marcellus's CCP.

Exhibit 78: HDFC Bank—distribution of annual returns

NEGATIVE RETURNS				POSITIVE RETURNS			
< -30%	**-20% to -30%**	**-10% to -20%**	**0% to -10%**	**0% to +10%**	**+10% to +20%**	**+20% to +30%**	**> +30%**
FY09	FY20	FY01	FY99	FY02	FY12	FY07	FY97
			FY03	FY16		FY11	FY98
						FY13	FY00
						FY14	FY04
						FY19	FY05
							FY06
							FY08
							FY10
							FY15
							FY17
							FY18

Source: Marcellus Investment Managers; Ace Equity

Exhibit 79: Asian Paints—distribution of annual returns

NEGATIVE RETURNS				POSITIVE RETURNS			
< -30%	**-20% to -30%**	**-10% to -20%**	**0% to -10%**	**0% to +10%**	**+10% to +20%**	**+20% to +30%**	**> +30%**
FY09		FY97	FY01	FY90	FY91	FY05	FY89
		FY99		FY93	FY95	FY11	FY92
				FY03	FY96	FY12	FY94
				FY16	FY98	FY14	FY00
				FY18	FY07	FY17	FY02
					FY20		FY04
							FY06
							FY08
							FY10
							FY13
							FY15
							FY19

Source: Marcellus Investment Managers; Ace Equity

As Vishnu took her through these charts featured in the book *The Victory Project*, Devika realized that:

- Positive returns occur with significantly greater consistency with CCP stocks than with the Sensex. Most companies which feature in the CCP delivered positive returns in 80 per cent of the years out of the past thirty-two years, i.e., in four out of five years, as opposed to 66 per cent for the Sensex.
- In the years in which returns were positive, these companies' returns were typically above 30 per cent per annum compared to the Sensex, in whose case majority of the positive returns were below thirty per cent per annum.
- The years in which these companies gave negative returns (such as in FY1999, FY2001 and FY2009) are typically followed by years in which these companies gave returns above 30 per cent per annum.

Being a businesswoman herself, Devika now asked Vishnu whether the stability and the consistency of Marcellus's CCP came at the cost of lower returns during bull markets. She had a hazy recollection of her professor from business school shouting in a lecture directed at MBA students that high-quality companies like Asian Paints and HDFC Bank give lower returns when the economy booms and the markets roar. Vishnu now showed her another couple of charts which underscored the fallacy of such theories emanating from business schools located in the western hemisphere.

The charts below show that using the CCP approach not only helps your investments outperform the Sensex in the vast majority of time periods, but it also (a) rarely gives you negative returns, and (b) in most time periods it generates significant positive returns.

Exhibit 80: Total shareholder return from the CCPs vs the Sensex on a one-year rolling basis[3]

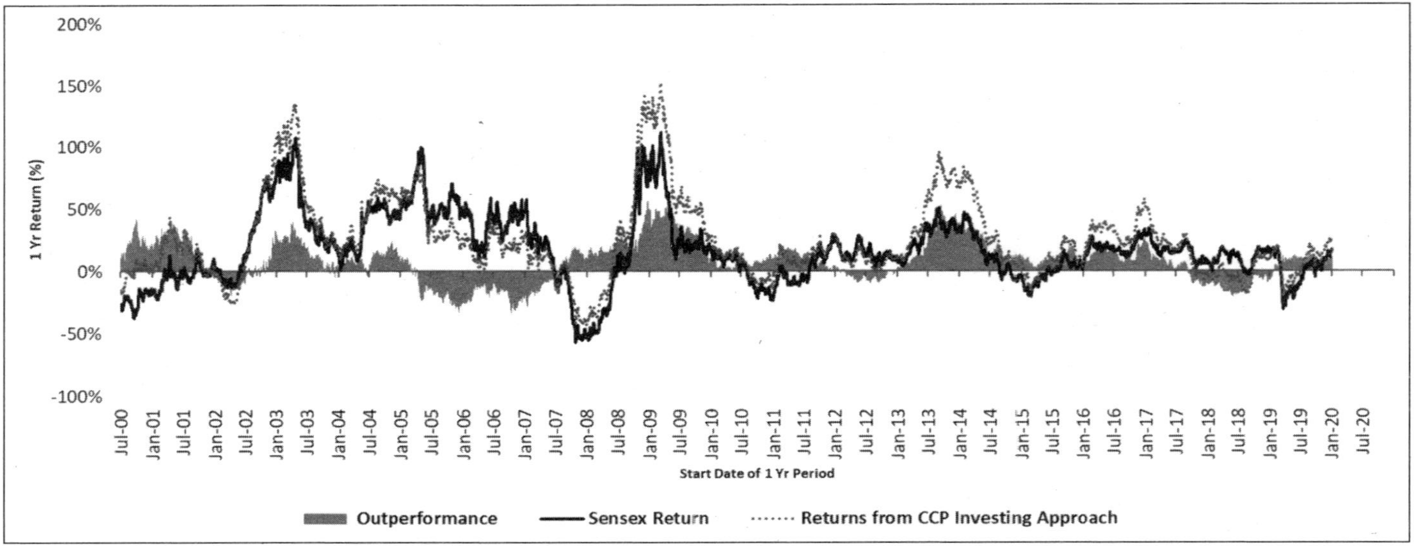

Source: Marcellus Investment Managers; Ace Equity

Exhibit 81: Total shareholder returns, CCPs vs the Sensex on a three-year rolling basis[4]

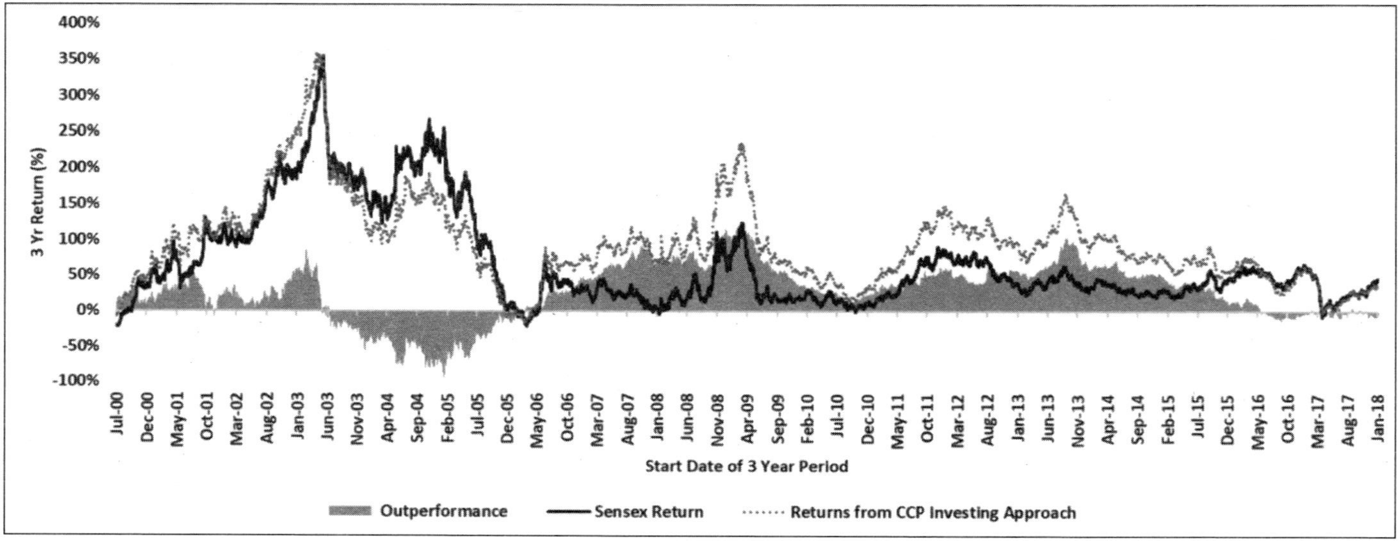

Source: Marcellus Investment Managers; Ace Equity

In fact, as Exhibit 81 shows, if you had followed this approach for a period of at least three years within the last twenty years, only on one occasion would you have got negative returns (namely in the three-year period starting 2006, i.e., the period characterized by the global financial crisis, when the Sensex more than halved in value in the space of nine months).

Devika could see in the two charts (Exhibits 80 and 81) the markedly lower volatility of returns generated from the CCP investment approach as compared with returns from the Sensex.

The meeting drew to a close, with Vishnu explaining to Devika that if she had invested 60 per cent of her corpus in the CCP ten years ago and the rest in tax-free government bonds, then over the past decade she would have earned 13 per cent returns per annum (post-tax, i.e., after paying capital gains tax).[5] Vishnu then pointed out that if, over the coming ten years, this blended portfolio delivered for her a significantly lower return than 13 per cent, even then she would be in a financially robust position going into retirement.[6]

The meeting ended with Devika requesting Vishnu to send her copies of the two books—*The Unusual Billionaires* (2016) and *Coffee Can Investing: The Low-Risk Route to Stupendous Wealth* (2018) written by Saurabh and his colleagues on how investors can consistently grow their wealth in India without having to take high levels of risk.

THE WAY FORWARD FOR RAJVEER

In the opening chapter of the book, we ran into Rajveer Bhatia, a graduate from one of India's premier business schools and a vice-president in an investment bank in Mumbai. Unfortunately, as we learnt in Chapter 1, Rajveer had first burnt his fingers by speculating in small-cap stocks and then by investing his and his parents' monies in a credit risk fund which had subsequently blown up.

Now thirty-year-old Rajveer found himself in a tight financial situation. He and his parents' total assets, excluding their primary residence, amounted to just Rs 5 crore (consisting of small-cap stocks worth Rs 3 crore and fixed deposits made by Rajveer's parents worth Rs 2 crore). Rajveer needed to finance his parents through retirement over the next fifteen years and he still aspired to buy a holiday home in Goa. Were these financial goals realistic?

Thankfully for Rajveer, one of his investment banking clients was Shineda Industries, and their CEO, Devika Patel, referred him to her investment advisor, Vishnu Krishnamurthy. Rajveer met Krishnamurthy on a weekday afternoon, at a coffee shop in the Bandra-Kurla Complex in Mumbai.

As Rajveer described his financial position, Vishnu assessed that given his youth and well-paid job, Rajveer was actually in a good position to take greater financial risks than Devika Patel. However, Rajveer still needed to make sure that his parents' retirement was paid for properly over the next fifteen years. Therefore, Vishnu advised Rajveer to divide his corpus into two parts.

The first bucket consisted of low-risk assets which would produce steady cash flows on an annual basis for Rajveer's parents. Vishnu advised Rajveer to invest Rs 2.5 crore in long-dated government of India bonds, and another Rs 2 crore in the fixed deposits of a leading private sector bank. Net of tax, Vishnu believed that this combination would give Rajveer's parents around Rs 25 lakh in income per annum.

The second bucket consisted of the residual Rs 50 lakh left in Rajveer's portfolio. Vishnu advised Rajveer to consider investing it in Marcellus's small-cap PMS, the Little Champs Portfolio (LCP). Rajveer immediately expressed his indignation at Vishnu's suggestion. Not only was Rajveer scarred by his small-cap adventures, but he also believed that if anybody could make money in small caps, it was he.

Vishnu asked Rajveer to consider whether he really had any spare time left in the day after dealing with his demanding day job and looking after his parents' needs. 'Let's be realistic here. We are meeting in a coffee shop on a weekday afternoon because your lunch hour is the only time you get to take a breather. If that's the case, then where will you find the time to diligence small-cap stocks?'

Vishnu then shared with Rajveer the research that Marcellus had published on small-cap stocks, showing that whilst the best small caps deliver staggering outperformance vis-à-vis large and mid-caps, the weakest small caps can incinerate shareholder wealth in less than a year.

Exhibit 82: The lowest-quartile returns in small caps can quickly erode investor wealth[7]

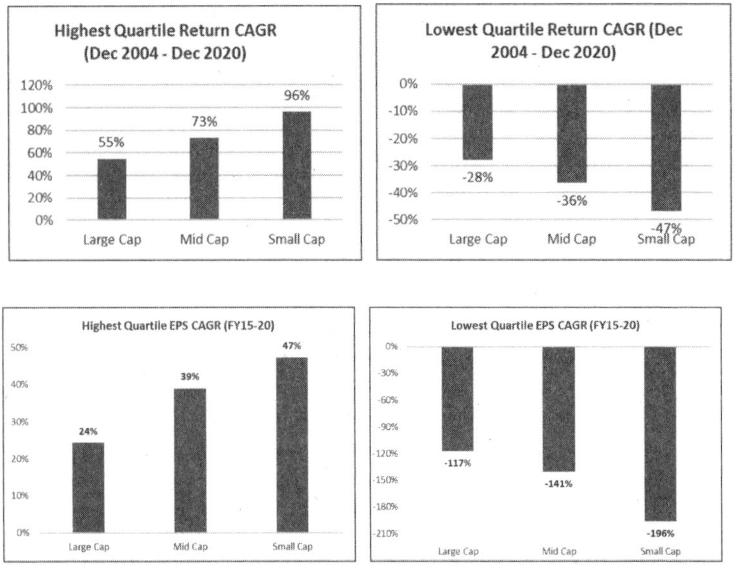

Source: Marcellus Investment Managers; Ace Equity

The key skill in small-cap investing, therefore, was investing in companies which: (a) do NOT cook their books; (b) allocate their capital and their free cash flows prudently to generate enhanced profits in the years ahead; and (c) build barriers to entry using their brands, business processes and relationships with customers, suppliers and employees. Vishnu told Rajveer that as an investment banker he would know how much diligence and market intelligence is required to establish comfort on these points for even a single small cap, let alone for a portfolio of fifteen such stocks.

He then invited Rajveer to go to Marcellus's website and watch their webinar on Little Champs Portfolio (LCP).[8] The once-bitten-twice-shy Rajveer spent an entire weekend going through Marcellus's videos and newsletters on LCP before requesting Vishnu to put him in touch with the team at Marcellus. When Vishnu asked Rajveer what prompted him to decide in favour of Marcellus, Rajveer's reply was, 'Look, after all the ups and downs I have been through, I am now left with only Rs 50 lakh. One of the reasons for my reverses is that I had built this mindset that to make money in small caps one has to punt on high-risk companies. Going through the material on the website, I realized that investing in small caps is actually the reverse—you have to look for well-run franchises, with clean and capable management teams, with strong balance sheets and healthy free cash flows and with proven competitive advantages. That was a real eye-opener for me. If I can invest in a group of high-quality small caps which can grow their business at around 20 per cent per annum, then fifteen years out I should have a corpus of around Rs 5-6 crore after paying capital gains taxes. That should allow me to build my dream villa in Goa fifteen years hence. And, by then, if I am a prolific dealmaker, I can host my clients and friends for weekend parties in Goa.'

Vishnu responded, 'Hopefully you will also remember to invite your financial advisor to these parties in Goa. Beyond my day job of identifying great investment strategies, I am also good at whipping up cocktails and mocktails, you know.'

KEY TAKEAWAYS

Financial planning is essential for an investor to ascertain her financial objectives and accordingly allocate her savings across various types of investment instruments.

- An investor's first allocation of her savings should relate to the quantum of funds required in the near term/for emergency purposes—also called rainy-day money. Since capital preservation is the only objective of this allocation (instead of wealth compounding), this investment should be in instruments such as tax-free government bonds.
- The equity allocation of an investor, regardless of whether it is in small caps or large caps, should be in a portfolio which has been thoroughly researched for: a) clean accounts; b) prudent and efficient capital allocation with strong free cash generation; and c) massive barriers to entry against competition.

* * *

Conclusion: Lessons from Rahul Dravid: Combining Technical Abilities with Behavioural Skills

'Gavaskar was a great defensive batsman who took on the best at their best and won. Tendulkar was blessed with outrageous talent that he never took for granted. Dravid perhaps had the strongest mind among the three, the largest mental reserves.'

—Sanjay Manjrekar in *Cricinfo* Magazine (2006)

'There is always a bat in the dressing room. I hold the bat in my hands and go through some of the shots that I might play. Before sleeping the previous night I spend 15 minutes running through the next day and how I would like it to pan out for me, structuring my thoughts.'

—Rahul Dravid[1]

While Dravid's technical proficiency as a Test batter was of a very high order, what really set him apart were the mental routines and mind conditioning regimen that he followed from his school days. This preparation, and his visualization techniques, not only allowed him to identify his own weaknesses but also gave him the capacity to remedy these weaknesses himself. Dravid's success was therefore driven as much by his behavioural traits as by his technical skills. In this regard, Dravid is a great role model for aspiring equity investors.

WHY IT IS SO HARD TO BE LIKE DRAVID

In the Introduction, we discussed how Dravid's outstanding record as a Test batter is built on simple principles like playing straight, staying at the crease for long periods, eschewing risky shots and staying fit. That, however, raises the conundrum of 'if it is so simple to be like Rahul Dravid, why are so few batsmen able to reach the standard set by this legend from Bengaluru?' In short, why is it so hard to be like Rahul Dravid? And the short answer is, human behaviour.

At the core of outsized success in any walk of life—including batting and investing—lies the ability of a small number of individuals to train their minds to achieve outcomes that appear to be beyond the reach of 99.99 per cent of the population. While what these individuals do might be simple, that does not mean it is easy. There are, broadly speaking, four reasons why it is not easy to bat like Rahul Dravid.

Firstly, Dravid's training and his basic mental conditioning began when he was around eight years old. That's when his coach, Keki Tarapore, started teaching him the importance of playing with a straight bat and the central role of relentless practice in attaining a high level of skill. Long before Malcolm Gladwell wrote about his famous '10,000 hours of practice' principle in *Outliers* (2008), scores of Indian coaches like

Keki Tarapore (for Dravid), Ramakant Achrekar (for Sachin Tendulkar) and Desh Azad (for Kapil Dev) trained their wards to follow this principle. As Fazal Khaleel, Dravid's teammate from his school cricket team, who also played Ranji Trophy cricket with Dravid, recollects:

> He paid attention to detail, especially the basics. If his form was not good he would go back to shadow-practice—to the hanging ball. When correcting our basics, our coach, Keki Tarapore, would tell us that if the bat did not come down straight, the ball would travel at an angle. Rahul never forgot the instruction. Interestingly, he never made any changes to his basic cricket or in his approach to the game. Right from his school days, he has played the same way. Playing in the V came naturally to him and he never altered it.

Whilst many middle-class schoolboys growing up in India's big metros might have access to the coaching and batting facilities that Dravid did, where Dravid really pulled away from his peers—both before and after he started playing international cricket—was in his appetite for practice. John Wright, who coached the Indian cricket team from 2000 to 2005, was the first to tell the world how seriously Dravid took net practice:

> I have never seen a more dedicated cricketer than Rahul in the nets. He was able to simulate a game situation, not just by going through the motions but by making every ball count. It was like he didn't want to get out even in the nets. In a situation when we had three or four bowlers going at him, he wanted to compete. He was always testing himself and worked on whatever needed the time, like his technique, or sorting out some kink.[2]

Not only was Rahul practising in the nets, he was also practising shots in his mind everywhere and all the time. His wife, Vijeta, discovered this fact shortly after they got married: 'When I went to Melbourne and Sydney [in January 2004] . . . I was still trying to get to know him, know his game. It was only then I began to notice how he would prepare: his routines, his obsession with shadow practice at all hours of the day, which I first found very weird . . .'[3]

Thus, through a combination of good coaching and relentless practice—in the nets and in his mind—by the time Dravid entered the Indian Test team, aged twenty-three, he had comfortably exceeded the 10,000 hours of practice required to perform at world-class level.

Secondly, in addition to these strengths, Rahul Dravid was one of the first Test cricketers to start using set routines and mental conditioning techniques to improve his game. The remarkable thing is that he seemed to have started these routines when he played cricket as a schoolboy. Fazal Khaleel says:

> As a room-mate, Rahul was difficult as well as easy to share with. He wanted a zen-like atmosphere in the room—everything peaceful and calm. He was quiet and meditative, would not watch TV much; he read books instead . . . He had his set routines and rituals, even in those days. He would do breathing exercises and clean his nostrils using the ancient practice of Jalneti. It was very boring.[4]

When asked by Sharda Ugra in 2012 as to how he started using meditation as a tool for preparation, Dravid responded:

> I took to it quite young. I was just drawn to it. I did it a couple of times at 18-19, some basic form of meditation. I think I got better with age. It started off with trying to do

> some relaxation, to calm myself down in some ways. And I've experimented with a few things . . . but I found that it was a handy way to relax and switch off.[5]

As the years went by and as Dravid rose up the cricketing pantheon, his mental conditioning techniques were perfected to a high level of proficiency. Vijeta talks about his meditation and other mind practices during their overseas tour sometime in 2006-07:

> When we began to travel with the kids . . . we made sure we got two rooms, next to each other. The day before every match, the boys were told that their father had to be left alone for a while, and he was. He would go into his room and meditate or maybe to do a few visualization exercises. On the morning of the game he would get up and do another session of meditation before leaving for the ground. I have tried meditation myself and I know that the zone Rahul is able to get into as quickly as he does takes a lot of years of training to reach.[6]

The sum total of everything we have discussed so far allows you to visualize not just a supremely skilled cricketer but also one whose mental conditioning has given him enormous reserves of mental strength. Dravid himself pulled the entire construct together in an interview he did for *Cricinfo* editor Sambit Bal in 2004:

> I try to have as many nets as possible in the last couple of days before the match. When I feel comfortable with my game, I stop. Then I start thinking about the match. I look at the wicket. I try to analyse the kind of bowlers I will be playing, their strengths and weaknesses. I replay in

> my mind the memories of my last encounter with them. I look at videos if they're available. If a bowler got me out last time, I try to think about how I got out, what mistake I committed.
>
> And I do my best to be in a relaxed state of mind, because that's when I play at my best. I try to slow things down a couple of days before the game. I have long lunches, do things in an unhurried way. The morning of the match, I always get up a couple of hours before we have to get to the ground, so that I have plenty of time to get ready. I take my time to have a bath, wear my clothes, eat breakfast. I never rush things, that sort of sets up my mood for the rest of the day. Then, if the facilities permit, I have a net at the ground.[7]

Thirdly, in addition, as his career progressed, David sought feedback from peers and introspected on it to understand his weaknesses. He figured out technical solutions to these weaknesses using his cricketing intelligence and then spent hundreds of hours at the nets fixing these issues. Finally, he implemented these technical fixes in live cricket matches against high-quality opposition. John Wright noted this before most other people:

> He never made the same mistake twice. He learnt hugely in one-day cricket—which probably was an area he had to work at a little bit more than others. He had been dropped from the Indian one-day team and then went on to come back and have a very good World Cup [in 2003] . . . He had all the shots but he worked hard at turning the strike over, getting the singles, and dropping the ball on the on side, when you normally might put it on the off side. At the start people would try to slow him down, but then he worked out a way so they couldn't do that.[8]

It is interesting—and inspiring—to know how Dravid sorted out his one-day cricket batting. Dravid's former teammate in the Indian team and India's opening batter in that memorable 2003-04 Australia tour, Aakash Chopra, has beautifully described this:

> When he started out, Dravid used to crouch a lot more in his stance, with his head falling over a bit towards the off side. His bat, coming from the direction of [the] gully, forced him make a huge loop at the top of the backlift. Both the backlift and the falling head allowed him to punish anything that was even marginally on his legs. His wide backlift also made him a good cutter of the ball, provided there was width on offer. On the flip side, it meant fewer front-foot shots on the off side . . .
>
> The knowledge of where his off stump was, coupled with immense patience, ensured that Dravid continued to score bucketfuls of runs in Test cricket, in spite of the bowlers finding him out. But though the runs were coming they were not coming as briskly as he would have liked. He had to stay longer at the crease to accumulate his runs, and that eventually cost him his place in the ODI team. He needed [to] find ways to open up his off-side play . . .
>
> An ardent follower of the Gavaskar school of batting, Dravid would, when he started out, go back and across before the ball was bowled and then further across to get behind the line of the ball. While this method worked well in Test cricket, it needed some tinkering in the shorter format. So instead of going back and across, he preferred going back and back, to ensure that he stayed beside the ball more often, which allowed him to free his arms while playing through the off. These tweaks were successful and Dravid went on to play his finest cricket in that period . . . It

> must have taken hundreds of hours of practice to get it into his system, so as to make it absolutely seamless. Dravid went through the grind.[9]

This ability to understand and acknowledge one's weaknesses, then to figure out a solution and finally to have the mental strength required to implement the fix in front of a global audience is very rare. It is unlikely that this suite of characteristics can be coached into a person; you need the individual to have the curiosity and the mindset to grow in this fashion. Dravid had that growth mindset from an early age. But where did that growth mindset—Dravid's fourth great strength—come from?

Greg Chappell, who was India's coach for much of Dravid's tenure as captain of the Indian team from 2005-07, said,

> Rahul is an avid reader, who reads in the search of knowledge with which to improve himself. He is a like a child in that he constantly asks questions and then asks why when you give him an answer . . . In that way, he was eminently coachable. He could take concepts and turn them into action because of his intelligence and a strong belief in his ability.[10]

Writing in January 2004, the noted sports journalist Rohit Brijnath highlighted Rahul Dravid's extensive reading of a variety of books:

> Last month, in *Wisden Asia Cricket* magazine, he wrote an article on books. He remembered his days as a young player, curled up on the wooden bunk as the train rattled its way to another match, reading 'To Kill a Mockingbird'. In Adelaide [in December 2003], 'Racers', the story of the dramatic 1996 Formula One Season, rested on his table. But there is one book he identifies with powerfully, perhaps the tale has

something in it for him. David Halberstam's 'The Amateurs' studies in detail the quest of American rowers for Olympic selection, dissecting their pain, their rage, the obsession of their journey . . . Dravid explains: 'It shows you true passion and true drive. It's what sport is about for people who play it. It's not about the accolades or the money, but about the personal battles, the sacrifice. It's about the process and I enjoy that.'[11]

Writing about Rahul Dravid in the *Mint Lounge* in March 2010, Rohit Brijnath said:

> When he came to Singapore once . . . What are you reading, he'd ask. What do you think, he'd ask. Not about cricket, but tennis, toughness, politics. He'd linger in bookshops, stroll into theatres, sit in wildlife parks. One year he opted to go and learn from a visual skills specialist in South Africa; last summer, he drove to Chelsea FC to wander through their Mind Room. From his wide interests emerged cricket's most interesting man.[12]

Dravid's wife Vijeta says that even if he had a bad day on the cricket field, his growth mindset would help him bounce back:

> At the end of the day's play, he may be thinking about it, his batting may bother him . . . but at that point he can compartmentalise his life very well. He won't order room service or brood indoors. He would rather go out, find something to do; go to a movie or watch musicals, which he loves. He will walk out to the sea or go to the bookstores.[13]

So, there you have it. It is very difficult to bat like Rahul Dravid because it very difficult to find in one person the confluence of so many rare traits—technical talent, a strong work ethic, the desire to mentally steel oneself for the toughest challenges in the game, the humility to acknowledge deficiencies, the intelligence to rectify these weaknesses and, finally, the courage to go out in front of a billion people and implement the solution to the weaknesses.

The final word on Rahul Dravid's greatness comes from the man himself: 'I have looked at all areas of my game and worked hard on all of them. I have really worked on my physical fitness. I think it's a question of everything coming together,' he told Sambit Bal for *Wisden Asia Cricket* magazine in January 2004.

As in Test cricket, so in investing, the most successful investors are those who not only work on their technical skill-set but also think deeply about the underlying workings of great companies. Such investors are then able to see the companies in a way that nobody else can i.e., these investors are able to gain insights into the functioning of these companies that no one else has. Furthermore, by introspecting and by reviewing their previous investment decisions, these investors are able to identify deficiencies in their investment toolset. Then, Dravid-like, these investors proceed to identify remedies to their deficiencies. The greatest investors, like the greatest Test cricketers, are a combination of strong technical skills and a growth mindset.

APPENDIX 1

The Marcellus Checklist

'. . . we need a different strategy for overcoming failure, one that builds on experience and takes advantage of the knowledge people have but somehow also makes up for our inevitable human inadequacies. And there is such a strategy—though it will seem almost ridiculous in its simplicity maybe even crazy to those of us who have spent years carefully developing ever more advanced skills and technologies. It is a checklist.'

—Atul Gawande[1]

Each of the three key components of Marcellus's formula—clean accounts, competitive advantages, and capital allocation—covers a wide array of subjects, including accounting, corporate strategy, industry analysis and corporate finance. To make it easier to keep track of the research process and monitor one's progress in identifying Consistent Compounders using Marcellus's formula, we have prepared a set of checklists. These checklists cover the major steps in the research process and will help readers arrive at the answer as to whether a company is a consistent compounder or not.

THE CHECKLIST

ACCOUNTING RATIOS

☐	Cash flow from operations/EBITDA	Check the trend of the ratio; a consistently low ratio indicates that revenues and operating profits are not getting converted to cash
☐	Volatility in depreciation rate	The depreciation rate is often modified to manipulate earnings; volatility of the same flags off such risks
☐	Change in reserves and surplus explained by the profit/loss for the year and dividends	To check if expenses have been written off directly from the balance sheet instead of being routed through P&L, thus inflating the profit
☐	Yield on cash and cash equivalents	A low yield could mean misstatement of cash and equivalents
☐	Contingent liabilities as percentage of net worth	Indicative of the extent of off-balance sheet risks
☐	CWIP to gross block	High ratio would indicate unsubstantiated capex
☐	Free cash flow (cash flow from operations + cash flow from investing) to median revenues	To check if cash generated by business is being siphoned off or whether reported revenue/earnings are believable
☐	Growth in auditors' remuneration to growth in revenues	Faster growth in auditors' remuneration vis-à-vis company's operations raises concerns surrounding auditors' objectivity

ADVANCED ACCOUNTING CHECKS

☐	Comparative common-sized income statement vs peers to analyse any significant divergence in P&L items vs peers
☐	Comparative Dupont analysis vs peers
☐	R&D capitalization vs charge to P&L
☐	Goodwill as percentage of net worth
☐	Frequent change of auditors

☐	Any significant adverse comment in the auditor's report
☐	Any significant portion of company's operations (such as subsidiaries) not audited by the principal statutory auditor
☐	Quality of audit committee (whether chaired by an independent director)
☐	Frequent changes in accounting periods

GOVERNANCE CHECKS

☐	Related-party transactions and their significance
☐	Other business interests of promoters (any significant stress in those business, etc.)
☐	M&A with promoter-owned entities
☐	Significant litigation surrounding promoters
☐	Promoter family structure, succession, etc.
☐	Pledge of promoter shareholding
☐	Insider buying and selling
☐	Remuneration to promoters
☐	Frequency and necessity of equity dilution

FORENSIC CHECKS FOR BANKS AND NBFCS

☐	Treasury income as percentage of NII	To check if treasury income is being booked aggressively
☐	Fee income as percentage of NII	Higher proportion of fee income vs peers may be because of aggressive lending practices to boost profitability at the cost of asset quality
☐	NPA volatility	Higher NPA volatility maybe due to inconsistency in NPA recognition

☐	Provision as percentage of NPA	A low ratio indicates inadequate provisioning and therefore artificially higher profitability
☐	Contingent liabilities to net worth	Indicative of the extent of off-balance sheet risk
☐	Growth in auditor remuneration vs total interest income	Faster growth in auditors' remuneration vis-à-vis company's operations raises concerns surrounding auditors' objectivity

COMPETITIVE ADVANTAGES CHECKS

☐	Is the long-term average return on capital employed (RoCE) greater than the cost of capital?
☐	How does the RoCE of the company compare with that of peers? Does it indicate dominance of the industry's profit pool?
☐	If a new competitor with deep pockets and ability to survive a loss on the income statement for a long time enters the market, will the incumbent lose market share?
☐	Does the company disrupt the industry business model at regular intervals, rather than getting disrupted by new competitors or peers?

SOURCES OF COMPETITIVE ADVANTAGE—INNOVATION

☐	Is the company consistently the first amongst peers to introduce new products, processes, technologies, revenue models, etc.?
☐	What is the importance attached to R&D and who leads the function in the company?
☐	Is there a culture of investing in innovation and to be 'ahead of the curve', with the knowledge that not all R&D investments will lead to a new product?

SOURCES OF COMPETITIVE ADVANTAGE—BRAND

☐	What differentiates a company's products from peers' that makes them distinct brands?
☐	Is there any dilution or muddling of the brand positioning?
☐	Are the advertising campaigns differentiated, do they break through the clutter and convey the core brand promises clearly?
☐	What are the talent recruitment strategies, training policies and retention tools used by the company?
☐	Is there a key-man risk and/or excessive reliance on the promoter?
☐	Is there a succession plan in place? How is the leadership team chosen?
☐	How rewarding is it to be a supplier to the company?
☐	What is the return on investment for a distributor/dealer of the company's products?

SOURCES OF COMPETITIVE ADVANTAGE—STRATEGIC ASSETS

☐	If a company operates with a licence (from the government, or from a foreign owner), what is the duration of the licence and the regional or product-wide exclusivity it enjoys?
☐	How long has been the relationship between the company and the licensor? A longer history is indicative of a healthy relationship
☐	Do the competitive advantages grant the company pricing power in the business?

CAPITAL ALLOCATION CHECKS

☐	Is the company generating positive operating cash flow and free cash flow on a consistent basis?
☐	What is the growth strategy being adopted—market penetration, product development, market development or diversification?
☐	What is the quantum of capital being allocated towards the growth strategy? How much is it as a proportion of the net worth?
☐	Does the growth strategy lead to a substantial increase in financial leverage?
☐	If growth is being pursued in international markets through acquisitions, what is the management's experience and track record in these geographies?
☐	Does the promoter group have other businesses also? If yes, what is their ownership of the other businesses?
☐	Are there other investments by the promoter group in capital-intensive businesses? If yes, what is the source of capital for these businesses?
☐	Is there a clear succession plan in place at all key leadership levels?
☐	Is there evidence of decentralization of power and authority—both for day-to-day business execution, as well as for implementing capital allocation decisions?
☐	What is the quality and tenure of CXOs in the organization?
☐	What is the involvement and independence of the board of directors—both in the context of decentralizing capital allocation decision making as well as in the recruitment of CXOs in the firm?
☐	What is the historical evidence of execution of succession at the CXO level without adverse impact on the organization?

TIMING AND PRICING CHECKS

☐	What is the consistency of free cash generation? In a rolling time-frame of three years, how many instances of negative free cash flows have been reported in the past ten/twenty years?
☐	What is the longevity of free cash flow generation? This question can be answered by consolidating the replies to all the question asked above.
☐	Does the company have clean accounts?
☐	Does the management have a consistent track record of prudent capital allocation?
☐	Does the company have sustainable competitive advantages?
☐	What is the DCF value of the free cash flow over the long-term period assessed in the question above?

* * *

APPENDIX 2

Sir John Kay's IBAS Framework[1]

SUSTAINABLE COMPETITIVE ADVANTAGE

'No formula in finance tells you that the moat is twenty-eight feet wide and sixteen feet deep. That's what drives the academics crazy. They can compute standard deviations and betas, but they can't understand moats. Maybe I'm being too hard on the academics.'

—Warren Buffett[2]

'I always try and spend the last few minutes . . . to touch on a competitor, or a company they do business with, such as a supplier or a customer. Although not all managements will talk about other companies, when they do, it can be very revealing. The ultimate commendation is when a company talks positively about a competitor. I always put a strong weight on such a view.'

—Anthony Bolton,[3] the legendary fund manager who ran the Fidelity Special Situations fund

Sustainable competitive advantages allow firms to add more value than their rivals and to continue doing so over long periods of time. But where do these competitive advantages come from? And why is it that certain firms seem to have more of these advantages than others? At Marcellus, we have been deeply influenced by the work of Sir John Kay on corporate strategy in general, and it is his framework that we use to assess the sustainable competitive advantages of companies.

In his 1993 book *Foundations of Corporate Success*, Kay states that 'sustainable competitive advantage is what helps a firm ensure that the value that it adds cannot be competed away by its rivals'. He goes on to say that sustainable competitive advantages can come from two sources: distinctive capabilities or strategic assets. Whilst strategic assets can be in the form of intellectual property (patents and proprietary know-how), legal rights (licences and concessions) or a natural monopoly, distinctive capabilities are more intangible in nature.

Distinctive capabilities, says Sir John, are those relationships that a firm has with its customers, suppliers or employees, which cannot be replicated by other competing firms and which allow the firm to generate more value additions than its competitors. He further divides distinctive capabilities into three categories:

- Brands and reputation
- Architecture
- Innovation

Let us delve into these in more detail, as understanding them is at the core of understanding the strength of a company's franchise.

BRANDS AND REPUTATION

> 'A product can be quickly outdated, but a successful brand is timeless.'
>
> —Stephen King, American novelist, author and TV producer

> 'Reputations are created in specific markets. A reputation necessarily relates to a product or a group of products. It is bounded geographically, too. Many reputations are very local in nature. The good plumber or doctor neither has nor needs a reputation outside a tightly defined area. Retailing reputations are mostly national. But an increasing number of producers of manufactured goods, from Coca-Cola to Sony, have established reputations worldwide, and branding has enabled international reputations to be created and exploited for locally delivered services in industries as diverse as accountancy and car hire.'
>
> —Sir John Kay[4]

In many markets, product quality, in spite of being an important driver of purchase decisions, can only be ascertained by the long-term experience of using that product. Examples of such products are insurance policies and healthcare. In many other markets, not only is the ticket price of the product high but customers can also assess the quality of the product only after they have parted with their cash. A few examples of such products would be cars and high-end TVs.

In both these markets, customers use the strength of the company's reputation as a proxy for the quality of the product or service. For example, people gravitate towards the best hospital in town for critical surgery and tend to prefer world-class brands whilst buying expensive home entertainment equipment. Since reputation for such high-end services or expensive equipment takes many years to build, reputation tends to be difficult and costly to create. This, in turn, makes it a very powerful source for a competitive advantage.

For products that are used daily, investors tend to be generally aware of the strength of a brand. In more niche products or B2B products (e.g., industrial cables, mining equipment, municipal water purification and semiconductors), investors often do not have first-hand knowledge of the key brands in the relevant markets. In such instances, to assess the strength of the brand, they turn to:

- Brand recognition surveys conducted by the trade press.
- Duration of the warranties offered by the firm (the longer the warranties, the more unequivocal the statement it makes about the firm's brand).
- The length of time the firm has been in that market (e.g., 'Established 1915' is a fairly credible way of telling the world that since you have been in business for over a century, your product must have something distinctive about it).
- How much the firm spends on marketing and publicity (a large marketing spend figure, relative to the firm's revenues, is usually a reassuring sign).
- How much of a price premium the firm is able to charge vis-a-vis its peers.

One way to appreciate the power of brands and their reputation to generate sustained profits and hence, shareholder returns, is to look at how some of India's most-trusted brands have fared over the last decade. One can take the annual *Economic Times* survey for this. As can be seen in Exhibit 83, over the past decade, the listed companies with the most powerful brands have comfortably beaten the most widely acknowledged front-line stock market index by a comfortable margin on revenues, earnings and share price movement.

In the table below, we have compared large FMCG companies and their popular brands (with their ranking in a brand survey) with the revenue growth, EPS growth and share price growth associated with them for the past decade. HUL, for example, which has seven brands in the top 40 (Horlicks, Surf, Dove, Lifebuoy, Pepsodent, Lux and Pond's), has revenue growth (8 per cent), EPS growth (13 per cent) and a stock price increase (23 per cent) that has outperformed the BSE Sensex (8.8 per cent). To reemphasize the point, companies with huge and successful brands have delivered strong financial returns and also beaten the BSE Sensex over the past decade.

Exhibit 83: Performance of listed companies with the most trusted brands

Company	Trusted Brands*	Ten-Year Growth (2011–20) (% CAGR)		
		Revenues	**EPS**	**Share price****
Hindustan Unilever	Horlicks (9), Surf (17), Dove (18), Lifebuoy (24), Pepsodent (28), Lux (30), Pond's (36) etc.	8%	13%	23%
Nestlé India	Maggi (13), KitKat (44) etc.	9%	12%	17%
Pidilite	Fevicol (10)	13%	15%	28%

Source: Marcellus Investment Managers; Ace Equity; figures in brackets indicate the brand's rank in the Economic Times' Most Trusted Brands 2020 list (source: https://brandequity.economictimes.indiatimes.com/news/industry/most-trusted-brands-2020/74800967); **share price performance measured from January 2011 to December 2020

ARCHITECTURE[5]

> 'Architecture is a system of relationships within the firm, or between the firm and its suppliers and customers, or both. Generally, the system is a complex one and the content of the relationships implicit rather than explicit. The structure relies on continued mutual commitment to monitor and enforce its terms. A firm with distinctive architecture gains strength from the ability to transfer firm product and market specific information within the organization and to its customers and suppliers. It can also respond quickly and flexibly to changing circumstances. It has often been through their greater ability to develop such architecture that Japanese firms have established competitive advantages over their American rivals.'
>
> —Sir John Kay[6]

> 'A dream you dream alone is only a dream. A dream you dream together is reality.'
>
> —Sir John Lennon

Architecture refers to the network of contracts, formal and informal, that a firm has with its employees, suppliers and customers. Thus, architecture would include the formal employment contracts that a firm has with its employees, and it would also include the more informal obligation it has to provide ongoing training to its employees. Similarly, architecture would include the firm's legal obligation to pay its suppliers on time and its more informal obligation to warn its suppliers in advance if it were planning to cut production in three months.

Such architecture is most often found in firms with a distinctive organizational style or ethos, because such firms tend to have a well-organized and long-established set of processes or routines for doing business. So, for example, if you have ever taken a home loan in India, you will find a marked difference in the speed and professionalism with which HDFC processes a home loan application as compared to other lenders. The HDFC branch manager asks the applicant more specific questions than other lenders, and this home loan provider's due diligence on the applicant and the property appears to be done more swiftly and thoroughly than most other lenders'.

So, how can investors assess whether the firm they are scrutinizing has architecture or not? In fact, whilst investors will often not know the exact processes or procedures of the firm in question, they can assess whether a firm has such processes and procedures by gauging these features:

- The extent to which the employees of the firm cooperate with each other across various departments and locations;
- The rate of staff attrition (sometimes given in the Annual Report; in the absence of detailed information in the Annual Report, a broad sense can be had from tracking the key management personnel's career progression on social media sites such as LinkedIn);
- The extent to which the staff in different parts of the firm give the same message when asked the same question; and
- The extent to which the firm is able to generate innovations in its products or services or production processes on an ongoing basis.

At the core of successful architecture is cooperation (within teams, across various teams in a firm, and between the firm and its suppliers) and sharing (of ideas, information, customer insights and, ultimately, rewards). Built properly, architecture allows a firm with ordinary people to produce extraordinary results.

Perhaps the most striking demonstration of architecture in India is the unlisted non-profit agricultural cooperative, Gujarat Cooperative Milk Marketing Federation Ltd (GCMMF), better known to millions of Indians as Amul.

Amul is India's legendary dairy company, and the man who engineered this remarkable enterprise's rise to glory is Verghese Kurien. Born into an affluent Syrian Anglican family in Kerala in 1921, Kurien excelled in academics and sports, first in Loyola College in Chennai, and then at the College of Engineering (Guindy) and, finally, in Michigan State University (where he was sent on an elite scholarship sponsored by the government of India). Upon his return to India in 1949, the government sent him to work at a run-down creamery[7] in Anand, in what was then part of Bombay State and is now part of Gujarat.

Kurien hated his government job in Anand, and when he quit a few months later, Tribhuvandas Patel, a prominent political leader of the local farmers, persuaded Kurien to stay and help run the Kaira District Co-operative Milk Producers' Union Limited (which came to be known popularly as Amul dairy). Twenty-five years later, this co-operative was merged into other co-operatives to create the now legendary Gujarat Co-operative Milk Marketing Federation Ltd (GCMMF).

Arguably, the most striking example of sustained co-operation on an epic scale in India, GCMMF generated revenues in FY2019 of Rs 33,000 crore (nearly $4.5 billion). That is three times as much as its closest competitor Nestlé India's revenues, and only 20 per cent shy of HUL's revenues. On this measure, GCMMF is India's second largest FMCG company. Not only is GCMMF big, it grows much faster than its rivals. Over the past decade, GCMMF has grown revenues at 17 per cent CAGR, compared with Nestlé's 9 per cent and HUL's 8 per cent. Over the last five years, the growth gap between GCMMF and its two largest rivals has got even bigger! In key FMCG-product categories such as butter, cheese and packaged milk, Amul has been the long-standing market leader in the face of sustained efforts by MNCs to break its dominance. GCMMF is also India's biggest exporter of dairy products.[8]

Growth aside, the scale on which GCMMF operates is astonishing. GCMMF's daily procurement of milk is 2.3 crore litres from more than 18,700 village milk co-operative societies (which include 36 lakh milk producer-members). The way GCMMF aggregates the milk produced by these members into the village co-operative dairy, and then further aggregates that into the district co-operative, which in turn feeds into the mother dairy unit, has been studied by numerous management experts. So, how does GCMMF give a fair deal to its farmers, its management team, its 10,000 dealers, its 1 million retailers and its hundreds of millions of customers? At the core of this pioneering co-operative's success appear to be four factors:

CAREFUL CULTIVATION OF THE BRAND

Its sixty-year-old brand, with its distinctive imagery of the little girl in the dress with the red polka dots, has been central to Amul's success. Cultivated with great effort and patience, numerous surveys have shown Amul to be one of the most trusted brands in the country. As Kurien says in his autobiography *I Too Had a Dream*:[9]

> . . . we had to make the products as attractive as possible to the market . . . We sought help from advertising professionals . . . In 1966 . . . the Amul account was given to the Advertising and Sales Promotion Company (ASP) with the brief that they should dislodge Polson from its 'premier brand'

position in Bombay. That was when Eustace Fernandes of ASP created the Amul mascot—the mischievous, endearing girl. The image of the Amul girl went down so well with consumers that very soon it became synonymous with Amul . . . Together, the team at ASP gave Amul butter its memorable and catchy campaign tagline 'Utterly, butterly, delicious'—which broke all records to become the longest-running campaign in Indian advertising history.

SUSTAINED ALIGNMENT WITH STAKEHOLDERS' INTERESTS

The practical concept—implemented daily in millions of homes—is that of a fair deal for the farmer and the linked idea of the disintermediation of the middleman. As Harish Damodaran explains in *India's New Capitalists: Caste, Business, and Industry in a Modern Nation*:[10]

> A farmer pouring buffalo milk with 6% fat content to a Gujarat co-operative 2004-05 would receive Rs 13-14 per litre, which is 25-30% more than the corresponding farmgate prices paid by dairies elsewhere in the country . . . Taking an average rate of Rs 13, the GCMMF dairies would in 2004-05 have pumped in around Rs 2,800 crore to their farm members, constituting 70% of their aggregate turnover of Rs 4,000 crore. By contrast, milk purchase costs are less than half of the value of product sales for a company like Nestlé India, marking the essential difference between a farmer controlled co-operative and an investor-owned concern.

POLITICAL AND REGULATORY BUY-IN

GCMMF and Kurien were able to co-opt almost every single politician of note in independent India to help them promote the cause of Gujarati farmers. As Kurien's autobiography shows, Sardar Patel, Jawaharlal Nehru, Lal Bahadur Shastri, Morarji Desai, T.T. Krishnamachari, YB Chavan, Indira Gandhi—basically, anyone who mattered in New Delhi or in the politics of west India—was brought to Anand, wowed by the scale of the miracle in Anand and converted to the cause of promoting Amul. Kurien explains in his autobiography how he repeatedly used his political clout to hurt his competitors by getting bans, embargoes, tariffs, etc., imposed on them. An interesting incident[11] dates to 1962, when, upon the Indian Army's request, Kurien stopped supplying butter in the open market and instead diverted all his output to the army. When a rival company, Polson, took advantage of this by increasing the prices of its butter, Kurien simply went to the government and had Polson's butter output frozen. When Polson's aggrieved promoter complained to the relevant minister in Ahmedabad, Kurien told him in front of the minister, 'You bloody bastard. You come here and speak lies to the Minister. I will castrate you.'[12]A more prosaic but equally effective example of architecture would be the way India's largest car manufacturer, Maruti Suzuki, is tied up in a common architecture with its suppliers. This company has around 250 local suppliers based in the vicinity of its plants on the outskirts of Delhi, and another twenty global suppliers.[13] Each of these 270-odd suppliers understands Maruti's design specifications for specific components and has its own Enterprise Resource Planning (ERP) software hooked into Maruti's. These suppliers have long-term contracts with the company and, as a result, they have been able to work in sync over the course of several decades.

Even more interestingly, several of these suppliers, in turn, will have smaller suppliers in the Gurgaon-Manesar region who supply them components which, when put together, make for a larger sub-system that goes into the making of a Maruti car. In spite of this complex web of interlinkages, Maruti's supply chain functions seamlessly. In the 1980s, Maruti used to give its suppliers thirty days' notice for the components it needed. Now, it instructs the supplier the previous night about the specific two-hour slot the next day when the components have to reach its assembly line. It takes a new entrant into the Indian auto market many years, sometimes decades, to create a supply chain as efficient as this. That's the power of architecture—it brings different companies together into a common network with a common goal in mind.

INNOVATION

> 'Some leaders push innovations by being good at the big picture. Others do so by mastering details. [Steve] Jobs did both, relentlessly.'
>
> —Walter Isaacson in *Steve Jobs*

Whilst innovation is often talked about as a source of competitive advantage, especially in the technology and pharmaceutical sectors, it is actually the most tenuous source of sustainable competitive advantage as:

- Innovation is expensive.
- Innovation is uncertain—it tends to be a hit-or-miss process.
- Innovation is hard to manage due to the random nature of the process.

Furthermore, even when the expensive innovation process yields a commercially useful result, the benefits can be competed away, as other firms replicate the innovator and/or employees who have driven the innovation process tend to extract the benefits of innovation through higher compensation.

In fact, innovation is more powerful when it is twinned with the two other distinctive capabilities described above—reputation and architecture. Apple is the most celebrated example of a contemporary firm which has clearly built a reputation for innovation (think of the slew of products from Apple over the past decade—first changing how people access music, then changing how they perceive phones and, finally, changing how they use personal computers).

STRATEGIC ASSETS

In contrast to the three distinctive capabilities discussed above, strategic assets are easier to identify as sources of competitive advantages. Such assets can come in different guises:

- Intellectual property, i.e., patents or proprietary know-how (e.g., the recipe for Coke's famous syrup, which is a closely held secret and kept in the company's museum in Atlanta, Georgia);
- Licences and regulatory permissions to provide a certain service to the public, e.g., in telecom, power, gas or public transport;
- Access to natural resources, such as coal or iron-ore mines;
- Political contacts, either at the national, state or city level
- Sunk costs incurred by the first mover, which results in other potential competitors deciding to stay away from that market, e.g., given that there already is a Mumbai-Pune highway operated by IRB, it does not make sense for anyone else to set up a competing road; and
- Natural monopolies, i.e., sectors or markets which accommodate only one or two firms. For example, the market for supplying power in Mumbai is restricted to one firm, Tata Power.

While strategic assets can come in different forms, all of them result in a lower per unit cost of production for the firm owning the asset relative to its competitors. For example, Tata Steel's decades-old access to coal and iron-ore from its captive mines allows it to make more money per tonne of steel produced than any other steel manufacturer in India. Total raw material costs for Tata Steel (including costs of mining) amount to approximately Rs 17,000 per ton, against Rs 22,000 per ton for JSW Steel, which does not have access to captive sources of key raw materials.

Unsurprisingly, therefore, among the top fifty companies by market cap in India since the Nifty50 was launched in 1995, there is only one conglomerate—Tata Sons—which has had three companies—i.e., Tata Power, Tata Steel and Tata Motors—featuring in the index more or less throughout to date.

In fact, the Tatas are almost a textbook case of how to build businesses—without being the most innovative players in town, they have combined architecture and brands to great effect, thereby creating robust sources of sustainable competitive advantages. The group seems to have created at least three specific mechanisms to ensure that these sources of competitive advantage endure:

Firstly, Tata Sons, an unlisted company (owned by several philanthropic trusts endowed by members of the Tata family), is the promoter of the major operating Tata companies and holds significant shareholdings in these companies. Tata Sons' patient, long-term orientation in terms of building large and robust businesses gradually, has played a major role in the stability of the listed Tata businesses.

Secondly, Tata Quality Management Services (TQMS), a division of Tata Sons, assists Tata companies in their business excellence initiatives through the Tata Business Excellence Model, Management of Business Ethics and the Tata Code of

Conduct. TQMS, quite literally, provides the architecture for harmonization of practices in various parts of the Tata empire.

Thirdly, Tata Sons is also the owner of the Tata name and several Tata trademarks, which are registered in India and around the world. These are used by various Tata companies under a licence from Tata Sons as part of their corporate name and/or in relation to their products and services. The terms of use of the group mark and logo by Tata companies are governed by the Brand Equity and Business Promotion (BEBP) agreement entered into between Tata Sons and Tata companies.

To sum up, to get ahead—and remain consistently ahead—of competition, companies should continuously invest in innovation and brands and in building strong architecture around their stakeholders. These sustainable competitive advantages are essentially the moats that companies build to remain ahead of the game. As ever, nobody explains the practical application of the sustainable competitive advantage construct better than Kay:

'BMW cars are not the most powerful, or the most reliable, or the most luxurious on the market, although they score well against all these criteria. No one has ever suggested that they are cheap, even for the high level of specification that most models offer. Although BMW rightly emphasises the quality and advanced nature of its technology, its products are not exceptionally innovative . . .. The achievements of BMW are built on two closely associated factors. The company achieves a higher quality of engineering than is usual in production cars. While most car assembly has now been taken over by robots or workers from low wage economies, BMW maintains a skilled German labour force. The company benefits, as many German firms do, from an educational system which gives basic technical skills to an unusually high proportion of the population. Its reputation has followed from these substantial achievements . . ..

'Yet BMW's success was neither easy nor certain . . . The turning point came when the firm identified a market which most effectively exploited its capabilities—the market for high-performance saloon cars, which has since become almost synonymous with BMW. The BMW 1500, launched in 1961, established a reputation for engineering quality in the BMW automobile brand. The brand in turn acquired a distinctive identity as a symbol for young, affluent European professionals. That combination—a system of production which gives the company a particular advantage in its chosen market segment, a worldwide reputation for product quality, and a brand which immediately identifies the aims and aspirations of its customers—continues to make BMW one of the most profitable automobile manufacturers in the world.

'Today, the BMW business is structured to maximise these advantages. Retail margins on BMW cars are relatively high. The company maintains tight control over its distribution network. This control supports the brand image and also aids market segmentation. BMW cars are positioned differently and priced very differently in the various national markets. The same tight control is reflected in BMW's relationships with suppliers, who mostly have continuing long associations with the company. BMW's activities are focused almost exclusively on two product ranges—high performance saloon cars and motor bikes which reflect its competitive strengths.

'BMW is a company with a well-executed strategy. It is a company which came—after several false starts—to recognise its distinctive capabilities and chose the market, and subsequent markets, which realised its full potential. Its dealings with its suppliers and distributors, its pricing approach, its branding and advertising strategies, are all built around that recognition and these choices. There was no master plan, no single vision which took BMW from where it was in 1959 to where it is today.'[14]

* * *

APPENDIX 3

Robert Kirby's Coffee Can Investing Method[1]

A LOW-RISK APPROACH TO INVESTING

> 'In investing, as in auto racing, you don't have to win every lap to win the race, but you absolutely do have to finish the race. While a driver must be prepared to take some risks, if he takes too many risks, he'll wind up against the fence. There are sensible risks—and there are risks that make no sense at all.'
>
> —Robert G. Kirby, Capital Group[2]

We have referenced the book *Coffee Can Investing: The Low-Risk Route to Stupendous Wealth* many times in the book. In this appendix we explain the concept in detail.

Headquartered in Los Angeles, Capital Group is one of the world's largest asset management firms, with assets under management in excess of $1.7 trillion. In the late 1960s, Capital Group set up an entity called Capital Guardian Trust Company, whose aim was to provide traditional investment counselling services to wealthy individuals. Robert Kirby joined Capital in 1965 as the main investment manager at Capital Guardian Trust, where his job involved advising high-net-worth clients on their investments and managing their portfolios. Nearly twenty years later, he wrote a remarkable article which introduced to the world the concept of the 'coffee can portfolio'.

In his article,[3] written in 1984, Kirby narrated an incident involving his client's husband. The gentleman had purchased stocks recommended by Kirby in denominations of $5,000 each but, unlike Kirby, did not sell anything from the portfolio. This process (of buying when Kirby bought but not selling thereafter) led to enormous wealth creation for the client over a period of about ten years. The wealth creation was mainly on account of one position transforming into a jumbo holding worth over $800,000, which came from 'a zillion shares of Xerox'. Impressed by the approach of 'buy and forget' followed by this gentleman, Kirby coined the term 'coffee can portfolio', in which the 'coffee can' harkens back to the times of the Wild West, when Americans, before the widespread advent of banks, saved their valuables in a coffee can and kept it under a mattress.

Although Kirby made the discovery of the 'coffee can' portfolio sound serendipitous, the central insight behind this construct—that in order to truly get rich, an investor has to let a sensibly constructed portfolio stay untouched for a long period of time—is as powerful as it is profound. After all, the instinctive thing for a hard-working, intelligent investor is to try to optimize his portfolio periodically, usually once a year. It is very, very hard for investors to leave a portfolio untouched for ten years. A retail investor will be tempted to intervene whenever he sees stocks in the portfolio sag in price. A professional investor will feel that he has a fiduciary responsibility to intervene if parts of the portfolio are underperforming. But Kirby's counter-intuitive insight is that an investor will make way more money if he leaves the portfolio untouched.

It is possible to recreate Kirby's coffee can investing approach for the Indian stock market, and this exercise has been described in detail in the book *Coffee Can Investing: The Low Risk Route to Stupendous Wealth (2018) by* Saurabh Mukherjea, Rakshit Ranjan and Pranab Uniyal. What follows is a summary of the approach described in that book.

ROBERT KIRBY'S CONSTRUCT APPLIED IN INDIA

We use straightforward investment filters to identify 10–25 high-quality stocks, and we then leave the portfolio untouched for a decade. Both in back-testing and in live portfolios, we find that this simple approach delivers consistently impressive results. In particular, the portfolio not only outperforms the benchmark consistently, but it also delivers healthy absolute returns and, more specifically, it performs extremely well when the broader market is experiencing stress.

Before we detail the returns delivered by this investment approach, let us explain the simple investment filters that can be used to build a portfolio which is aligned to Kirby's philosophy of buying great companies and leaving them alone in your portfolio for long periods of time. To begin with, we limit our search to companies—from the approximately 6,000 ones listed in India—with a minimum market capitalization of Rs 100 crore, as the reliability of data on companies smaller than this is somewhat suspect. There are around 1,500 listed companies (either on the Bombay Stock Exchange or the National Stock Exchange) in India with a market cap above Rs 100 crore. Within this universe we look for companies that, over the preceding decade, have grown sales each year by at least 10 per cent, alongside generating return on capital employed (pre-tax) of at least 15 per cent.

WHY RETURN ON CAPITAL EMPLOYED (RoCE)?

We have highlighted the relevance and importance of RoCE earlier in this book. A company deploys capital in assets, which in turn generate cash flows and profits. The total capital deployed by the company consists of equity and debt. RoCE is a metric that measures the efficiency of capital deployment for a company, calculated as a ratio of 'earnings before interest and tax' (EBIT) in the numerator and capital employed (sum of debt liabilities and shareholder's equity) in the denominator. The higher the RoCE, the better is the company's efficiency of capital deployment.

WHY USE AN RoCE FILTER OF 15 PER CENT?

We use 15 per cent as a minimum because we believe that is the bare minimum return required to beat the cost of capital. Adding the risk-free rate (approximately 6.2 per cent in India in early-2021) to the equity risk premium[4] of 7–7.5 per cent gives an expected rate of return/cost of capital broadly in that range. The equity risk premium, in turn, is calculated as 4 per cent (the long-term US equity risk premium) plus 2.5–3 per cent to account for India's credit rating (BBB, as per S&P). A country's credit rating affects the risk premium, as a higher rating (e.g., AAA, AA) indicates greater economic stability in the country, which lowers the risk premium for investing in that country. A lower credit rating indicates comparatively lower economic stability which, in turn, raises the risk premium for investing in that country.

WHY USE A REVENUE GROWTH FILTER OF 10 PER CENT EVERY YEAR?

India's nominal GDP growth rate has averaged 13 per cent over the past ten years. Nominal GDP growth is different from real GDP growth, in that unlike the latter, nominal GDP growth is *not* adjusted for inflation. In simple terms, it is gross domestic product (GDP) evaluated at current market prices (GDP being the monetary value of all finished goods and services produced within a country's borders in a specific time period). A credible firm operating in India should therefore be able to deliver sales growth of at least that much every year. However, very few listed companies—only six out of the nearly 1,500 firms screened by Marcellus Investment Managers—have managed to achieve this! Therefore, Marcellus has reduced this filter rate modestly to 10 per cent, i.e., he looks for companies that have delivered revenue growth of 10 per cent every year for ten consecutive years.[5]

For financial services stocks, we modify the filters of return on equity (RoE) and sales growth as follows:

RoE OF 15 PER CENT

We prefer return on equity (RoE) [6] over return on assets (RoA)[7] because this is a fairer measure of the ability of banks and non-bank lenders to generate higher income efficiently on a given equity capital base over time.[8]

LOAN GROWTH OF 15 PER CENT

Given that nominal GDP growth in India has averaged 13 per cent over the past ten years, a loan growth of at least 15 per cent is an indication of a bank's ability to lend over business cycles.

Now, let us look at the results. Detailed back-testing of this investment approach, based on data going back to 1991, shows that *such a portfolio beats benchmarks across most time periods*. The portfolio also performs admirably well during stressful periods (like the Lehman crisis in 2008 and the COVID pandemic in 2020) when the overall stock market nosedived. If invested for over a decade with no churn, this portfolio generates returns that are substantially higher than the benchmark (median compounded annualized outperformance over the last nineteen years of 7 percentage points).

Exhibit 84: Kirby's approach has outperformed benchmark indices over all but one of its twenty iterations[9]

		CCP Start		CCP End		CCP TSR	SENSEX TSR	Out performance
Kick-off Year	No. of Stocks	Date	Value	Date	Value	CAGR	CAGR	relative to Sensex
2000	5	01-Jul-00	500	30-Jun-10	3,831	22.6%	16.0%	6.6%
2001	6	01-Jul-01	600	30-Jun-11	9,802	32.2%	20.5%	11.7%
2002	8	01-Jul-02	800	30-Jun-12	7,631	25.3%	20.2%	5.1%
2003	9	01-Jul-03	900	30-Jun-13	10,117	27.4%	20.2%	7.2%
2004	10	01-Jul-04	1,000	30-Jun-14	16,880	32.7%	19.7%	12.9%
2005	9	01-Jul-05	900	30-Jun-15	6,659	22.2%	16.1%	6.0%
2006	10	01-Jul-06	1,000	30-Jun-16	6,376	20.4%	11.4%	9.0%
2007	15	01-Jul-07	1,500	30-Jun-17	9,030	19.7%	9.3%	10.3%
2008	11	01-Jul-08	1,100	30-Jun-18	7,442	21.1%	12.2%	8.9%
2009	11	01-Jul-09	1,100	30-Jun-19	5,950	18.4%	12.0%	6.4%
2010	7	01-Jul-10	700	30-Jun-20	1,982	11.0%	8.7%	2.2%
2011	14	01-Jul-11	1,400	31-Dec-20	3,750	10.9%	11.9%	-0.9%
2012	22	01-Jul-12	2,200	31-Dec-20	13,336	23.6%	14.1%	9.5%
2013	18	01-Jul-13	1,800	31-Dec-20	9,449	24.7%	14.1%	10.6%
2014	17	01-Jul-14	1,700	31-Dec-20	5,856	20.9%	11.5%	9.4%
2015	20	01-Jul-15	2,000	31-Dec-20	4,432	15.5%	11.6%	4.0%
2016	17	01-Jul-16	1,700	31-Dec-20	3,346	16.2%	14.7%	1.5%
2017	13	01-Jul-17	1,300	31-Dec-20	2,224	16.6%	14.5%	2.0%
2018	9	01-Jul-18	900	31-Dec-20	1,373	18.4%	14.0%	4.4%
2019	9	01-Jul-19	900	31-Dec-20	1,358	31.5%	14.4%	17.1%

Source: Marcellus Investment Managers; Ace Equity

For any stock, and indeed for any portfolio, one can disaggregate the source of investment returns into two sources: (a) growth in profits; and (b) growth in the price/earnings (P/E) multiple. Even more interesting than the ability of Kirby's approach to consistently outperform the Sensex is the source of this outperformance—namely, healthy profit growth (measured by earnings per share (EPS CAGR in Exhibit 85) rather than P/E rerating of the stocks in the portfolios. As the final three columns of the table show, in the vast majority of the iterations the dominant driver of returns is profit growth (measured by EPS growth).

Exhibit 85: Disaggregating the returns from Kirby's investment approach into profit growth (measured by EPS CAGR) and P/E growth[10]

Date	Value	Date	Value	EPS CAGR	P/E CAGR	TSR CAGR
2000	500	2010	3,831	19.0%	3.1%	22.6%
2001	600	2011	9,802	17.3%	12.8%	32.2%
2002	800	2012	7,631	16.8%	7.3%	25.3%
2003	900	2013	10,117	19.2%	6.9%	27.4%
2004	1,000	2014	16,880	18.6%	11.9%	32.7%
2005	900	2015	6,659	15.3%	6.0%	22.2%
2006	1,000	2016	6,376	18.7%	1.4%	20.4%
2007	1,500	2017	9,030	15.6%	3.5%	19.7%
2008	1,100	2018	7,442	11.7%	8.4%	21.1%
2009	1,100	2019	5,950	12.8%	5.0%	18.4%
2010	700	2020	1,982	8.0%	2.7%	11.0%
2011	1,400	2020	3,750	2.4%	8.3%	10.9%
2012	2,200	2020	13,336	5.6%	17.0%	23.6%
2013	1,800	2020	9,449	8.3%	15.2%	24.7%

Date	Value	Date	Value	EPS CAGR	P/E CAGR	TSR CAGR
2014	1,700	2020	5,856	10.7%	9.3%	20.9%
2015	2,000	2020	4,432	10.5%	4.6%	15.5%
2016	1,700	2020	3,346	7.5%	8.1%	16.2%
2017	1,300	2020	2,224	10.0%	5.9%	16.6%
2018	900	2020	1,373	12.5%	5.2%	18.4%
2019	900	2020	1,358	13.0%	16.4%	31.5%

Source: Marcellus Investment Managers; Ace Equity

In the next exhibit, we have analysed the performance of these twenty historical iterations of our application of Kirby's approach, with each portfolio lasting for up to ten years of holding period, i.e., over 150 years of cumulative portfolio investments. The median portfolio return[11] (compounded and annualized) has remained robust at 22–23 per cent historically for holding periods over three years. Moreover, this investment approach also delivers an extremely low level of volatility in these annualized returns for all holding periods—a necessary condition for investors to have a large exposure to equities in their net worth.

In more technical terms, analysis of the numbers behind the tables in Exhibit 84 and Exhibit 85 shows that over the past twenty years, the returns generated from this approach are positive for all holding periods of five years or more, and have been in excess of 6 per cent per annum for all holding periods of five years or more. In simple terms, it means that Kirby's approach offers more than a 95 per cent probability of generating a positive return, as long as investors hold the portfolio for at least three years. If held for at least five years, there is more than 95 per cent probability of the investor generating a return greater than 6 per cent.

Exhibit 86: Returns from Kirby's investment approach have been robust across various holding periods (X-axis), with limited volatility in these returns, as depicted by the height of vertical bars, which measure two standard deviations (95 per cent confidence interval) of returns[12]

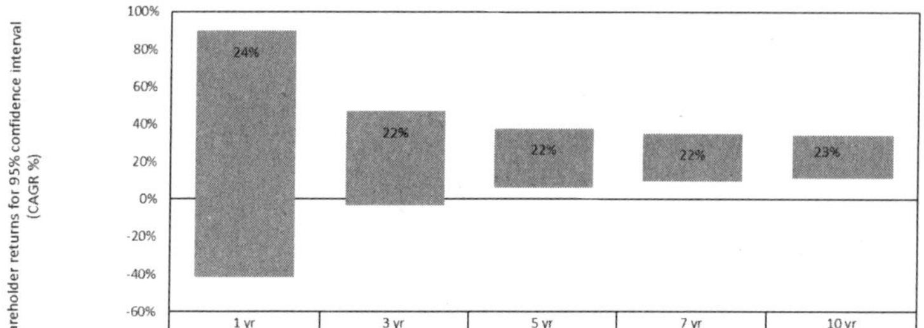

	1 yr	3 yr	5 yr	7 yr	10 yr
Upper Bound of 95%	90%	47%	38%	35%	34%
Median	18%	21%	22%	22%	23%
Mean	24%	22%	22%	22%	23%
Lower Bound of 95%	-42%	-3%	6%	10%	12%

Source: Marcellus Investment Managers; Ace Equity

Just to emphasize the importance of 18–23 per cent CAGR returns, a run-rate of 26 per cent return per annum results in the portfolio growing in size to ten times in ten years, 100 times in twenty years and 1,000 times in thirty years.

EMULATE ROB KIRBY AND CREATE YOUR OWN PORTFOLIO

Having discussed the virtues of Kirby's investment approach, if in July 2020 one were to screen the entire spectrum of listed companies with market cap greater than Rs 100 crore using our twin filters of revenue growth (or loan book growth for banks) and profitability every year over FY2011–20, we get the list of seven stocks, listed in Exhibit 87.

Exhibit 87: Applying Kirby's investment approach in 2020

Company Name	Amt. Invested (₹)	Mcap (₹ Mn)*	Mcap ($ Mn)*
Abbott India Ltd	100	3,35,082	4,587
Caplin Point Laboratories Ltd	100	38,305	524
Dr Lal Pathlabs Ltd	100	1,92,131	2,630
HDFC Bank Ltd	100	79,10,648	1,08,286
Bajaj Finance Ltd	100	31,90,820	43,678
Neogen Chemicals Ltd.	100	16,962	232
V-Mart Retail Ltd.	100	46,210	633

Source: Marcellus Investment Managers, Ace Equity;* as on 31 December 2020

As discussed in the preceding pages, a portfolio constructed today using this approach needs to be invested equally in all the stocks mentioned in this list. This portfolio should be left untouched for the next ten years, regardless of how well or badly it does in a short-term period within this ten-year holding period. Will such a portfolio make money for you? There are no guaranteed returns when it comes to equity investments, but if we go by the historical track record of this form of investing, Exhibit 84 shows that investing based on Kirby's approach outperforms the Sensex in the vast majority of time periods. Moreover, it (a) rarely gives you negative returns, and (b) in most time periods it generates significant positive returns.

* * *

Glossary

Term	Meaning
Discounted Cash Flow	A method of valuing assets (including companies) by calculating the net present value of all cash inflows and outflows from that asset over its lifetime
Present Value	The value of a future stream of cash flows today; usually expressed with reference to a discount rate. For example, if invested at a rate of 10 per cent, Rs 100 will be Rs 110 after a year. Therefore, the Present Value of Rs 110 today is Rs 100
Competitive Advantage	What enables a business to outperform its competitors and allows a company to achieve relatively healthy returns for its shareholders
Correlation	A statistic that measures the degree to which two variables move in relation to each other
Yield to Maturity	The total return earned on a bond if it is held until maturity with the interest received reinvested at the same rate.
Mark-to-Market	Measuring the fair value of an asset, typically using its market price
Barriers to Entry	The high initial costs or other hurdles that prevent new competitors from easily entering an industry or area of business
Cost of Capital	Interest rate on debt and/or the return expected by shareholders on equity capital

Term	Meaning
Price to Book Value (P/B)	A valuation ratio measuring the stock price as a multiple of the book value or net worth per share
Price Earnings (P/E)	A valuation ratio measuring the stock price as a multiple of the profit/earnings per share
Return on Capital Employed (RoCE)	The returns earned per unit of capital employed in the business. Calculated as EBIT/Capital Employed
Return on Equity (RoE)	The profit earned as a percentage of the net worth of the company
Compounded Annual Growth Rate (CAGR)	A measure of the annualized rate of return on an investment from one point to another, assuming all profits are reinvested
Market Capitalization	The market value of a company, measured as the number of shares outstanding multiplied by the market price
Cash Flow from Operations (CFO)	The cash profit after adjusting for changes in working capital
Capital Work in Progress	The portion of spending on building fixed assets which are not ready for use and therefore are not recognized/capitalized as Fixed Assets in the books of accounts
Gross Block	The aggregate book value of all Fixed Assets of the company
Dupont analysis	An analytical tool to break down Return on Equity into its key drivers. The formula used is Dupont Analysis = Net Profit Margin x Asset Turnover x Equity Multiplier. Asset Turnover in turn is calculated as Sales / Total Assets and Equity Multiplier is Total Assets / Net worth
Earnings Before Interest Depreciation and Amortisation (EBITDA)	Revenues reduced by all operating costs
Gross debt / Equity	Total debt by the net worth
Net debt / Equity	Total debt less cash and cash equivalents by the net worth

Term	Meaning
Goodwill	An intangible asset created when a company purchases another company for a price that is higher than the net value of assets of the company being acquired
Qualified Institution Placement (QIP)	An issue of shares by a listed company to institutional investors such as mutual funds, insurance companies, foreign institutional investors
BIFR	The Board for Industrial and Financial Reconstruction, an agency of the Government of India for revival and/or winding up of sick (bankrupt) companies. It is no longer in existence
Ind-AS	Accounting Standards applicable to Indian companies
PMS	Portfolio Management Services
Internal Rate of Return (IRR)	The rate at which the NPV of a stream of cash flows is zero
EV/EBITDA	A valuation ratio measuring the Enterprise Value of a company by its EBITDA. Enterprise Value is the market capitalization of the company plus its new debt

* * *

Notes

INTRODUCTION

1. *Rahul Dravid—Timeless Steel: Collected Writings on Indian Cricket's Go-to Man* (The Walt Disney Company, 2012).
2. https://www.bbc.com/news/world-asia-india-17308981.
3. Sambit Bal's interview with Rahul Dravid first published in *Wisden Asia Cricket Magazine* (2004).
4. Devendra Prabhudesai, *A Biography of Rahul Dravid: The Nice Guy Who Finished First* (Rupa, 2019).
5. https://www.youtube.com/watch?v=3at5EHBXe9s
6. Aakash Chopra, 'Chapter 11: Redemption and Immortality', in Devendra Prabhudesai, *A Biography of Rahul Dravid: The Nice Guy Who Finished First* (Rupa, 2019).
7. Jason Gillespie, speaking to Nagraj Gollapudi, 'I can't recall beating him more than one ball in a row', ESPNcricinfo, 9 March 2012.
8. Rohit Brijnath, 'Twin Treatises in Courage', *Rahul Dravid—Timeless Steel: Collected Writings on Indian Cricket's Go-to Man* (The Walt Disney Company, 2012).
9. Sambit Bal's interview with Rahul Dravid, first published in *Wisden Asia Cricket Magazine,* 2004.
10. Rohit Brijnath, 'Twin Treatises in Courage', *Rahul Dravid—Timeless Steel: Collected Writings on Indian Cricket's Go-to Man* (The Walt Disney Company, 2012).
11. https://www.bbc.com/news/world-asia-india-17308981.
12. https://www.espncricinfo.com/story/rahul-dravid-stats-analysis-india-s-overseas-hero-and-much-more-556766
13. https://www.sportskeeda.com/cricket/top-five-indian-batsmen-with-highest-average-overseas-conditions/6.

14. https://www.espncricinfo.com/story/rahul-dravid-stats-analysis-india-s-overseas-hero-and-much-more-556766.
15. https://www.espncricinfo.com/story/samir-chopra-on-meeting-rahul-dravid-620920.
16. https://www.bbc.com/news/world-asia-india-17309801.
17. https://www.espncricinfo.com/story/jason-gillespie-i-can-t-recall-beating-dravid-more-than-one-ball-in-a-row-556792.
18. Sambit Bal, 'The Man Who Acquired Greatness', *Rahul Dravid—Timeless Steel: Collected Writings on Indian Cricket's Go-to Man* (The Walt Disney Company, 2012).
19. Rahul Bhattacharya, *Pundits from Pakistan: On Tour with India* (Penguin India, 2004).
20. Virender Sehwag, in Devendra Prabhudesai, *A Biography of Rahul Dravid: The Nice Guy Who Finished First* (Rupa, 2019).

CHAPTER 1: THE FOUR MOST DAMAGING MYTHS IN INDIAN INVESTING

1. Monika Halan, *Let's Talk About Money: You've Worked Hard for It, Now Make it Work for You* (HarperBusiness, 2008).
2. https://rbidocs.rbi.org.in/rdocs/PublicationReport/Pdfs/HFCRA28D0415E2144A009112DD314ECF5C07.PDF.
3. https://residex.nhbonline.org.in/#:~:text=NHB%20RESIDEX%2C%20India's%20first%20official,stakeholders%20from%20the%20housing%20market.
4. https://www.globalpropertyguide.com/rental-yields.
5. https://www.livemint.com/Money/0FkDebceEB43YSoZuPQorJ/Debt-funds-are-not-riskfree-Tread-carefully.html.
6. https://marcellus.in/blogs/nifty-indian-gdp-a-complete-breakdown-in-relationship.
7. http://aswathdamodaran.blogspot.com/2020/.
8. https://www8.gsb.columbia.edu/sites/valueinvesting/files/files/Buffett1984.pdf.
9. https://www.investopedia.com/terms/c/capm.asp.
10. Price impact refers to the change in stock prices as a result of buying or selling of shares. For thinly traded shares, the impact tends to be higher.
11. Source: World Bank

12. Saurabh Mukherjea, Rakshit Ranjan and Pranab Uniyal, *Coffee Can Investing: The Low-Risk Road to Stupendous Wealth* (Penguin India, 2018).
13. Benjamin Graham and David L. Dodd, *Security Analysis* (Mc-Graw Hill, 1934).
14. https://www8.gsb.columbia.edu/sites/valueinvesting/files/files/Buffett1984.pdf.

CHAPTER 2: WHAT TO BUY—PART 1: ACCOUNTING QUALITY

1. Berkshire Hathaway, Chairman's letter, 1988.
2. Letter dated 7 January 2009 from B. Ramalinga Raju to the board of Satyam Computer Services Ltd.
3. 'Satyam scam: All you need to know about India's biggest accounting fraud', *Hindustan Times*, 9 April 2019.
4. BSE, Marcellus Investment Managers.
5. Howard M Schilt, *Financial Shenanigans: How to Detect Accounting Gimmicks and Fraud in Financial Reports* (Mc-Graw Hill, first edition, 1993; currently in its fourth edition, 2018).
6. Capital work in progress (CWIP) refers to that portion of spending on building fixed assets which are not ready for use and therefore are not recognized/capitalized as fixed assets in the books of accounts.
7. https://indiaoutbound.info/market-analysis/a-royal-downfall-of-cox-kings/.
8. https://www.indiatoday.in/magazine/economy/story/19970915-ratan-tata-proves-his-supremacy-by-ousting-ajit-kerkar-from-taj-group-of-hotels-830570-1997-09-15.
9. Gross Block Turnover, calculated as Net Sales divided by the Fixed Assets. The ratio measures the revenues generated for every unit of investment in Fixed Assets.
10. https://mumbaimirror.indiatimes.com/mumbai/other/cox-kings-says-staff-caused-company-loss-of-rs-5564-cr/articleshow/78084391.cms.
11. Tamal Bandyopadhyay, 'Banks to blame for Amtek Auto's bloated debt', *Livemint*, 7 December 2015.

CHAPTER 3: ACCOUNTING QUALITY: SPOTTING THE NAUGHTY LENDERS

1. Mary Buffett and David Clark, *Warren Buffett and the Interpretation of Financial Statements* (Scribner, 2008).
2. Based on Marcellus's accounting quality framework.
3. DHFL's FY13 Annual Report.
4. DHFL's FY16 Annual Report.
5. Project loans are the long-term financing of infrastructure and industrial projects based on the projected cash flows of the projects rather than the balance sheets of their sponsors.
6. Tamal Bandyopadhyay, *Pandemonium—The Great Indian Banking Tragedy* (Roli Books, 2020).
7. https://www.financialexpress.com/industry/banking-finance/dhfl-claims-cross-rs-1-lakh-crore/1907431/.

CHAPTER 4: WHAT TO BUY—PART 2: GREAT FRANCHISES

1. From Warren Buffet's answer to a question (number 23) at the 2003 Berkshire Hathaway Annual Meeting.
2. Bruce Greenwald and Judd Kahn, *Competition Demystified* (Portfolio, 2007).
3. http://www.johnkay.com/1993/06/01/the-structure-of-strategybusiness-strategy-review-1993.
4. Marcellus' discussions with ex-employees of Asian Paints.
5. https://www.garwarefibres.com/norway/x12-lice-shield-the-proven-patented-sea-lice-solution/; https://www.garwarefibres.com/wp-content/uploads/2020/01/fish-farmer-magazine.pdf.
6. http://www.johnkay.com/1993/06/01/the-structure-of-strategybusiness-strategy-review-1993.
7. Saurabh Mukherjea, *The Unusual Billionaires* (Penguin India, 2016).
8. https://www.thehindubusinessline.com/markets/stock-markets/hdfc-mf-recovers-entire-investment-in-essel-group-ncds/article31976941.ece.
9. HDFC AMC disclosures.
10. HDFC AMC annual reports.

11. http://www.johnkay.com/1993/06/01/the-structure-of-strategybusiness-strategy-review-1993.
12. Saurabh Mukherjea and Anupam Gupta, *The Victory Project: Six Steps to Peak Potential* (Penguin, 2020).
13. Marcellus's discussions with Pidilite's distribution channel partners.
14. https://economictimes.indiatimes.com/there-is-enough-opportunity-in-adhesive-segment-madhukar-parekh-pidilite/articleshow/6811400.cms?from=mdr.
15. http://www.johnkay.com/1993/06/01/the-structure-of-strategybusiness-strategy-review-1993.
16. Saurabh Mukherjea, *The Unusual Billionaires* (Penguin India, 2016).
17. http://www.gmmpfaudler.com/content/Investor_Presentation_Sep_2020.pdf.
18. Ibid.
19. Marcellus's discussions with pharma industry participants.
20. Data sourced from Ace Equity.
21. https://brandequity.economictimes.indiatimes.com/news/industry/most-trusted-brands-2020/74800967.
22. Data sourced from Ace Equity.
23. Peter Thiel, *Zero to One: Notes on Startups, or How to Build the Future* (Currency, 2014).
24. Data sourced from Bloomberg and Ace Equity.
25. AIL's Annual Report FY2018–19.
26. AIL's Annual Report FY2011.
27. AIL's Annual Report FY2011.
28. AIL annual reports and Marcellus research
29. https://fortune.com/2015/04/03/how-abbott-labs-is-crushing-it-in-asia/.
30. https://fortune.com/2015/04/03/how-abbott-labs-is-crushing-it-in-asia/.
31. https://www.forbesindia.com/article/india-rich-list-2019/indias-richest-2019-divis-journey-into-the-elite-league-of-drug-makers/56291/1.
32. https://www.forbesindia.com/article/india-rich-list-2014/murali-divi-the-accidental-chemist/38771/1.
33. Cheminor was a subsidiary of Dr Reddy's Laboratories (later acquired by DRL) to serve as its contract manufacturing arm.

Murali Divi was managing director of Cheminor before setting up Divi's Laboratories.

34. https://www.forbesindia.com/article/india-rich-list-2014/murali-divi-the-accidental-chemist/38771/1.
35. Marcellus's discussions with Asian Paints' ex-employees.
36. Marcellus's discussions with Asian Paints' distribution channel partners.
37. https://www.cognizant.com/perspectives/asian-paints-the-digital-odyssey-of-a-serial-reinventor.
38. https://new.abb.com/cpm/industry-specific-solutions/consumer-fine-chemicals/one-of-world-s-largest-dcs-and-mes-projects-for-integrated-paint-process.
39. https://sightmachine.com/pr/asian-paints-deploys-sight-machine-for-digital-transformation-of-manufacturing/.
40. Marcellus's discussions with industry participants.
41. Marcellus investment managers' research.

CHAPTER 5: WHAT TO BUY—PART 3: MASTERS OF CAPITAL ALLOCATION

1. William N. Thorndike, Jr., *The Outsiders : Eight Unconventional CEOs and their Radically Rational Blueprint for Success* (Harvard Business School Press India Limited, 2012).
2. Earnings Before Interest and Tax (including other income).
3. https://brandequity.economictimes.indiatimes.com/news/marketing/how-kelloggs-is-taking-on-the-breakfast-challenge/73142223.
4. Kellog's annual report, https://www.sec.gov/Archives/edgar/data/55067/0000950124-95-000907.txt.
5. Conference calls with Info Edge (India) Ltd. and Matrimony.com Ltd.
6. https://www.hul.co.in/news/press-releases/2020/glaxosmithkline-consumer-healthcare-limited-merges-with-hindustan-unilever-limited.html.
7. Society of Indian Automobile Manufacturers.
8. Marcellus investment managers' research.
9. https://www.coca-colaindia.com/newsroom/coca-cola-india-launches-ready-drink-flavoured-milk-offering-vio-bangalore.

10. https://www.moneycontrol.com/news/business/milk-it-coca-cola-plans-to-re-enter-dairy-business-with-vio-brand-2795521.html.
11. https://www.coca-colaindia.com/newsroom/beat-the-heat-this-summer-with-vio-spiced-buttermilk-a-refreshi.
12. Capital employed in overseas businesses is calculated as consolidated capital employed less standalone capital employed less investment in subsidiaries; operating cash flows are considered for the period over which the acquisitions have been made.
13. Wherever a firm has written off intangibles directly against reserves, instead of routing them through P&L, we have added back the intangibles to the capital employed—the largest being Marico's adjustment of Rs 723 crore worth of intangibles against reserves in FY2014. Standalone RoCE has been calculated after excluding investments in subsidiaries and associates from the capital employed. This adjustment has been made to get a sense of the RoCE generated by the firm's standalone business *before* the effect of capital allocated towards the non-standalone business.
14. Tata Steel Annual Reports
15. https://www.worldsteel.org/steel-by-topic/statistics/steel-data-viewer/C_asu_per_capita_cse/KOR/CHN.
16. https://www.worldsteel.org/steel-by-topic/statistics/steel-data-viewer/C_asu_per_capita_cse/KOR/CHN.
17. Tata Steel annual reports; Ace Equity.
18. Marcellus Investment Managers, based on management interviews and investor conference calls.
19. Pidilite annual reports, including those of its subsidiary companies.
20. https://www.bseindia.com/xml-data/corpfiling/AttachLive/1cd804fa-dbce-4749-a3f1-fd1248177b8f.pdf.
21. https://www.huntsman.com/investors/newsroom/news-releases/detail/460/huntsman-announces-the-sale-of-its-india-based-diy-consumer.
22. Letter dated 7 January 2009 from B. Ramalinga Raju to the Board of Satyam Computer Services Ltd.
23. https://www.hindustantimes.com/business/satyam-scam-all-you-need-to-know-about-india-s-biggest-accounting-fraud/story-YTfHTZy9K6NvsW8PxIEEYL.html.
24. John C. Maxwell, *The 21 Irrefutable Laws of Leadership: Follow Them and People Will Follow You* (HarperCollins Leadership, 2007).

25. https://www.asianpaints.com/about-us.html.
26. https://www.hdfcbank.com/personal/about-us/overview/board-of-director.

CHAPTER 6: WHEN TO BUY?

1. John C. Bogle, *Common Sense on Mutual Funds: New Imperatives for the Intelligent Investor* (John Wiley & Sons, 2000)
2. Charlie Munger, 'The Art of Stock Picking', http://csinvesting.org/wp-content/uploads/2013/01/Charlie-Munger-Art-of-Stock-Picking.pdf.
3. Ben Carlson, *A Wealth of Common Sense—Why Simplicity Trumps Complexity in Any Investment Plan* (Bloomberg Press, 2015).
4. https://www.spglobal.com/spdji/en/documents/spiva/spiva-india-year-end-2019.pdf.
5. Saurabh Mukherjea, Rakshit Ranjan, Pranab Uniyal, *Coffee Can Investing: The Low Risk Road to Stupendous Wealth* (Penguin India, 2018).
6. https://www8.gsb.columbia.edu/articles/columbia-business/superinvestors.
7. Free Cash Flow to Equity (FCFE) is the residual cash flow that remains after spending on capital expenditure (both maintenance as well as growth/expansion) and after payments to debt holders (interest as well as principal repayments). Since we are valuing the equity of the company, the FCFE is the more relevant measure compared to Free Cash Flow to Firm (FCFF), which is the free cash before debt service. For a visual representation of the cash flow waterfall, refer Exhibit 60.
8. Returns up to December 2020, which is three months short of twenty-five years.

CHAPTER 7: PREPARING AN INVESTMENT PLAN

1. https://www.sebi.gov.in/sebiweb/other/OtherAction.do?doRecognisedFpi=yes&intmId=13.
2. https://marcellus.in/video/marcellus-consistent-compounders-philosophy-www-marcellus-in/.

3. Marcellus Investment Managers, Ace Equity. The returns from the CCP investment approach are taken as the average of all live portfolio iterations during the period. Total shareholder return is the stock price change plus cash returned to shareholders in the form of dividends and buybacks.
4. Ibid.
5. Assuming 6 per cent returns on the government bonds and assuming 18 per cent returns (post-tax) on CCP.
6. As explained in Chapter 1, Devika needs to compound her wealth at 9 per cent per annum over the next decade to have a healthy corpus going into retirement.
7. (1) We classify companies with market cap of > Rs 15,000 crore as large cap, of between Rs 3,000 crore and Rs 15,000 crore as mid-cap, and of below Rs 3,000 crore as small cap; (2) Returns calculated for three baskets (large, mid- and small cap) with equal allocation to each stock within those baskets. Stocks rebalanced annually at July-end based on market-cap criteria; (3) No dividends, transactions costs and other charges considered in the above returns calculations. (4) 2) Earnings growth calculated for three baskets (large, mid- and small cap) with equal allocation to each stock within those baskets.
8. https://marcellus.in/video/marcellus-webinar-introducing-little-champs-marcellus-small-cap-pms/.

CONCLUSION: LESSONS FROM RAHUL DRAVID: COMBINING TECHNICAL ABILITIES WITH BEHAVIOURAL SKILLS

1. Sambit Bal's interview with Rahul Dravid, first published in *Wisden Asia Cricket* (2004)
2. John Wright, India's coach between 2000 and 2005, speaking to Sharda Ugra of ESPNcricinfo in *Rahul Dravid Timeless Steel: Collected Writings on Indian Cricket's Go-to Man* (The Walt Disney Company, 2012).
3. https://www.espncricinfo.com/story/vijeeta-dravid-on-her-husband-rahul-556979.
4. Fazal Khaleel was interviewed by Nagraj Gollapudi of ESPNcricinfo and the interview appeared in *Rahul Dravid Timeless Steel: Collected*

Writings on Indian Cricket's Go-to Man (The Walt Disney Company, 2012).

5. Rahul Dravid's interview with Sharda Ugra appeared on ESPNcricinfo on 29 March 2012.
6. https://www.espncricinfo.com/story/vijeeta-dravid-on-her-husband-rahul-556979.
7. Sambit Bal's interview with Rahul Dravid, first published in *Wisden Asia Cricket* magazine (2004).
8. John Wright, India's coach between 2000 and 2005, speaking to Sharda Ugra of ESPNcricinfo in *Rahul Dravid Timeless Steel: Collected Writings on Indian Cricket's Go-to Man* (The Walt Disney Company, 2012).
9. https://www.espncricinfo.com/story/aakash-chopra-on-rahul-dravid-s-evolution-as-a-batsman-557698.
10. Greg Chappell, in *Rahul Dravid Timeless Steel: Collected Writings on Indian Cricket's Go-to Man* (The Walt Disney Company, 2012).
11. Rohit Brijnath, in *Rahul Dravid Timeless Steel: Collected Writings on Indian Cricket's Go-to Man* (The Walt Disney Company, 2012).
12. Ibid.
13. https://www.espncricinfo.com/story/vijeeta-dravid-on-her-husband-rahul-556979.

APPENDIX 1: THE MARCELLUS CHECKLIST

1. Atul Gawande, *The Checklist Manifesto: How to Get Things Right* (Picador, 2011).

APPENDIX 2: SIR JOHN KAY'S IBAS FRAMEWORK

1. This appendix is an updated version of Appendix 1 of *The Unusual Billionaires* (2016) by Saurabh Mukherjea. Saurabh has also written about Sir John's work in some of his columns which appear in the media e.g., http://www.moneycontrol.com/news/features/3-bookschanged- ambit-ceo- saurabh-mukherjeas-life_1157700.html.
2. http://www.thebuffett.com/quotes/How-to-Think-About-Businesses.html#i92.

3. Anthony Bolton, *Investing Against the Tide: Lessons from A Life of Running Money* (Financial Times, 2009).
4. http://www.johnkay.com/1993/06/01/the-structure-of-strategy-business-strategy-review-1993.
5. Some of the material in this sub-section is taken from Chapter 7 of *The Victory Project: Six Steps to Peak Potential* by Saurabh Mukherjea and Anupam Gupta (2020).
6. http://www.johnkay.com/1993/06/01/the-structure-of-strategy-business-strategy-review-1993.
7. A creamery is an establishment where butter, cheese, cream and milk are prepared and sold.
8. Annual reports for Nestlé and HUL, and GCMMF's website for the GCMMF-related data.
9. Verghese Kurien, as told to Gouri Salvi, *I Too Had a Dream* (Lotus Collection, 2005).
10. Harish Damodaran, *India's New Capitalists: Caste, Business, and Industry in a Modern Nation* (Palgrave Macmillan, 2008).
11. Verghese Kurien, *I Too Had a Dream* (Lotus Collection, 2005).
12. Ibid., p. 75.
13. http://indiatransportportal.com/a-peek-into-maruti%E2%80%99s-supply-chain-management-3024.
14. http://www.johnkay.com/1993/06/01/the-structure-of-strategy-business-strategy-review-1993.

APPENDIX 3: ROBERT KIRBY'S COFFEE CAN INVESTING METHOD

1. This appendix is an updated version of section from Chapter 9 of *The Victory Project: Six Steps to Peak Potential* (2020) by Saurabh Mukherjea and Anupam Gupta. Saurabh has also written about Rob's work in his previous books, *The Unusual Billionaires* (2016) and *Coffee Can Investing; the Low Risk Route to Stupendous Wealth* (2018).
2. Charles D. Ellis, *Capital: The Story of Long-Term Investment Excellence* (Hoboken: John Wiley & Sons, 2004).
3. Robert G. Kirby, 'The Coffee Can Portfolio', *Journal of Portfolio Management* 11, No. 1 (1984), pp. 76–80.

4. The equity risk premium denotes the additional return that the investor expects over and above the risk-free rate of return, for investing in equity.
5. It is important to note that we are *not* looking for companies which have grown sales over a ten-year period at a compounded annualized rate of at least 10 per cent. Instead, we *are* looking for companies which have grown sales every single year for ten consecutive years by at least 10 per cent.
6. RoE is the amount of profits earned (after paying corporate taxes) as a percentage of shareholders' equity.
7. RoA gives a sense of how efficient a management team is at using its assets to generate earnings. It is calculated by dividing a company's annual profits (after paying corporate taxes) by its total assets.
8. The assets of a bank are its equity plus the amount of money the bank has borrowed. Therefore, by looking at RoE, rather than RoA, we are not only able to measure a bank's ability to lend money profitably but also measure its ability to gauge exactly how much money the bank should borrow.
9. All stock prices are as of 31 December 2020. 'CCP Start Value' denotes an equal allocation of Rs 100 to the stocks qualifying to be in the portfolio for that year. The portfolio kicks off on 30 June of every year. The CAGR returns for all the portfolios since 2011 have been calculated until 31 December 2020, since they are yet to complete a ten-year cycle. Both portfolio returns and Sensex returns have been computed using TSR, i.e., total shareholder return, which includes dividends. The 2020 iteration, which started on 1 July 2020, has not completed a full year and hence its returns have not been computed. The sales growth filter has been relaxed to 9.5 per cent in FY2018 to include Astral Limited, because it was part of the 2017 iteration and missed the filter by a very narrow margin.
10. All stock prices in this table are as of 31 December 2020. EPS CAGR and P/E CAGR have been calculated for the April–March period due to inconsistency of trailing twelve-month EPS data for various stocks, whereas TSR CAGR is for the July–June period. TSR, i.e., total shareholder return, is the stock price change plus cash returned to shareholders in the form of dividends and buy-backs.

11. Median denotes the mid-point of returns, such that there is an equal probability of returns falling above or below it.
12. The period under consideration is July 2000 to December 2020. The investment horizons are calculated on a weekly rolling basis. For instance, the standard deviation of one-year return is the standard deviation of returns generated by considering 6,855 one-year periods (for all the CCP iterations) including 01/07/2000 to 01/07/2001, 08/07/2000 to 08/07/2001, and so on.

Acknowledgements

The concepts and the ideas contained in this book come from the twice weekly half-day long research meetings of the team at Marcellus Investment Managers. The forensic accounting ratios used in Chapters 2 and 3, the analysis of company-specific competitive advantages contained in Chapter 4, the study of capital allocation in Chapter 5 and the conceptualization of the Indian investors' challenges as laid out in Chapters 1 and 6—all this and more arises from the intellectual ferment of Marcellus. The three of us—Saurabh, Rakshit and Salil—are fortunate to be part of these meetings and, in this book, we have tried our best to convey these concepts and ideas as clearly as we could. Our thanks to the team at Marcellus for giving us the support and opportunity to turn the team's cutting-edge research into a coherent narrative.

We would like to specifically thank Ashvin Shetty, Tej Shah, Sudhanshu Nahta, Deven Kulkarni, Harsh Shah, Minali Bafna and Omkar Sawant for the time and the effort they spent on meticulously crafting the case studies which sit at the heart of this book.

Manish Kumar was the editor at Penguin Random House who commissioned Saurabh to write his previous bestseller, *The Victory Project: Six Steps to Peak Potential* (co-authored by Anupam Gupta, 2020). He was equally receptive when we approached him with the idea for this book. Even as he battled COVID-19 himself, Manish provided us with invaluable assistance not only in putting together this book but also in dealing with our myriad requests around the look and feel of the book. Thank you very much, Manish. In addition to Manish's inputs, the book has benefited from the fastidious copyediting of Saloni Mital. We are also thankful to Gunjan Ahlawat for turning a vague idea in our minds into a stunning cover page.

Many of the concepts in this book were first fleshed out in Marcellus's newsletters. Clients and friends of the firm responded to these newsletters with insightful comments. Those inputs helped us sharpen our thinking further. We are grateful to the staff, clients and friends of Marcellus Investment Managers for the manner in which they have supported the development of this book.

Our friends at Motilal Oswal Financial Services and IIFL Securities helped us in sourcing much of the data that we have analysed in this book. We thank them for their help and support.

Saurabh's family—Sarbani, Jeet and Malini—were initially horrified to hear that he was breaking his habit of writing a book every other year (*The Victory Project* was published in 2020 and hence *Diamonds in the Dust* should, in the normal course of affairs, have been scheduled for 2022). However, they soon realized that writing was the best way to keep Saurabh sane through the extended COVID-19 lockdown that everybody in India had to endure. Many thanks to Sarbani, Jeet and Malini for their patience, their support and their love. Saurabh would also like to thank his parents, Chaitali and Prasanta Mukhopadhyay, who taught him to appreciate merit rather than money.

Rakshit would like to thank his wife, Roohani, and the munchkins, Ruchir and Rishaan for tolerating his incessant disappearances into his home office and for their endless love and encouragement. Rakshit is also grateful to his parents, Dr Savita Ranjan and Dr K. K. Ranjan, for their unwavering support.

Salil would like to thank his wife Nancy for being his inspiration and his anchor and for her solid support while he spent long hours at his home–office desk over the past many months. Salil also thanks his son Jahaan for understanding why his father was home all the time, but not available to spend as much time with him. Salil is grateful to his late father, Bharat Desai, for nurturing his love of books and reading and to his mother, Hema Desai, for her infinite love, support and blessings.

The authors thank Pranab Uniyal for his permissions to use concepts from the bestselling book he co-authored with Saurabh and Rakshit, *Coffee Can Investing: The Low-Risk Road to Stupendous Wealth*.

We also thank Anupam Gupta for allowing us to use ideas and cases from *The Victory Project: Six Steps to Peak Potential*, which he co-authored with Saurabh.

The authors also thank Harsh Mariwala, Sanjeev Bikhchandani, Mark Mobius, Monika Halan, Harish Bhat and Sir John Kay for taking time to review the material in *Diamonds in the Dust* and give the book their endorsement.

The authors can be contacted at the following address: salil@marcellus.in.